D1265546

GRAPHIS DESIGN 89

The International Annual on Design and Illustration

Das Internationale Jahrbuch über Design und Illustration

Le Répertoire International de Design et Illustration

Edited by/Herausgegeben von/Réalisé par

B. Martin Pedersen

Editor and Art Director: B. Martin Pedersen

Assistant Editors: Annette Crandall, Heinke Jenssen

Designers: Marino Bianchera, Martin Byland, Udi Nadiv

Photographer: Walter Zuber

Graphis Press Corp, Zurich (Switzerland)

GRAPHIS PUBLICATIONS

GRAPHIS, International bi-monthly journal of graphic art and photography

GRAPHIS DESIGN ANNUAL, The international annual on design and illustration

GRAPHIS PHOTO, The international annual of photography

GRAPHIS POSTER, The international annual of poster art

GRAPHIS PACKAGING VOL. 5, An international survey of packaging design

GRAPHIS DIAGRAM VOL. 2, The graphic visualization of abstract, technical and statistical facts and functions

GRAPHIS COVERS, An anthology of all GRAPHIS covers from 1944-86 with artists' short biographies
and indexes of all GRAPHIS issues

GRAPHIS ANNUAL REPORTS, An international compilation of the best designed annual reports

FILM + TV GRAPHICS 2, An international survey of the art of film animation

GRAPHIS-PUBLIKATIONEN

GRAPHIS, Die internationale Zweimonatszeitschrift für Graphik und Photographie

GRAPHIS DESIGN ANNUAL, Das internationale Jahrbuch über Design und Illustration

GRAPHIS PHOTO, Das internationale Jahrbuch der Photographie

GRAPHIS POSTER, Das internationale Jahrbuch der Plakatkunst

GRAPHIS PACKUNGEN BAND 5, Internationaler Überblick der Packungsgestaltung

GRAPHIS DIAGRAM BAND 2, Die graphische Darstellung abstrakter, technischer und statistischer Daten und Fakten

GRAPHIS COVERS, Eine Sammlung aller GRAPHIS-Umschläge von 1944-86 mit Informationen über die Künstler
und Inhaltsübersichten aller Ausgaben der Zeitschrift GRAPHIS

GRAPHIS ANNUAL REPORTS, Ein internationaler Überblick der Gestaltung von Jahresberichten

FILM + TV GRAPHICS 2, Ein internationaler Überblick über die Kunst des Animationsfilms

PUBLICATIONS GRAPHIS

GRAPHIS, La revue bimestrielle internationale d'arts graphiques et de la photographie

GRAPHIS DESIGN ANNUAL, Le répertoire international de la communication visuelle

GRAPHIS PHOTO, Le répertoire international de la photographie

GRAPHIS POSTER, Le répertoire international de l'art de l'affiche

GRAPHIS EMBALLAGES VOL. 5, Répertoire international des formes de l'emballage

GRAPHIS DIAGRAM VOL. 2, La représentation graphique de faits et données abstraits, techniques et statistiques

GRAPHIS COVERS, Recueil de toutes les couvertures de GRAPHIS de 1944-86 avec des notices biographiques
des artistes et le sommaire de tous les numéros du magazine GRAPHIS.

GRAPHIS ANNUAL REPORTS, Panorama international du design de rapports annuels d'entreprises

FILM + TV GRAPHICS 2, Un panorama international de l'art du film d'animation

PUBLICATION No. 192 (ISBN 3-85709-188-6)

© Copyright under Universal Copyright Convention

Copyright 1988 by Graphis Press Corp., 107 Dufourstrasse, 8008 Zurich, Switzerland

No part of this book may be reproduced in any form without written permission of the publisher

Printed in Japan by Toppan

Typeset in Switzerland by Setzerei Heller, Zurich

Typefaces: Garamond ITC Light Condensed, Futura Extra Bold

O
NC
997
.A1
G73
1989

DABNEY LANCASTER LIBRARY
LONGWOOD COLLEGE
FARMVILLE, VIRGINIA 23901

ABBREVIATIONS

AUSTRALIA	AUS
AUSTRIA	AUT
BELGIUM	BEL
BRAZIL	BRA
CANADA	CAN
DENMARK	DEN
FRANCE	FRA
GERMANY (WEST)	GER
GREAT BRITAIN	GBR
INDIA	IND
ITALY	ITA
JAPAN	JPN
MEXICO	MEX
NETHERLANDS	NLD
NORWAY	NOR
PHILIPPINES	PHI
POLAND	POL
SPAIN	SPA
SWEDEN	SWE
SWITZERLAND	SWI
TURKEY	TUR
USA	USA

ABKÜRZUNGEN

AUSTRALIEN	AUS
BELGIEN	BEL
BRASILIEN	BRA
DÄNEMARK	DEN
DEUTSCHLAND (BRD)	GER
FRANKREICH	FRA
GROSSBRITANNIEN	GBR
INDIEN	IND
ITALIEN	ITA
JAPAN	JPN
KANADA	CAN
MEXIKO	MEX
NIEDERLANDE	NLD
NORWEGEN	NOR
ÖSTERREICH	AUT
PHILIPPINEN	PHI
POLEN	POL
SCHWEDEN	SWE
SCHWEIZ	SWI
SPANIEN	SPA
TÜRKEI	TUR
USA	USA

ABRÉVIATIONS

ALLEMAGNE OCCIDENTALE	GER
AUSTRALIE	AUS
AUTRICHE	AUT
BELGIQUE	BEL
BRÉSIL	BRA
CANADA	CAN
DANEMARK	DEN
ESPAGNE	SPA
ETATS-UNIS	USA
FRANCE	FRA
GRANDE-BRETAGNE	GBR
INDE	IND
ITALIE	ITA
JAPON	JPN
MEXIQUE	MEX
NORWÈGE	NOR
PAYS-BAS	NLD
PHILIPPINES	PHI
POLOGNE	POL
SUÈDE	SWE
SUISSE	SWI
TURQUIE	TUR

ERRATUM

On page 216 of the Graphis Design Annual 87/88, we incorrectly listed the credits for the two men's toiletries flacons depicted. The Art Director and Designer for these flacons was Yumi Arakawa. Kazumi Akutagawa was the Art Director and Designer for the flacons shown on page 217. We regret this error and offer our sincere apologies to Mr. Arakawa.

ABKÜRZUNGEN

ERRATUM

Im Graphis Design Annual 87/88 haben wir auf Seite 216 falsche Künstlerangaben zu den abgebildeten Glasflakons für eine Herrenkosmetiklinie gemacht. Art Director und Designer dieser Flakons war Yumi Arakawa. Kazumi Akutagawa war der Art Director und Designer der auf Seite 217 gezeigten Flakons. Wir bedauern diesen Irrtum.

ERRATUM

A la page 216 du Graphis Design Annual 87/88, il convient de rectifier la mention de crédit relative aux deux flacons. C'est à Yumi Arakawa que reviennent le design et la direction artistique de ces flacons. Quant à Kazumi Akutagawa, il est le directeur artistique et concepteur des flacons qui figurent à la page 217. Nos lecteurs voudront bien excuser cette méprise.

REMARKS

■ We extend our heartfelt thanks to contributors throughout the world who have made it possible for us to publish a wide and international spectrum of the best work in this field.

■ Entry instructions may be requested at:
Graphis Press Corp., Dufourstrasse 107,
8008 Zurich, Switzerland

ANMERKUNGEN

■ Unser herzlicher Dank gilt den Einsendern aus aller Welt, die es uns durch ihre Beiträge möglich gemacht haben, ein breites, internationales Spektrum der besten Arbeiten zu veröffentlichen.

■ Teilnahmebedingungen:
Graphis Verlag AG, Dufourstrasse 107,
8008 Zurich, Schweiz

ANNOTATIONS

■ Toute notre reconnaissance va aux artistes du monde entier dont les envois nous ont permis de constituer un vaste panorama international des meilleurs travaux.

■ Modalités d'envoi de travaux:
Editions Graphis SA, Dufourstrasse 107,
8008 Zurich, Suisse

Whoever lives in today's Western world is continuously confronted with an ever-increasing flood of information. The results of a survey conducted in the seven largest industrial nations show that an average of 5,000 "chunks" of information are showered on us daily.

Included in all of this are items such as the hijacking of a Kuwaiti airliner, Nancy Reagan's astrological passion, the latest song of Michael Jackson, mastering of the office's new computer program, and an underworld murder – as well as the sudden death of Uncle Charles or Alice's favorite recipe.

The survey also indicates that even more complex types of information are structured into comprehensible units, that which remains is still an endless amount which no one can digest. And no one wants to digest.

Several years ago, some forty percent of this amount was absorbed. Today it is barely two percent. The remainder simply passes unnoticed.

From this it is obvious that the subject matter of the communications devised for services and products – in other words, advertising – is not at the top of the interest list. The competition as it is described above is too strong.

However, it is the framework within which our industry must function. It thus becomes a question of adhering to that two percent which is taken seriously. One possibility of doing so is with ample money and the recourse of sheer quantity, browbeating the public with the same repetitive message.

Only the largest and wealthiest of corporations can afford this approach. Advertising budgets in any case represent a ridiculously low amount when compared to the total effort and expenditures invested in promotion. In addition, total spending increases from year to year as more and more firms invest in professional communications. They have come to realize that without this, they essentially have no chance.

If we want to be seen and heard under these conditions, we need a new generation of advertising.

The request for advertising which informs as objectively as possible, and only objectively, has led to an absurdum.

First of all, as we have seen, this information could no longer be absorbed. And secondly, the information concerned was for the most part information long familiar to everyone.

By now we know that toothpaste is basic to brushing teeth, that almost every detergent launders to the same intensity of whiteness, and that coffee is not cacao. And we are also aware of the fact that no reputable firm can afford to bring an inferior product on the market – at least not if it wants to maintain its good name.

In the future, good arguments will not suffice to put our customers in the forefront. We must go beyond them and evoke the public's sympathy for their services and products.

Information in itself can only be successful if we have something truly innovative or extraordinary to describe. And in the meantime, that alone is seldom enough.

In the near future we will have to return to an essential. That essential is an image.

The concept of image has long become familiar, but it has lost its original meaning. Tomorrow's advertising must restore its significance.

A corporation, a product, or a service does not have a good or bad layout. They have neither good nor bad typography. They do not have good or bad slogans. They have neither good nor bad photographs, good nor bad illustrations.

Companies, services and products either have a good image or a bad image.

The definition and promotion of an image will become the goal of communications in the future. We must thus conceive for our customers a precise image of their companies, their services and their products.

It will no longer suffice to visualize verbal concepts. We must create visual concepts. The large four-color illustration can no longer fulfill the requirements of communication.

A new language of image and of portrayal must be designed.

That means visual statements which are expressive enough to transmit a given message.

That means visual statements which are direct enough to be recognized in a matter of seconds.

That means visual statements which are new enough to immediately distinguish that which we are promoting from that of our competitors.

That means visual statements which are strong enough to awaken an emotional identification with their contents.

Information which is transmitted via the emotions will not only be more quickly perceived, but will also have a more lasting effect.

Only a few firms have conceived their advertising programs in this way. Benetton with its youngsters worldwide, Esso's "Tiger in the Tank", Silk Cut with its slitted silk, and Marlboro's cowboys. As in the case of Silk Cut, the reason for the new generation of advertising is often legal in nature. Great Britain has restricted the explicit promotion of cigarettes to a point of near ineffectiveness. Or it is conceived for an international campaign and thus must function with limited reliance on the written word.

The outlook for us as consumers is most pleasant. Soon it will no longer be necessary for us to let ourselves be talked into something. We can quietly enjoy the appeal which is made to our emotions and our sympathies.

It will also be nice for all of those who can think in images.

FRANCIS SULZER, born 1949, is Creative Director and co-proprietor of the advertising agency Sulzer, Sutter in Zurich, Switzerland.

Wer heute in der westlichen Welt lebt, ist einer täglich steigenden Informationsflut ausgesetzt. Eine Untersuchung in den sieben grössten Industrienationen der Welt ergab, dass jeden Tag im Durchschnitt fünftausend Informationseinheiten auf uns niederprasseln.

Dazu gehören die Geiselnahme einer kuwaitischen Maschine, die Sternguckerei Nancy Reagans, der neueste Song von Michael Jackson, das Erlernen eines neuen Computerprogramms im Geschäft, der Mord im Milieu genauso wie der plötzliche Tod von Onkel Karl oder das interessante Kuchenrezept von Alice.

Auch wenn komplexere Informationen bei der Untersuchung in mehrere Einheiten zerlegt wurden, bleibt eine unendliche Fülle, die niemand mehr verdauen kann. Und auch niemand mehr verdauen will.

Vor einigen Jahren wurden noch vierzig Prozent dieser Informationsmenge aufgenommen. Heute sind es noch knapp zwei Prozent. Der Rest geht unter.

Und dass die Kommunikation für Dienstleistungen und Produkte, also die Werbung, dabei nicht die interessanteste ist, scheint klar. Die Konkurrenz, wie oben beschrieben, ist zu gross.

Das also ist das Umfeld, in dem sich unsere Branche bewegt. Doch was tun, wenn man zu den zwei Prozent gehören will, die wahrgenommen werden? Man kann es natürlich, wenn man genug Geld hat, mit der Masse versuchen. Das Publikum mit der immer gleichen Information sozusagen breitschlagen.

Das jedoch können sich nur die grössten und kapitalkräftigsten Unternehmen leisten. Ein durchschnittliches Werbebudget ist, gemessen an den Gesamt-Werbeaufwendungen, sowieso ein lächerlicher Betrag. Zudem steigen die Gesamtausgaben von Jahr zu Jahr. Denn immer mehr Unternehmen investieren in professionelle Kommunikation, da sie wissen, dass sie ohne diese Kommunikation kaum mehr Chancen haben.

Um in dieser Situation gehört und gesehen zu werden, brauchen wir eine neue Generation von Werbung.

Die Forderung nach Werbung, die möglichst objektiv und nur objektiv informiert, hat genau diese Werbung ad absurdum geführt. Erstens, weil, wie wir gesehen haben, diese Information gar nicht mehr aufgenommen werden kann. Und zweitens, weil es je länger je mehr meist Informationen sind, die jedermann schon lange kennt.

Jeder weiss doch inzwischen, dass man zum Zähneputzen Zahnpaste braucht. Dass praktisch jedes Waschmittel gleich weiss wäscht. Dass Kaffee kein Kakao ist. Und dass kein angesehenes Unternehmen es sich heute leisten kann, ein schlechtes Produkt auf den Markt zu bringen, wenn es ein angesehenes Unternehmen bleiben will.

Wir werden in Zukunft also nicht mehr nur mit guten Argumenten für unsere Kunden kämpfen können. Wir werden um Sympathien für ihre Dienstleistungen und Produkte werben müssen.

Denn mit Information pur werden wir nur noch Erfolg haben, wenn wir wirklich etwas Innovatives oder Aussergewöhnliches zu sagen haben. Und das ist inzwischen selten genug.

Wir werden uns deshalb in nächster Zukunft wieder auf etwas Wesentliches besinnen müssen. Und dieses Wesentliche heisst Image. Dieser Begriff, inzwischen in aller Munde, hat seine ursprüngliche Bedeutung verloren. Die Werbung von morgen wird ihm seine Bedeutung zurückgeben müssen.

Denn ein Unternehmen, ein Produkt, eine Dienstleistung haben nicht ein gutes oder schlechtes Layout. Sie haben keine gute oder schlechte Typographie. Sie haben keinen guten oder schlechten Slogan. Sie haben kein gutes oder schlechtes Photo. Und auch keine gute oder schlechte Illustration.

Unternehmen, Dienstleistungen und Produkte haben entweder ein gutes oder ein schlechtes Image.

Image wird die Kommunikation der Zukunft sein. Wir werden unseren Kunden ein präzises Bild von ihrem Unternehmen, von ihren Dienstleistungen und ihren Produkten machen müssen.

Es wird nicht mehr genügen, verbale Konzepte zu visualisieren. Wir werden visuelle Konzepte erfinden müssen. Ein grosses, vierfarbiges Bild wird nicht mehr reichen, um die kommunikatorischen Anforderungen zu erfüllen.

Neue Bildsprachen müssen erfunden werden.

Das heisst Bilder, die aussagekräftig genug sind, um die gewünschte Botschaft zu vermitteln.

Das heisst Bilder, die stark genug sind, um in Sekundenschnelle aufgenommen zu werden.

Das heisst Bilder, die neu genug sind, um das, was wir bewerben, von der Konkurrenz zu unterscheiden.

Das heisst Bilder, die emotional genug sind, um Sympathien zu wecken.

Denn Information, die über Emotion transportiert wird, wird nicht nur schneller aufgenommen, sie wirkt auch anhaltender.

Wenige Unternehmen werben schon so. Benetton mit der Jugend der Welt. Esso mit dem Tiger im Tank. Silk Cut mit dem Schnitt in der Seide. Und Marlboro mit seinen Cowboys. Zu oft noch sind die Gründe für das Entstehen dieser neuen Generation von Werbung wie bei Silk Cut rechtlicher Natur. In Grossbritannien dürfen in der Zigarettenwerbung kaum mehr Aussagen gemacht werden. Oder sie entsteht, weil eine Kampagne international und damit ohne viel Worte funktionieren muss.

Für uns als Konsumenten meine ich: Schöne Aussichten. Denn bald brauchen wir uns nichts mehr aufschwatzen zu lassen. Bald können wir ruhig geniessen, wie man um unsere Sympathie wirbt.

Schön auch für alle, die in Bildern denken können.

FRANCIS SULZER (geb.1949) ist Creative Director und Mitinhaber der Werbeagentur Sulzer, Sutter in Zürich, Schweiz.

Quiconque habite en Occident aujourd'hui se voit confronté à un afflux d'informations qui croît de jour en jour. Une enquête effectuée dans les sept grandes nations industrielles démontre que cinq mille informations différentes déferlent sur nous chaque jour.

Il peut s'agir du détournement d'un avion koweïtien, des penchants astrologiques de Nancy Reagan, du nouveau tube de Michael Jackson, de l'assimilation d'un nouveau programme d'ordinateur au bureau ou d'un meurtre crapuleux aussi bien que de la mort subite de l'oncle Charles ou d'une bonne recette de gâteau d'Alice.

Même en tenant compte du fait que des informations complexes ont été décomposées en fragments mieux discernables pour les besoins de l'enquête, il n'en reste pas moins une somme inimaginable de stimuli que personne ne peut plus espérer traiter dans son cerveau. Et que personne ne veut plus traiter non plus.

Il y a quelques années, le taux de rétention était encore de 40% environ. Il plafonne aujourd'hui à 2%. Les 98% restants constituent du «bruit» sans signification.

Or, il est évident que la communication relative aux prestations de services et aux produits, soit la publicité, ne compte pas nécessairement parmi les informations les plus captivantes. Comme nous venons de le voir, la concurrence est de taille.

Voici donc l'environnement où opère notre industrie. Que faut-il donc faire pour faire partie des 2% réellement perçus? A condition de disposer de pas mal d'argent, on peut bien sûr essayer la quantité. Répéter interminablement la même information jusqu'à ce que le public mette les pouces.

Ce mode de faire n'est à la portée que des très grandes entreprises aux reins financiers solides. Le budget publicitaire moyen est de toute façon ridiculement étriqué quand on le compare à l'ensemble des dépenses publicitaires. Et puis, les dépenses globales augmentent d'année en année. C'est qu'un nombre croissant d'entreprises investissent dans la communication, sachant que sans cette communication elles ne peuvent plus guère escompter aucun impact.

Si l'on veut encore être entendu et vu dans cette situation, il nous faut une nouvelle génération publicitaire.

La publicité courante, celle qui entend renseigner aussi objectivement que possible et sur le seul plan de l'objectivité, cette publicité-là fait du surplace. Primo parce que, nous l'avons vu, ce genre d'information n'a plus de chance d'être perçu. Secundo parce qu'avec le temps la plupart de ces informations s'avèrent connues de tout le monde depuis belle lurette.

Tout le monde a fini par savoir qu'il faut de la pâte dentifrice pour se brosser les dents. Que pratiquement chaque lessive lave blanc, et tout aussi bien qu'une autre. Que le café, ce n'est pas du cacao. Et qu'aucune entreprise qui se respecte ne peut plus se permettre le luxe de mettre un mauvais produit sur le marché dans la mesure où elle veut garder son image d'entreprise respectable.

A l'avenir, nous ne pourrons donc plus nous contenter de nous battre pour nos clients avec de bons arguments. Nous allons devoir briguer les sympathies du public pour leurs services et leurs produits.

L'information en soi ne nous vaudra le succès que lorsque nous aurons vraiment quelque chose de nouveau ou d'extraordinaire à affirmer. Et ça, c'est plutôt rare de nos jours.

Dans un proche avenir, il va donc falloir se rappeler quelque chose d'essentiel. Cette chose essentielle, c'est l'image. Ce concept, dont tout le monde raffole aujourd'hui, a perdu son sens initial. La publicité de demain devra le lui restituer.

C'est qu'une entreprise, un produit, un service n'ont pas une bonne ou une mauvaise maquette. Une bonne ou une mauvaise typo. Un bon ou un mauvais slogan. Une bonne ou une mauvaise photo. Ni non plus une bonne ou une mauvaise illustration.

Les entreprises, services et produits ont soit une bonne, soit une mauvaise image.

L'image sera la communication de l'avenir. Nous allons devoir dresser pour nos clients un tableau précis de leur entreprise, de leurs services et de leurs produits.

Il ne suffira plus de visualiser des concepts verbaux. Nous devrons inventer des concepts visuels. Une image quadrichrome au grand format ne suffira plus pour satisfaire aux exigences de la communication. Il faudra inventer de nouveaux langages visuels.

C'est-à-dire des images qui soient assez expressives pour transmettre le message souhaité.

C'est-à-dire des images qui soient assez puissantes pour être perçues en une fraction de seconde.

C'est-à-dire des images qui soient assez neuves pour distinguer ce que nous prônons de ce que fait la concurrence.

C'est-à-dire des images qui soient assez chargées d'émotions pour susciter la sympathie.

Car l'information transportée par l'emotion n'est pas seulement perçue plus rapidement, elle exerce aussi un effet plus durable.

Rares sont les entreprises à faire déjà ce genre de publicité. Benetton avec la jeunesse du monde. Esso avec le tigre dans le moteur. Silk Cut avec la coupure dans la soie. Et Marlboro avec ses cow-boys. Trop souvent encore, les raisons d'être de l'apparition de cette nouvelle génération publicitaire sont juridiques, comme dans le cas de Silk Cut. C'est qu'en Grande-Bretagne, on n'a plus guère le droit de passer un message en faisant de la réclame pour les cigarettes. Ou bien cette nouvelle publicité doit son origine à l'internationalisme d'une campagne qui doit se passer de l'expression verbale dans la mesure du possible.

Pour nous autres consommateurs, j'estime que ce sont là d'alléchantes perspectives. Car bientôt nous n'aurons plus besoin de nous laisser entuber. Bientôt nous pourrons savourer le plaisir d'être courtisés.

Ce sera également alléchant pour tous ceux qui sont capables de penser en image.

FRANCIS SULZER, né en 1949, est Directeur créatif et copropriétaire de l'agence publicitaire Sulzer, Sutter à Zurich, Suisse.

ADVERTISING

ANNONCES

ANZEIGEN

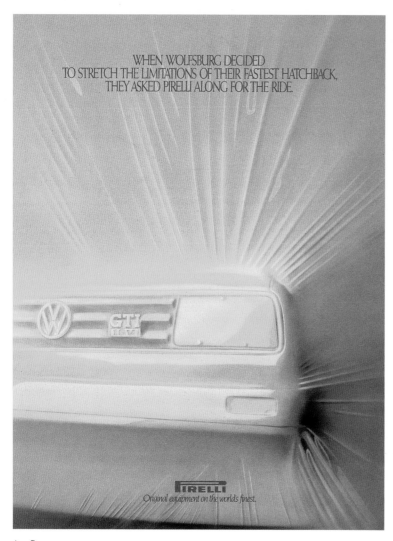

WHEN WOLFSBURG DECIDED
TO STRETCH THE LIMITATIONS OF THEIR FASTEST HATCHBACK,
THEY ASKED PIRELLI ALONG FOR THE RIDE.

PIRELLI
Original equipment on the world's finest.

IN ITS MOST POTENT FORM,
THE CAR HAILED AS "THE BEST HANDLING PRODUCTION SPORTS CAR IN AMERICA"
IS EQUIPPED WITH TIRES OF EQUAL CALIBRE.

Pirelli. Original equipment on the world's finest

ART DIRECTOR:
Michael Arola

PHOTOGRAPHER:
Gene Allison

COPYWRITER:
Kip Klappenback

AGENCY:
Cochrane Chase,
Livingstone & Co.

CLIENT:
Pirelli Tire Corporation

■ 1, 2

GM AM.

9 horas.
É bom começar o dia no
conforto de um Chevrolet.
10 horas.
Avenida Paulista:
reunião de negócios.
13 horas.
Almoço nos Jardins:
follow up.
15 horas.
Centro Empresarial:
apresentação do projeto.
17 horas.
Negócio fechado.
18:15 horas.
Home sweet home.

GM PM.

20 horas.
Sala de apartamento:
replay do dia, compacto.
21 horas.
Sushi-bar da moda:
sashimi, sushi misto e chá
para dois.
22:30 horas.
Jazz e vinho branco.
23:30 horas.
Jazz e vinho branco.
24:01 horas.
É bom começar outro dia no
conforto de um Chevrolet.
24:30 horas.
Home sweet home.

GM BRASIL / Chevrolet
TECNOLOGIA A SERVIÇO DO HOMEM

ART DIRECTOR:
Murilo Felisberto
PHOTOGRAPHER:
Marcos Magaldi
COPYWRITER:
Luis Toledo
AGENCY:
DPZ Propaganda S.A.
CLIENT:
General Motors
■ 3

■ 1, 2 Advertisements for *Pirelli* tires to promote their
image in automotive magazines. The *VW-GTI-16V* and the
Porsche 944 Turbo exemplify the theme of readiness for the
most demanding requirements. (USA)

■ 3 Advertisement with the story of a day and a night in
the life of a *Chevrolet*. (BRA)

■ 1, 2 Inserate für *Pirelli*-Autoreifen, aus einer Image-
kampagne in Autozeitschriften. Einsatz für höchste
Ansprüche – hier für *VW-GTI-16V* und den *Porsche 944
Turbo* – ist das Thema. (USA)

■ 3 Inserat für *Chevrolet*, mit Beschreibung des Ablaufs
eines Tages und einer Nacht – mit *Chevrolet*. (BRA)

■ 1, 2 Annonces pour les pneus *Pirelli*. Campagne de prestige dans les revues spécialisées sur le thème des performances maximales, pour la *VW-GTI-16V* et la *Porsche 944
Turbo*. (USA)

■ 3 Annonce pour les modèles *Chevrolet*. On y évoque un
jour et une nuit passés en *Chevrolet*. (BRA)

Is uw reserve 'n goeie invaller?

Voor banden maakt het 'n groot verschil of u in uw eentje naar de zaak rijdt of bepakt en bezakt naar het zonnige Zuiden jakkert.

Daarom moet u, voor u op vakantie gaat, de spanning van die banden afstemmen op de lading van uw auto en de rij-omstandigheden in het buitenland.

Want te hard of te zacht gepompte banden leiden tot een minder vaste wegligging en een auto die moeilijker bestuurbaar wordt. En tevens tot snellere slijtage en een hoger brandstofverbruik.

MICHELIN MXV BAND

Maar ook het vijfde wiel aan de wagen, de reserveband, dient in prima staat te zijn.

Want is dat niet het geval, dan kan een lekke band op een afgelegen plek tot letterlijk ontroerende vakantietaferelen leiden.

Vandaar dat Michelin u aanraadt om vóór de vakantie te kontroleren of al uw banden de juiste spanning hebben. En te zorgen voor banden waar u onder alle omstandigheden op kunt vertrouwen. Bijvoorbeeld banden uit de serie M van Michelin.

Een serie die loopt van standaard tot extra breed en laag. En die het resultaat is van jarenlang testen, testen en nog eens testen.

Reden waarom de meeste autofabrikanten de serie M van Michelin 'af fabriek' monteren. Is dat bij u niet het geval, laat dat dan doen als uw huidige banden aan vervanging toe zijn. Uw bandenleverancier zal u daarbij graag helpen.

Een Michelin komt pas op de weg als-ie door 'n hel is gegaan. **MICHELIN**

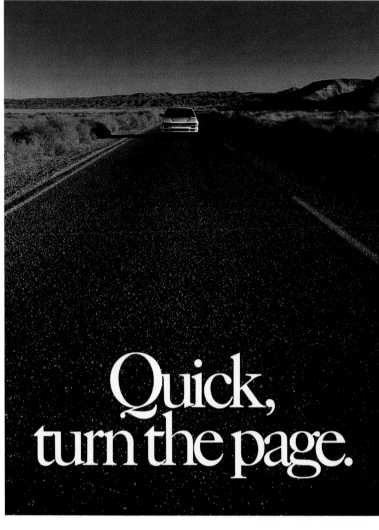

Quick, turn the page.

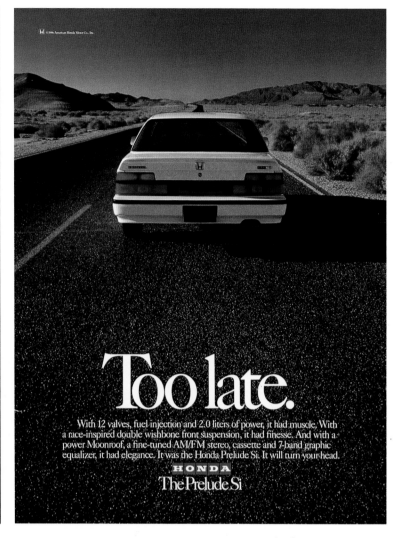

Too late.

With 12 valves, fuel injection and 2.0 liters of power, it had muscle. With a race-inspired double wishbone front suspension, it had finesse. And with a power Moonroof, a fine-tuned AM/FM stereo, cassette and 7-band graphic equalizer, it had elegance. It was the Honda Prelude Si. It will turn your head.

HONDA
The Prelude Si

ART DIRECTOR:
GERARD VAN DER HART
PHOTOGRAPHER:
WILL VAN DER VLUGT
COPYWRITER:
RON WALVISCH
AGENCY:
NOORDERVLIET &
WINNINGHOFF/LEO BURNETT
CLIENT:
MICHELIN
◀■4

ART DIRECTOR:
RICHARD KILE
PHOTOGRAPHER:
BOB STEVENS STUDIO
COPYWRITER:
DAVID HUDSON
AGENCY:
RUBIN POSTAER & ASSOC.
CLIENT:
HONDA MOTOR CO., INC.
■5, 6

■ 4 Newspaper advertisement for *Michelin* tires. It refers to the importance of correct pressure for all tires, including the spare tire, for a trip to the south, and emphasizes the good quality of *Michelin* tires. (NLD)

■ 5, 6 Front and back sides of an advertisement for *Honda* automobiles. The slogan alludes to their speed. (USA)

■ 4 Zeitungsanzeige für *Michelin*-Reifen. Es wird auf die Bedeutung des richtigen Drucks für alle Reifen – auch des Reservereifens – bei der Fahrt in den Süden hingewiesen, sowie auf die gute Qualität der *Michelin*-Reifen. (NLD)

■ 5, 6 «Schlagen Sie die Seite schnell um. Zu spät.» – Vor- der- und Rückseite eines Inserats für *Honda*. (USA)

■ 4 Annonce de journal pour les pneus *Michelin*. On y relève la bonne tenue des pneus de cette marque et l'impor- tance qu'il y a à les gonfler à la pression correcte en cas de voyage au sud, sans oublier la roue de secours. (NLD)

■ 5, 6 «Tournez vite la page. Trop tard!» Recto et verso d'une annonce *Honda*. (USA)

ART DIRECTOR:
Hans Goedicke
PHOTOGRAPHER:
Michael Steenmeijer
AGENCY:
Snabilie, Goedicke, Floor
CLIENT:
Iveco Belgium N.V.
■ 7–9

■ 7–9 "When speed counts, then it's Iveco's *TurboDaily*". Examples from a series of advertisements for transport vehicles from Iveco. (BEL)

■ 7–9 «Wenn es auf Schnelligkeit ankommt, *TurboDaily* von Iveco.» Beispiele aus einer Serie von Anzeigen für Transporter von Iveco. (BEL)

■ 7–9 Exemples d'annonces utilisées dans une campagne publicitaire en faveur des camionnettes *Iveco*. L'accent est mis sur leur rapidité. (BEL)

ALS HET ER BESLIST SNEL MOET ZIJN NEEM JE DE TURBODAILY VAN IVECO.

QUAND RAPIDITÉ OBLIGE: TURBODAILY D'IVECO.

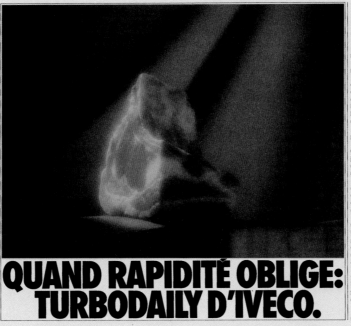

QUAND RAPIDITÉ OBLIGE: TURBODAILY D'IVECO.

ART DIRECTOR:
Cees van Asperen
PHOTOGRAPHER:
Henry ter Hall
COPYWRITER:
Klaas Slooten
AGENCY:
Prad B.V.
CLIENT:
Mercedes-Benz
► ■ 10, 11

■ 10, 11 From an advertising campaign for various *Mercedes* models. The slogans read: "This model also looks great fully clothed" and "Like a good insurance policy". (NLD)

■ 10, 11 Inserate aus einer einheitlich gestalteten Kampagne für verschiedene *Mercedes*-Modelle. Die Slogans: «Angezogen ist auch schön» und «Wie eine gute Versicherung». (NLD)

■ 10, 11 Annonces pour une campagne homogène destinée à faire connaître différentes *Mercedes*. Slogans: «C'est pas mal d'être habillé»; «Comme une bonne assurance». (NLD)

Aangekleed is ook mooi.

Het model dat u hier ziet afgebeeld is even zeldzaam als laten we zeggen een Playmate. Met dit verschil dat de Mercedes 190E 2.3-16 bij voorkeur gekleed gaat. Maar, laten we eerlijk zijn, sommige modellen worden er alleen maar verleidelijker door.

Toch zijn skirts, front- en hekspoiler er niet alleen voor de uiterlijke schijn. Ze zijn bij deze auto even functioneel als de wielen. Deze lichaamsbouw is tekenend voor het sportieve karakter van de auto. De motor, een 4-cilinder met 16 kleppen, geeft een vermogen van 136 kW (185 pk). De 100 km p/u wordt bereikt in ca. 8 sec. De topsnelheid bedraagt zo'n 230 km. Behalve het indrukwekkende accelereren merkt de bestuurder er weinig van. Het onderstel is erop gemaakt om de

ontwikkelde krachten op te vangen. Wendbaarheid, koersvastheid en stabiliteit zijn ingebouwde zekerheden. Zoals ook veiligheid een onvervreemdbare eigenschap van de auto is. Het uithoudingsvermogen is onuitputtelijk. De 190E 2.3-16 heeft drie lange-afstandsrecords stukgereden. Niemand die dat tot op heden heeft kunnen evenaren. Rijden in dit model is sportiviteit ten top. Maar dan in alle rust bedreven. Omdat het comfort dat van de 'grote Mercedessen' evenaart. Een ieder die zich nu aangesproken voelt door de 2.3-16 dient nog een ding te weten: het model beweegt zich uitsluitend in uitdagend zilver of opwindend zwart. **Mercedes-Benz 190E 2.3-16.**

MERCEDES-BENZ NEDERLAND BV. REACTORWEG 25, 3542 AD UTRECHT TELEFOON 030-451911.

Vergelijk het met een goede verzekering.

Er zijn weinig automobielen waar het fundamentele begrip veiligheid zo grondig gestalte gekregen heeft als bij de 200D-300E. Maar om nu te zeggen dat deze Mercedes daardoor even weinig inspirerend is als bijv. de kleine lettertjes in een polis. Nee, daarvoor is een Mercedes teveel Mercedes-Benz. Dus sportieve kracht gekoppeld aan eigenzinnige perfectie. Vooruitstrevend en 'ontevreden' met wat was, vond Mercedes-Benz al in 1951 de veiligheidskooi met kreukelzones uit. Anno nu zijn meer dan 1000 wagens in crash tests beproefd om de best mogelijke bescherming van de inzittenden te realiseren. En om andere verbeteringen uit te proberen. Zoals het in 1978 door Mercedes-Benz ontwikkelde en vandaag

de dag zo veel toegepaste ABS-remsysteem. Maar ook de Airbag en de electronische gordelspanners zijn typische Mercedes innovaties. Zelfs de pedalen zijn bijzonder. Want deze buigen bij een botsing weg van de bestuurder. Zodat ze geen beenletsel veroorzaken. Oog voor detail dus. Als bij het ruime, rustgevende comfort. Luxe zonder onnodige en gebruikersonvriendelijke zaken. Geen batterij van kleine lampjes, wel grote goed afleesbare klokken. Functionele oplossingen voor die eventualiteiten. Kortom, de 200D-300E-serie biedt een hele waarborg. Een waarvan u zich gewoonweg zou moeten verzekeren. **Mercedes-Benz 200D-300E.**

200-230E-260E-300E-200D-250D-300D. MERCEDES-BENZ NEDERLAND BV. REACTORWEG 25, 3542 AD UTRECHT TELEFOON 030-451911.

■ 12–14 Styling and unlimited endurance, freedom and dreams of vacation, adventure and individualism are the themes designed to appeal to young men in these advertisements from a campaign for *BMW* motorcycles. (GER)

■ 15–17 Several examples from a series of advertisements for different models of the German *BMW* motorcycle. Each describes not only the technical specifications and advantages, but also refers to the styling and reliability. Their evaluation, as published in cycling journals, is quoted in part. (USA)

■ 12–14 Inserate aus einer Werbekampagne für *BMW*-Motorräder. Stil und zeitlose Robustheit, Freiheit und Ferienträume, Abenteuer und Individualismus sind die Themen dieser an junge Männer gerichteten Werbung. (GER)

■ 15–17 «Das Motorrad, mit dem Nebenstrassen zum besten Weg werden, Amerika zu sehen.» «Dieses Jahr werden 500 wilde Individualisten ein Motorrad besitzen, das sowohl wild als auch individuell ist.» «Geformt nach den Gesetzen der Physik, nicht nach den Launen der Mode.» Aus einer Kampagne für *BMW*-Motorräder. (USA)

■ 12–14 Annonces d'une campagne en faveur des motos *BMW* axée sur les besoins qui sont au cœur des jeunes: posséder une machine qui défie le temps par son style et sa robustesse, être libre, vivre l'aventure en individualiste. (GER)

■ 15–17 «La moto qui fait des routes secondaires la voie royale pour explorer l'Amérique.» «Cette année, 500 individualistes farouches posséderont une moto à leur image.» «Façonné d'après les lois de la physique, pas d'après les caprices de la mode.» Annonces vedettes d'une campagne pour les motos *BMW*. (USA)

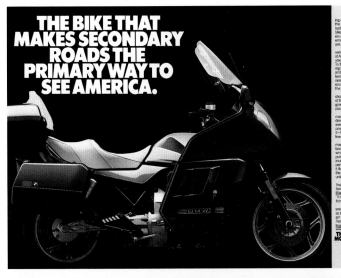

THE BIKE THAT MAKES SECONDARY ROADS THE PRIMARY WAY TO SEE AMERICA.

You've seen them rolling down the interstate by the score—those broad-backed behemoth touring bikes. Supplying their owners endless views of government-landscaped medians and broken white lines.

For a distinctly more varied and memorable look at America, however, we'd advise you to turn to Bavaria. To the BMW K100LT. A touring bike with enough heft and power to cruise the interstates with ease. Yet nimble and light enough to encourage you to seek out the narrowest back roads.

How can the K100LT show you so much more of the U.S.A.? Obsessive engineering would be a good place to begin.

An obsessiveness that made the K100LT two hundred pounds lighter than its average rival. Yet abundantly powerful where you need it—90% of its torque is at a low 3,500 rpm.

An obsessiveness that made the K100LT a textbook in aerodynamics. Its wind-tunnel tested fairing reduces wind and rain while increasing the bike's overall performance. And earned it the longest warranty in the business—3 years and unlimited mileage.*

An obsessiveness, finally, that produced a motorcycle so versatile, Rider Magazine was moved to say, "it could change the direction of motorcycle touring."

A direction which, if you're as inclined to byways as to highways, should begin with a trip to your BMW motorcycle dealer.

THE LEGENDARY MOTORCYCLES OF GERMANY.

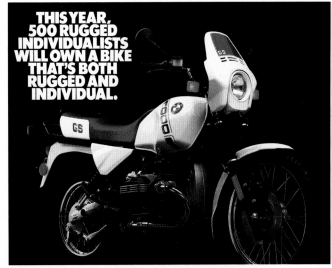

THIS YEAR, 500 RUGGED INDIVIDUALISTS WILL OWN A BIKE THAT'S BOTH RUGGED AND INDIVIDUAL.

In setting the standards for motorcycling over the past 65 years, BMW has resolutely gone its own way. Thus making us highly sympathetic with motorcyclists who share that point of view.

That sympathy has found its most vivid expression in BMW's unique new R100GS.

A motorcycle that bestows on the individualist the freedom to get up in the morning and follow his instincts—not his bike's limitations.

The R100GS accomplishes this by offering a contemporary steel bike rugged enough to handle the rocks and roads of even the most forbidding canyons.

Yet light and nimble enough to negotiate inner-city jungles with equal ease.

And whatever terrain your heart leads you to, the GS assures you unparalleled comfort getting there. Equipped with BMW's revolutionary Paralever Suspension—found on no other motorcycle in the world—it ensures a phenomenal roadholding ability on a variety of road surfaces.

What's more, such unparalleled comfort is enhanced by unparalleled confidence. The GS is driven by BMW's legendary 1000cc horizontally opposed twin engine. Time-and perfected over the last 65 years and possessing a minimum of moving parts, it is arguably the most reliable engine ever built.

To inspire your confidence yet further, BMW's unique three-year warranty is good for unlimited mileage. Rugged, or otherwise.*

If you feel the R100GS's profile clearly matches your own, you should make a point of going to your nearest BMW motorcycle dealer.

It may be the first time you see rugged individualists standing in line.

THE LEGENDARY MOTORCYCLES OF GERMANY.

SCULPTED FROM THE LAWS OF PHYSICS, NOT THE WHIMS OF FASHION.

A perusal of the motorcycle world quickly reveals what the whims of fashion have wrought: mass-produced, look-alike machines, created as much to bolster the rider's self-image as to enhance the joy of riding.

The laws of physics, on the other hand, have produced something far rarer and far less transitory: the BMW K75S. A stunning European sport bike whose real beauty lies in the riding.

To that end, BMW engineers have perfected the K75S's liquid-cooled, fuel-injected 3-cylinder engine. A power source proclaimed by Motorcyclist to be "as smooth as anything on the market."

An engine whose broad power band makes touring equally easy, whether on the autobahn or in the Alps.

Meanwhile, the rider exercising this abundance of power is the beneficiary of a frame-mounted fairing whose design emerged from relentless hours in BMW's wind tunnel. A design that affords you a cool indifference to foul weather as well as an increase in the K75S's overall performance.

Finally, in experiencing the results of a taut sports suspension—a pure product of applied physics—he will see exactly why the editors of both Cycle and Motorcyclist call the K75S "the best-handling BMW ever."

All with something else not exactly fashionable in motorcycling: a 3-year, limited warranty—the longest in the industry.*

Which makes the decision to buy a K75S anything but a whim.

*See warranty at your motorcycle dealer for details
© 1988 BMW of North America, Inc. The BMW trademark and logo are registered.

THE LEGENDARY MOTORCYCLES OF GERMANY.

ART DIRECTOR:
Ulli Bergob

PHOTOGRAPHER:
Thilo Ziemssen

COPYWRITER:
Gert Müller

AGENCY:
Spiess & Ermisch

CLIENT:
BMW Motorrad GmbH + Co.

◀■ 12–14

ART DIRECTOR:
Marcus Kemp/William Hartwell/Alain Briere

CREATIVE DIRECTOR:
Clem McCarthy/Rav Friedel

PHOTOGRAPHER:
Jeff Zwart

COPYWRITER:
Paul Wolfe

AGENCY:
Ammirati & Puris, Inc.

CLIENT:
BMW of North America/ Motorcycles

▲■ 15–17

ART DIRECTOR:
Clem McCarthy/Alain Briere/Yvonne Smith

PHOTOGRAPHER:
Jeff Zwart

COPYWRITER:
Rav Friedel/Paul Wolfe 18
Bill McCullam 19
Martin Puris/ Paul Wolfe 20

AGENCY:
Ammirati & Puris, Inc.

CLIENT:
BMW of North America

■ 18–20

THE ULTIMATE TANNING MACHINE.

There are cars without roofs. And then there's the BMW 325i convertible.

Created for the exhilaration of sunworshippers and high-performance devotees throughout the world, the BMW 325i convertible is, first and foremost, a BMW.

Second and foremost, it is a true, structurally integrated convertible built from the ground up—"unlike some non-factory, sawed-off roof jobs on other makers' cars" (Motor Trend magazine).

Thus, it offers classic BMW roadholding and handling, whether chasing the sun up twisted mountain passes or cruising in the glow of a summer-lit highway.

To experience some hair-raising performance—literally—and enjoy a demonstration of "the most perfect go-away roof yet" (Road & Track), visit your local authorized BMW dealer.

He'll show you how to go from 0 to 60 in 8.6 seconds. (Note: from pale to tan will take you slightly longer.)

THE ULTIMATE DRIVING MACHINE.

"A MAN SHOULD DO THREE THINGS IN HIS LIFE AND DRIVING THIS CAR IS ONE OF THEM."

THE NEW BMW 750iL.

The BMW 750iL has been greeted by the European press as "the superstar of the luxury class" and "not just a milestone in German automotive history, but its crowning achievement."

It was a well-known American automotive editor, however, who offered the spirited appraisal quoted on the opposite page.

Back when mighty Duesenbergs and Bugattis ruled the roadways, he explained, it was said that every man should enjoy three experiences in life: planting a tree, raising a son, and driving a 12-cylinder car.

The new flagship of BMW's 7-Series, he reports, makes the third endeavor more satisfying than ever imagined.

When you sit in the handstitched leather driver's seat, you command not merely an abundance of power but a seamless, unhesitating flow of power that never raises its voice above a whisper.

Your mastery of the most unruly roads is assured by the 750iL's even weight distribution and stable aerodynamics combined with a patented fully-independent suspension

and gas-pressure shocks.

The car is long, spacious, and uncannily quiet. Its amenities are astonishing—a cellular telephone, for example, is standard equipment—and it evinces a level of workmanship that is elsewhere close to extinction.

Your authorized BMW dealer can confirm the truth of this by arranging a thorough test drive of the 750iL.

The noblest transformation that 4,235 pounds of steel, aluminum, glass, and leather have ever undergone.

THE ULTIMATE DRIVING MACHINE.

OF COURSE THERE ARE LESS EXPENSIVE IMITATIONS. THE QUESTION IS, WOULD YOU REALLY WANT TO OWN ONE?

If ever you find yourself lured by the car makers claiming to be "just as good as a BMW but cheaper," keep in mind the old nugget of folk wisdom: "Cheap is expensive."

Because in choosing an imitation over an authentic BMW 325, you will be foregoing an investment so sound, it is projected to hold its value better than 90% of all cars sold this year.*

But the purchase of an imitation is not just expensive at resale time. It's costly every time you turn the key.

It costs you the stirring response of BMW's ingenious 2.7-liter eta engine. Which, by delivering outstanding torque at low rpms, makes the BMW 325 as efficient in

the city as it is exuberant in the country.**

It costs you an internationally-patented, fully-independent suspension born to take the twists and turns of the Bavarian Alps.

Most importantly, it costs you something more easily experienced than articulated: the fit, finish and feel of a true sports sedan, perfected over the years on the great racecourses of Europe. Not overnight in the boardrooms of business.

If you are in the market for a high-performance sedan, your local authorized BMW dealer will be happy to see that you don't become penny-wise and exhilaration-foolish.

THE ULTIMATE DRIVING MACHINE.

ART DIRECTOR:
Kees Janzen/
Jan van de Ven
PHOTOGRAPHER:
Henry ter Hall
COPYWRITER:
Gejus van Diggele
AGENCY:
Geudeker Oerlemans/RSCG
CLIENT:
Citroën Nederland
■ 21

ART DIRECTOR:
Bob Barrie
DESIGNER:
Bob Barrie
PHOTOGRAPHER:
Rick Dublin
COPYWRITER:
Mike Lescarbeau
AGENCY:
Fallon McElligott
CLIENT:
Continental Illinois Bank
■ 22

■ 18-20 Examples from a series of double-spread magazine advertisements for *BMW.* Technical advancement and reliability, comfort, efficiency, and reference to its Bavarian homeland are mentioned in the texts. (USA)

■ 21 "What more can be said for the *Citroën CX?*" Newspaper advertisement for Citroën Netherlands. (NLD)

■ 22 With this advertisement an Illinois bank appeals to the whims of middle-aged men. (USA)

■ 18-20 Anzeigen für *BMW:* «Die vollendete Bräunungsmaschine»; «Ein Mann sollte drei Dinge im Leben tun, eines davon ist, dieses Auto zu fahren»; «Es gibt natürlich billigere Imitationen. Möchten Sie wirklich eine besitzen?». (USA)

■ 21 «Gibt es über den *Citroën CX* noch etwas Neues zu berichten?» Zeitungsinserat für Citroën Nederland. (NLD)

■ 22 Inserat für eine Bank: «Lassen Sie uns Ihre Midlife-Krise finanzieren.» (USA)

■ 18-20 Annonces pour *BMW:* «la machine à bronzer nec plus ultra»; «un homme devrait faire trois choses dans sa vie; l'une, c'est de conduire cette voiture»; «il en existe bien entendu des imitations bon marché; en voudriez-vous?» (USA)

■ 21 «Y a-t-il du nouveau en ce qui concerne la *Citroën CX?*» Annonce de la Citroën Nederland. (NLD)

■ 22 Annonce d'une banque: «Laissez-nous financer votre crise de la quarantaine.» (USA)

■ 23 Advertisement for Cassina, the Italian manufacturer of contemporary furniture and of the authorized reproductions of designers such as Le Corbusier and Mackintosh. (ITA)

■ 24-26 *Conran's*, the New Yorker furniture store, offers good design at reasonable prices as proclaimed in this series of advertisements. (USA)

■ 23 Anzeige für Cassina, den Hersteller von zeitgenössischen Designermöbeln und von Nachbaumodellen der Klassiker wie z.B. von Le Corbusier und Mackintosh. (ITA)

■ 24-26 Beispiele aus einer Inseratenkampagne für das New Yorker Möbelgeschäft *Conran's*, das «gutes Design zu erschwinglichen Preisen» anbietet. (USA)

■ 23 Annonce pour Cassina, le fabricant d'ameublements contemporains, y compris la réédition autorisée des créations de stylistes tels que Le Corbusier et Mackintosh. (ITA)

■ 24-26 Exemples d'annonces conçues pour les ameublements *Conran's*, New York, qui proposent un «design de qualité à des prix abordables». (USA)

ART DIRECTOR:
TITTI FABIANI/FABIO LISCA
PHOTOGRAPHER:
ORIO RAFFO
COPYWRITER:
RIO RAIKES/ERIKA FERRARI
AGENCY:
B COMMUNICATIONS
CLIENT:
CASSINA
■ 23

The importance of aging well.

1956. The 356 Porsche Speedster.

1932. The Zippo Lighter.

1925. Art Deco Lamp.

GOOD DESIGN IS TIMELESS.
Good design transcends Modern or Traditional or Victorian. Instead of going out of fashion, it will, much like a great Broadway actor, span the years with grace and character.

Good design, whenever possible, uses materials that improve with the years as well.

Materials that look better than new, even when they aren't. (Interestingly, some of the most unlikely materials can become more beautiful with time.

Who would have guessed we would now appreciate many early plastic objects?)

Good design is honest. The intentions of both the manufacturer and the designer remain clearly honorable; ten, twenty, fifty years after it comes off the drawing board. Design with integrity, no matter what its age, wears well.

TIMELESS VERSUS TIMELESSNESS.
At Conran's, we believe contemporary design and design that's timeless aren't mutually exclusive.

Certainly, many of the things we sell are distinctly of the Eighties.

But, through careful selection, we believe they will someday feel equally at home in the Nineties and beyond. Much the same way many of our traditional pieces are comfortable in today's contemporary, more urban settings.

GOOD DESIGN, LIKE GOOD WRITING, REQUIRES A GOOD EDITOR.
At Conran's, the actual styling of a piece is not nearly as important to us as its quality of design and construction.

Some of our pieces are originals. Some aren't. Some designs are exclusive. Some are universally available.

Our only real criteria are that it is well made. That it does, what it was intended to do.

This careful editing process has its roots in Great Britain and Europe where Terence Conran opened his first stores 23 years ago.

What it means to you, here and now, is a highly refined selection of furniture,

housewares, toys and other home furnishings from all over the world.

The best of the best for people who are concerned with making their living space comfortable by their own standards, not someone else's.

The kind of place where you can buy a sofa that, twenty-five years from now, will look as good in your living room as a Porsche Speedster will look in your garage.

conran's
SERIOUS DESIGN AT AFFORDABLE PRICES

Good design in a sofa is 98% guts.

In the early 70's, Robert Pirsig doggedly pursued the meaning of quality in a 412-page philosophical journey, Zen and The Art of Motorcycle Maintenance.

It was an exercise that ultimately drove him, as well as many of his readers, crazy.

At Conran's, the pursuit of quality sometimes drives us crazy, too.

But here we became obsessed with the nature of quality in practical, rather than philosophical, terms.

Some of the more important things we look for:

The Frame. To prevent warping and twisting, we insist on kiln-dried hardwood that's free of knots and other imperfections. Well-seasoned maple, ash or oak are ideal.

Softer woods like pine and fir are unacceptable.

Springs. Good springing adds resilience and prevents sagging. Well-made sofas generally use one of four types: Continuous-coil springing, Flexolator springing, Eight-way hand-tied springing. Or drop-in cone springing.

Padding and Filling. Almost every state requires a label listing the contents of fillings used. The best: urethane foam, cotton batting, goose feather and down, and man-made fiberfill such as Dacron or Fortrel.

Upholstery. An upholstered piece that looks exceptionally well-tailored usually indicates high

quality inside, too. Check for tight welting, good cushion fit and straight patterns and seams.

And, above all, remember it's perfectly all right to question a sales person about the type of construction and quality of materials used. Because, even though it takes guts to

build a good sofa, it shouldn't take guts to buy one.

Conran's Custom Upholstered Furniture comes in eight different style frames. Each with multiple options, which include sofa, chair, love seat, sofa bed and ottoman. Your fabric or ours.

conran's
SERIOUS DESIGN AT AFFORDABLE PRICES

ART DIRECTOR:
DEAN HANSON

PHOTOGRAPHER:
RICK DUBLIN

COPYWRITER:
PHIL HANFT

AGENCY:
FALLON McELLIGOTT

CLIENT:
CONRAN'S

■ 24-26

Take this simple taste test.

1. Can you tell the $85 china from the $4.95 plate?

Some people become obsessed with good design.

Often to the extreme of sacrificing quality of life for tasteful things they cannot really afford.

At Conran's, we don't buy the notion that if it isn't expensive, it isn't good taste.

We've found that a sensible balance of quality and price is not only reasonable, but perfectly realistic.

To accomplish this,

we've developed a highly-refined editing process.

This process dates back 23 years to Great Britain

where Terence Conran opened his first stores.

The style of a piece isn't nearly as important

to us as its quality of design and construction.

Some of our pieces are originals. Some aren't. Some are exclusive. Some are universally available.

But all must, without exception, pass the Terence Conran Standard Test Of Good Design:

They must do the job intended.

They must be well made and durable.

And they must be both pleasing to use and pleasing to look at.

Finally, the price should be of this world.

Because people with good taste almost always possess a measure of good sense as well.

2. Which is a better chair design?

A.

B.

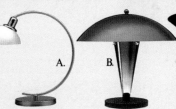

A.   B.   C.

3. Which of these lamps was designed in 1925?

Answers

1. Both are traditional Danish designs. The one from Royal Copenhagen (left) costs $80 more than the one from Conran's (right). Obviously, you can buy a lot of fresh pasta for $80.

2. A trick question. Because "better" design is what you like better. The interesting thing is how well each chair adapts to many different decorative environments. The traditional Windsor (C) can comfortably mix with very contemporary, urban styles. The contemporary Italian design (B) will fit nicely with many traditional furnishings.

3. Actually, none of the lamps were designed in 1925. But all three are inspired by designs first introduced at the 1925 Exposition Internationale in Paris. And each represents well the Conran ideal. That good design transcends periods and styles to "live" long after its creators have departed.

C.

SERIOUS DESIGN AT AFFORDABLE PRICES

ART DIRECTOR:
Wayne Gibson

PHOTOGRAPHER:
Jim Erickson 27
Jay Ahrend 28, 29

COPYWRITER:
Daniel Buss 27
Mike Hughes 28, 29

AGENCY:
The Martin Agency

CLIENT:
Ethyl Corporation

■ 27–29

■ 27–29 Ethyl, the chemical concern, publicizes the meticulous and extensive work of its research and development program in this advertising campaign. (USA)

■ 27–29 Inseratenkampagne des Chemiekonzerns Ethyl, mit der auf die sorgfältige und ausgedehnte Forschungs- und Entwicklungsarbeit hingewiesen wird. (USA)

■ 27–29 Campagne d'annonces de la société chimique Ethyl axée sur le travail de recherche et de développement systématique et important du groupe. (USA)

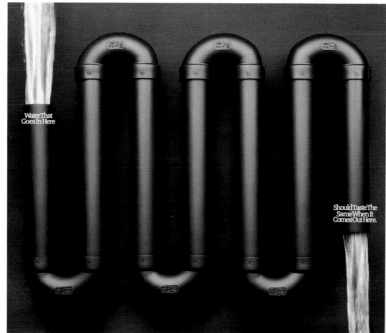

Water That
Goes In Here

Should Taste The
Same When It
Comes Out Here.

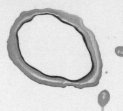

Where Would You Go If You Needed A Chemical That Would Eat Through This Page But Not The One Under It?

Are We Being Too Hard On Ourselves With Our New Quality Control Standards?

ART DIRECTOR:
JAN FORSBERG
PHOTOGRAPHER:
BJÖRN KELLER
COPYWRITER:
GÖRAN ÅKESTAM
AGENCY:
BO AGGERBORG AB
CLIENT:
TENO CONSUMER
■ 30, 31

■ 30, 31 The Swedish company Teno Consumer demonstrates the qualities of its dishcloths *Wettex* in a style suggestive of instruction in biology and physics. (SWE)

■ 30, 31 Im Stil der genannten Unterrichtsfächer Biologie und Physik wird in diesen Anzeigen über die Qualitäten des *Wettex*-Wischtuches informiert. (SWE)

■ 30, 31 Les qualités des chiffons *Wettex* sont exposées dans ces annonces dans le style des branches scolaires nommées ici, la biologie et la physique. (SWE)

Naturlära.

Av naturen har människan utrustats med ett visst mått av fumlighet. Somliga mer, andra mindre. Från naturen har Wettexduken utrustats med bomull och cellulosa. Suger mer, läcker mindre. Naturen kan vi inte ändra på, bara lära oss umgås med. Köp hem Wettex.

Fysik.

En egenskap som är typisk för många vätskor är att de snabbt sprider sig över en plan yta. Detta synes särskilt vanligt bland vätskor som mer av en tillfällighet än av mening hamnat på nämnda yta. Denna fysikaliska regel har dock ett undantag: Förvaras hushållsduken Wettex i anslutning till vätskan, kan den fysikaliska processen inte bara minska utan helt upphöra.

BOLLA. THE ITALIAN CLASSIC.

There's an Italian Classic that's been brightening lives every day for years. It's Bolla Wine. We've been producing classic premium wines for over a century.

Imported by Brown-Forman Beverage Company, Louisville, KY.

In fact, Bolla is the only family owned and operated winery in all of Northern Italy, the richest grape producing region in the world.

It's this heritage that enables us to produce a Valpolicella, Soave, Trebbiano and Bardolino that continue to taste exactly as they should year after year.

Maybe that's one reason the most popular premium wine from Italy is Bolla. And why you may begin seeing Bolla in a slightly different light.

ART DIRECTOR:
MARK MOFFETT
PHOTOGRAPHER:
CHRISTOPHER BROADBENT
COPYWRITER:
RODNEY UNDERWOOD
AGENCY:
AMMIRATI & PURIS, INC.
CLIENT:
BROWN FORMAN
▲■32

ART DIRECTOR:
SHARON L. OCCHIPINTI
DESIGNER:
SHARON L. OCCHIPINTI
PHOTOGRAPHER:
STUART HEIR 33
JIM PORTO 34
COPYWRITER:
SUSAN LIEBER
AGENCY:
DDB NEEDHAM
CLIENT:
COLOMBIAN COFFEE
▼■33, 34

Cream good enough for Colombian Coffee isn't exactly easy to find.

100% Obsessed.

JACK DANIEL'S TENNESSEE COOLER

ART DIRECTOR:
PAT BURNHAM
PHOTOGRAPHER:
JIM MARVY/CRAIG PERMAN
COPYWRITER:
BILL MILLER
AGENCY:
FALLON McELLIGOTT
CLIENT:
JACK DANIELS
■ 35

■ 32 Magazine advertisement for wines imported from northern Italy. (USA)

■ 33, 34 Double-spread advertisement to introduce the logo for *Columbian Coffee*. (USA)

■ 35 Example from an advertising campaign for Jack Daniel's *Tennessee Cooler*. The black-and-white photographs, with the witty and dry dialogue between the two men, appear in all versions. The campaign alludes to a series for *Bartles & James Wine Cooler*, well-known advertisements in which two other elderly men, Frank and Ed, are featured. (USA)

■ 32 Zeitschriftenanzeige für importierte Weine aus Norditalien. (USA)

■ 33, 34 Doppelseitige Anzeigen zur Bekanntmachung des Logos für *Columbian Coffee*. (USA)

■ 35 Beispiel aus einer Anzeigenkampagne für Jack Daniel's *Tennessee Cooler*. Schwarzweissphotos mit witzigen, trockenen Dialogen zwischen den beiden abgebildeten Männern erscheinen in allen Inseraten. Die Kampagne bezieht sich auf erfolgreiche Anzeigen für *Bartles & James Wine Cooler*, in der ebenfalls zwei alte Männer, Frank und Ed, auftreten. (USA)

■ 32 Annonce de magazine pour des vins importés d'Italie du Nord. (USA)

■ 33, 34 Annonces double page pour le lancement du nouveau logo des cafés colombiens, *Columbian Coffee*. (USA)

■ 35 Exemple tiré d'une campagne d'annonces en faveur du *Tennessee Cooler* de Jack Daniel. On y trouve partout des photos noir-blanc émaillées d'un dialogue survolté d'ironie entre les deux hommes qui y figurent. La campagne se réfère à celle du *Bartles & James Wine Cooler*, qui, mettant également en scène deux vieux, Frank et Ed, a connu un grand succès. (USA)

ART DIRECTOR:
MATT HALIGMAN
PHOTOGRAPHER:
PERRY OGDEN 36, 37, 39
ANNIE LEIBOVITZ 38
COPYWRITER:
JOE O'NEILL
AGENCY:
AMMIRATI & PURIS, INC.
CLIENT:
ROSE'S LIME JUICE
■ 36-39

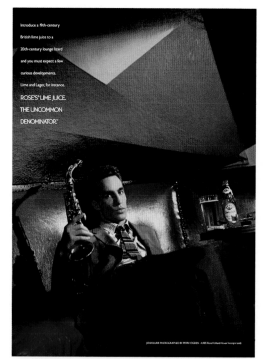

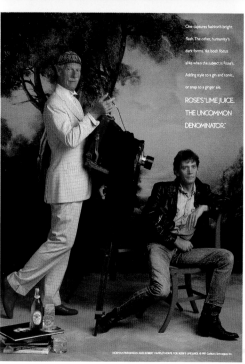

■ 36-39 Well-known people were commissioned for this advertising campaign for *Rose's Lime Juice.* These examples show saxophonist and actor John Lurie, painter James Mathers, the photographers Norman Parkinson and Robert Mapplethorpe, and rock singer Carmel Johnson. (USA)

■ 40-42 "Milk, the white motor" - examples from an advertising campaign to promote milk as an attractive and modern drink which gives energy everywhere and all the time. Target group of these ads were young people. (NLD)

■ 36-39 Der Saxophonist und Schauspieler John Lurie, der Maler James Mathers, die Photographen Norman Parkinson und Robert Mapplethorpe sowie die Rocksängerin Carmel Johnson wurden für diese Anzeigenkampagne für *Rose's Lime Juice* verpflichtet. (USA)

■ 40-42 «Milch, der weisse Motor» - Beispiele aus einer Anzeigenkampagne, deren Ziel es war, Milch bei den jungen Konsumenten als attraktives und modernes Getränk darzustellen, das überall und immer Energien gibt. (NLD)

■ 36-39 Le saxo et comédien John Lurie, le peintre James Mathers, les photographes Norman Parkinson et Robert Mapplethorpe et la chanteuse de rock Carmel Johnson ont prêté leur concours à cette campagne d'annonces pour la limonade *Rose's Lime Juice.* (USA)

■ 40-42 «Le lait, ce moteur blanc» - annonces utilisées dans une campagne de promotion laitière notamment auprès des jeunes, pour une boisson séduisante, moderne, et qui fournit de l'énergie en toutes circonstances. (NLD)

ART DIRECTOR:
Frans Hettinga
PHOTOGRAPHER:
Ruud Posthuma
COPYWRITER:
Harry Kramp
AGENCY:
PPGH/Moussault
CLIENT:
Nederlands Zuivelbureau
■ 40–42

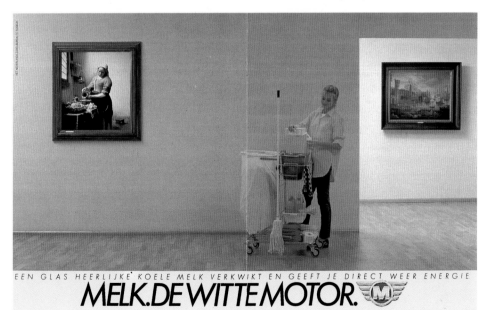

ART DIRECTOR:
ROY GRACE
PHOTOGRAPHER:
BRUNO
COPYWRITER:
DIANE ROTHSCHILD
AGENCY:
GRACE & ROTHSCHILD
CLIENT:
THE PADDINGTON CORP.
■ 43, 44

ART DIRECTOR:
YVONNE SMITH
DESIGNER:
YVONNE SMITH
PHOTOGRAPHER:
JIM HALL/SCOTT SMITH
COPYWRITER:
LAURIE BRANDALISE
AGENCY:
KEYE, DONNA, PEARLSTEIN
CLIENT:
MICROSOFT
■ 45

It's a whole new animal.

Introducing the amazing new mouse from Microsoft.

So superior to others of its kind, it will practically sell itself. Just put a customer in front of it.

You'll find that PC users—all those proud new PS/2™ owners included—can't wait to get their hands on its sleek high-tech body.

Which, by the way, has been carefully redesigned to increase pointing accuracy and significantly decrease wrist movement.

With this mouse in their corner, your customers can use all the hottest software. Like Microsoft® Word 4.0, Windows and Aldus Pagemaker.® Not to mention a few hundred other programs we're sure you won't mind selling them.

And our new mouse can be configured to fit virtually any MS-DOS® machine. From IBM® PCs and XTs to ATs and PS/2s. Of course, there is one thing

about our latest specimen that isn't new: the family name. Over half a million serious PC users have already adopted earlier versions of this Microsoft tool— making it by far the most popular mouse line in the business.

And now for three final selling points. To make our new mouse even more attractive to more people, we've packaged it three different ways. With three different software packages at

three different price points.

There's a choice of EasyCAD,™ Windows 2.0 and PC Paintbrush® for Windows, or Microsoft Paintbrush and Mouse Menus.

So contact your Microsoft representative as soon as you can.

You'll find the only problem you'll have with the new Microsoft mouse is keeping enough of them in your stockroom.

The New Microsoft Mouse.

Microsoft and MS-DOS are registered trademarks of Microsoft Corporation. Pagemaker is a registered trademark of Aldus Corporation. IBM is a registered trademark and   PS/2 is a trademark of International Business Machines Corporation. EasyCAD is a trademark of Evolution Computing. Paintbrush is a registered trademark of ZSoft Corporation.

■ 46, 47 From a publicity campaign in trade journals for the *Code-A-Phone* telephone answering machine. (USA)

■ 48 If the electrical current is interrupted, it is still possible to telephone with the *Alcatel 300SA,* as promised by the Alcatel telephone switching systems. (USA)

■ 49 Double spread announcing the introduction of five new models from Code-A-Phone. (USA)

■ 46, 47 Aus einer Inseratenkampagne in Fachzeitschriften für den *Code-A-Phone*-Telephonbeantworter. (USA)

■ 48 Alcatel, Produzent von Telephon-Schaltsystemen, verspricht in dieser Anzeige, dass es dank *Alcatel 300SA* möglich ist, trotz Stromunterbruch zu telephonieren. (USA)

■ 49 Mit diesem doppelseitigen Inserat gibt Code-A-Phone die Einführung von fünf neuen Modellen bekannt. (USA)

■ 46, 47 Annonces parues dans la presse spécialisée en faveur des répondeurs *Code-A-Phone.* (USA)

■ 48 Le fabricant de centraux téléphoniques Alcatel promet la poursuite d'une conversation téléphonique en cas de panne de courant, grâce à l'*Alcatel 300SA.* (USA)

■ 49 Cette annonce double page présente cinq nouveaux modèles de répondeurs *Code-A-Phone.* (USA)

ART DIRECTOR:
MATT MYERS
PHOTOGRAPHER:
STEVE BONINI 46, 47
GARY NOLTON 49
COPYWRITER:
PAMELA SULLIVAN
AGENCY:
BORDERS, PERRIN &
NORRANDER, INC.
CLIENT:
CODE-A-PHONE CORP.
■ 46, 47, 49

ART DIRECTOR:
DIANE COOK TENCH
PHOTOGRAPHER:
STEVE BRONSTEIN
COPYWRITER:
JOHN MAHONEY
AGENCY:
THE MARTIN AGENCY
CLIENT:
ALCATEL CORP.
► ■ 48

This used to be the best telephone answering device for the home.

In the fifties there was somebody always home. And a Code-A-Phone answering machine was something you found in the office. But today over half of all women work outside the home. And today we make a dozen machines to answer for them. As well as the latest business equipment, like voice mail. Where do we go from here? Wherever there's a call for us.

CODE·A·PHONE
A SUBSIDIARY OF CONRAC CORPORATION

There's a place for companies that ignore the market.

Some of the most venerable names in American business were folding in the late fifties, just as we were getting under way. So for thirty years we've made it a practice to find out what the customer wants before we produce it. Continually researching the market is time-consuming and expensive, and anyone who hasn't been around for a while might try to take a shortcut. But you don't have to go along for the ride.

CODE·A·PHONE
A SUBSIDIARY OF CONRAC CORPORATION

Portland, Oregon

NOW YOUR REMOTE PHONE CUSTOMERS WON'T NOTICE A LITTLE PROBLEM AT THE CENTRAL OFFICE.

It's impossible to predict just what will disrupt phone service between your central office and your remote customers.

But, as sure as there are bad Japanese horror movies, one day something will.

Luckily, now there's a Digital Loop Carrier that will help you put your foot down and stamp out the problem once and for all.

Introducing the Alcatel 300SA.

The 300SA is the only DLC that provides emergency stand-alone capability. So, no matter what disasters may strike the link with the main office, up to 240 of your customers will be able to keep on talking within their community.

But the 300SA is good for a lot more than emergencies; it's also an efficient substitute for a Remote Service Unit. It can be installed at between 50 and 75% of the cost, generate more income and fit nicely into your present telephone network.

If you'd like to know more about the Alcatel 300SA, just call 919-850-6000 or write to us at 3128 Smoketree Court, Raleigh, NC 27604.

ALCATEL
NETWORK SYSTEMS
©1987 Alcatel Corp.

Success is great, but you'd better be ready to follow it up.

Last year our first line of mass-market answering machines sold phenomenally. This year we have five new lines, including feature phones. Give us a whirl. **CODE·A·PHONE**
A SUBSIDIARY OF CONRAC CORPORATION

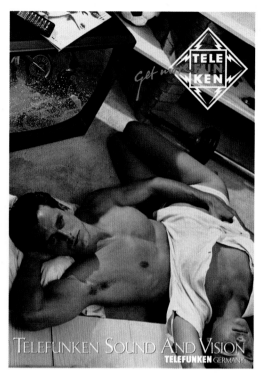

ART DIRECTOR:
Bernd Kracke/Fritz Haase
PHOTOGRAPHER:
Bruce Weber
COPYWRITER:
Bernd Kracke/Jan Ganser/
Bernd Imgram
AGENCY:
MA Media Productions GmbH
■ 50–52

ART DIRECTOR:
Hans Goedicke
PHOTOGRAPHER:
Aernout Overbeeke
AGENCY:
Snabilie, Goedicke, Floor
CLIENT:
E.C.I. Bookclub
▼■ 53

ART DIRECTOR:
Henny van Varik
PHOTOGRAPHER:
Ronald van Teunenbroek/
Peter Bos
COPYWRITER:
Ron Meijer/Raymond Nuyten
AGENCY:
GGK Amsterdam
▼■ 54

KOOP EEN REISBOEK, WAAR U DROOMT VAN VERRE LANDEN.

De echte lezer gaat het liefst op reis nog voor z'n koffers gepakt zijn.

Beleeft avonturen bij voorkeur met een kop koffie naast zich.

En laat plaatsbeschrijvingen graag op zich inwerken terwijl de hond aan z'n voeten ligt te slapen.

Dus gewoon in z'n eigen makkelijke stoel.

Maar gek genoeg staat lang niet elke lezer er bij stil dat je vanuit

diezelfde makkelijke stoel ook heel plezierig boeken kunt kopen.

Door lid te worden van ECI. Want ECI selecteert elk kwartaal uit het gigantische aanbod ruim vijfhonderd titels voor u.

Dus of u nu het debuut van Rudi van Dantzig, 'n mooie Milan Kundera, een verrassende Büch, een onthullende Le Carré of een handig doe-het-zelf boek zoekt, bij ECI vindt u het.

Elke gids van ECI is als 't

ware een winkel boordevol boeken.

Hebt u uw keus gemaakt dan vult u de bestelkaart in, belt met ECI of stapt naar één van de ECI clubwinkels.

U bestelt zoals 't u het best uitkomt.

Makkelijker kan niet. En voordeliger kunt u ook nauwelijks ergens terecht.

Wat niet zo vreemd is als u weet dat ECI met ruim één miljoen leden de grootste boekenclub is.

ECI kan daardoor groot en dus uiterst scherp inkopen.

Maar dat merkt u snel genoeg als u nu lid wordt.

U kunt daarvoor gratis bellen met de ECI klantenservice: 06-0221717.

Dan hoort u ook meteen wat de welkomstaanbieding is.

Een goed boek koop je makkelijker bij ECI.

Van Mozart tot Madonna in 1,3 sec.

Dit keer eens niet over het acceleratievermogen onder de motorkap, maar onder het kofferdeksel.

Want daar hoort de Sony CDX A20. Een perfecte CD-speler met wisselaar voor tien CD's. Waardoor u in luttele seconden overschakelt van Mozart naar Madonna, of van Buddy Miles naar Miles Davis.

Gewoon, door een simpele druk op de knop van het afstandsbedieningspaneel. Het enige onderdeel dat zich in de buurt van het dashboard bevindt en dat eenvoudig in het handschoenenkastje kan worden opgeborgen.

Terwijl de rest van de apparatuur stevig verankerd - en onzichtbaar - in de kofferruimte zit. (Een knappe dief, die daar nog brood in ziet.)

Bovendien vormt de CDX A20 een uitstekende combinatie met de XR 7300. Met deze stereo radio-

cassettespeler kunt u de CD-wisselaar automatisch sturen. De XR 7300 is uitgerust met een vermogen van 4 x 30 watt, u kunt hem automatisch afstemmen en er kunnen 18 FM en 6 MG voorkeuzestations in het geheugen worden opgeslagen. Het apparaat wordt inclusief anti-diefstalslede geleverd.

Wie dus niet alleen zijn ogen maar ook z'n oren wil strelen, rust z'n paradepaardje uit met de CDX A20 en de XR 7300.

En bij aanschaf kunt u natuurlijk gebruik maken van The Card van Sony. De Sony dealer kan u daar alles over vertellen. Brandsteder Electronics B.V., Jan van Gentstraat 119, 1171 GK Badhoevedorp. SONY.

Vergelijk en Sony wint.

Wanneer er, waar ook ter wereld, digitaal wordt opgenomen, gemonteerd of afgewerkt, gebeurt dat in meer dan 90% van de gevallen met de professionele digitale apparatuur van Sony.

Als je dat eenmaal weet, weet je eigenlijk ook van wie je een CD-speler zou moeten hebben.

Want wie het er perfect op weet te krijgen, weet het er natuurlijk ook weer perfect af te halen. Het mooiste voorbeeld is 't paradepaardje van Sony, de CDP 555 ESD.

Met viervoudige oversampling, gescheiden DA-converters voor het linker- en het rechter-kanaal en het zogeheten Gibraltar chassis.

Genoemd naar de rots van Gibraltar, omdat het is gemaakt van een materiaal dat elke vorm van trilling of resonantie uitsluit.

Om diezelfde reden is het zenuwcentrum van de CD, 't optische blok, bij de CDP 555 ESD in een trillingsvrij ceramisch chassis gebouwd. Met als resultaat een nog zuiverder geluid.

De digitale voorsprong van Sony vindt u uiteraard ook terug in de andere CD-spelers. 17 Zijn het er. Voor in de huiskamer, voor in de auto of voor buiten. Allemaal met 'n digitaal filter. Vanaf f 599,-.

Met de keuze uit vele boeiende extra's als Shuffle play, afstandsbediening en talloze programmeermogelijkheden. U kunt zelfs kiezen uit wisselaars voor vijf of tien CD's.

En wilt u het gemak van kopen met een credit card, dan kunt u betalen met 'The Card' van Sony. De Sony dealer kan u daar alles over vertellen.

Reden te meer om alleen op uw wensen, uw oren en de experts af te gaan. Bel voor het allerlaatste CD-nieuws, de Sony CD-nieuws-lijn, 06-91091099 (50 cent per minuut). SONY

Vergelijk en Sony wint.

Als je eenmaal weet waarmee CD's worden opgenomen, weet je eigenlijk ook waarmee je ze moet afspelen.

ART DIRECTOR:
Henny van Varik
PHOTOGRAPHER:
Peter Bos
COPYWRITER:
Ron Meijer
AGENCY:
GGK Amsterdam
CLIENT:
Brandsteder Electronics
■ 55

Industrial Design Study: WORKSTATION by *frogdesign*, Germany 0-7453/7071, California (408) 866-1801, Japan (03) 442-5558 (Photo by Dietmar Henneka)

Divide et impera.

Industrial Design for Apple: II GS system by **frogdesign**, Germany (07453) 8000, California (408) 866-1801, Japan (03) 442-5558 (Photo by Dietmar Henneka)

Industrial Design for The Helen Hamlyn Foundation: Remote Control by **frogdesign**, California (408) 8 66-18 01 and Germany 0-74 53/70 71 (Photo by D. Henneka)

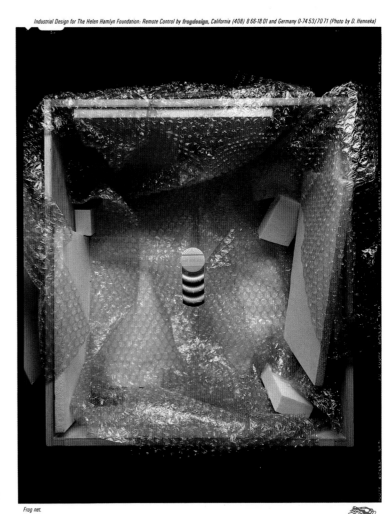

Per aspera ad astra.

Frog net.

ART DIRECTOR:
ANDREAS STEPHAN
PHOTOGRAPHER:
DIETMAR HENNEKA
AGENCY:
FROGDESIGN
■ 56-58

■ 56–58 Ads for several industrial designs created by frog-design: *56* shows a portable workstation used for self-promotion; *57* is a computer system designed for Apple and *58* a remote control for the Helen Hamlyn Foundation. (USA)

■ 56–58 Anzeigen für verschiedene Gegenstände, die von der Firma frogdesign entworfen wurden: *56* zeigt eine tragbare «Arbeitsstation», *57* ein Computersystem, das für Apple entwickelt wurde, und *58* eine Fernsteuerung. (GER)

■ 56–58 Pour divers designs industriels réalisés par frog-design. *56:* bureau portable, autopromotion; *57:* système informatique conçu pour les ordinateurs Apple; *58:* télé-commande créée pour la Helen Hamlyn Foundation. (USA)

■ 59–62 Examples from a publicity campaign for *Skiathlom*, a watch manufactured by Timex and primarily designed for skiers. The over-sized knobs permit even those wearing gloves to easily switch from time indicator to thermometer or stop-watch. (USA)

■ 59–62 Beispiele einer Inseratenkampagne für *Skiathlom*, eine Uhr, die in erster Linie für Skifahrer entworfen wurde. Übergrosse Knöpfe ermöglichen die Umstellung von der Zeitangabe auf das Thermometer oder den Chronographen, auch wenn man Handschuhe trägt. (USA)

■ 59–62 Exemples d'annonces publiées dans une campagne *Skiathlom* - une montre destinée en premier lieu aux skieurs. Des boutons surdimensionnés assurent le passage à la fonction thermomètre ou chronographe même pour un skieur empêtré dans ses gants ou mitaines. (USA)

ART DIRECTOR:
HOUMAN PIRDAVARI
PHOTOGRAPHER:
TERRY HEFFERNAN
COPYWRITER:
BRUCE BILDSTEN
AGENCY:
FALLON McELLIGOTT
CLIENT:
TIMEX
■ 59–62

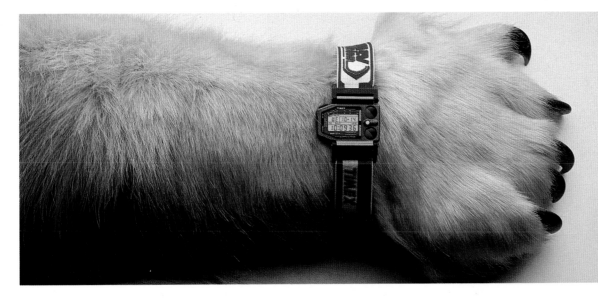

A ski watch should fit over your coat.

We not only designed the Timex Skiathlom* to fit the way you ski, but also to fit the way you dress while skiing.

It comes with two interchangeable straps. There's a high-tech resin strap, as well as an adjustable elastic one designed to fit over a parka or any part of your arm.

Even its buttons were designed oversized, so you can call up data from its sophisticated chronograph or thermometer with your gloves on.

For the Timex Skiathlom dealer that's nearest you, call 1-800-FOR-TIMEX. And we'll tell you where you can get your mitts on one. **TIMEX Skiathlom**

A ski watch should tell you how cold it is.

With its goggle-like strap and over-sized buttons, The Timex Skiathlom* is not only a true ski chronograph, it's a ski thermometer.

As a chronograph it's precise to 1/100th of a second, with selectable split or lap modes.

As a thermometer it's capable of readouts in Fahrenheit or Celsius, with both a digital and a bar-graph display. Plus, there's a 24-hour countdown timer, daily alarm, backlight and hourly chime.

If you'd like to see a Timex Skiathlom on your wrist, you're getting warmer. Call 1-800-FOR-TIMEX for your dealer. **TIMEX Skiathlom**

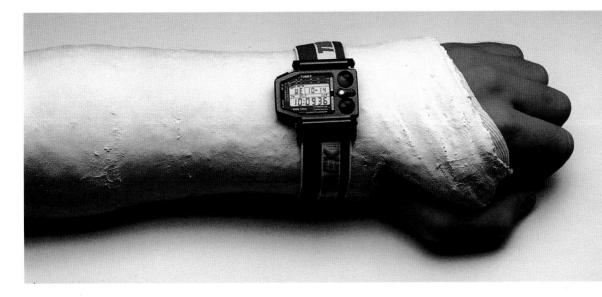

A ski watch should be hard to break.

With its sophisticated chronograph and built-in thermometer, the new Timex Skiathlom* is not only designed specifically for skiing. It's built for the punishment your body takes while skiing.

The falls. The cold. The wet.

Its case is water-resistant to 50 meters. Its elastic strap stretches to fit over bulky skiwear. Even its battery is designed to last four long years.

Call 1-800-FOR-TIMEX for the dealer that's nearest you. And be kind to yourself for a change. **TIMEX Skiathlom**

ART DIRECTOR:
HOUMAN PIRDAVARI
PHOTOGRAPHER:
STEVE UMLAND
COPYWRITER:
TOM MCELLIGOTT
AGENCY:
FALLON MCELLIGOTT
CLIENT:
WOLVERINE
■ 63, 64

We reluctantly admit that there are some tennis problems the Brooks Nouveau KW can't solve.

The new Brooks® Nouveau KW can't control the weather. Or your forehand. Or for that matter, your emotions. But one thing it can help keep under control is tennis injuries.

How? A major technological breakthrough called the Kinetic Wedge.™ A patented feature available only in Brooks tennis shoes for men and women.

To learn how the Kinetic Wedge can help reduce injuries and increase comfort, visit your athletic shoe store. Or call 1-800-233-7531 for a free technical bulletin.

BROOKS.

Nouveau KW

Unfortunately, there are some running problems even the Brooks Triad can't solve.

The new Brooks® Triad cannot stop dogs, rain or city smog. But it can help stop the one thing that takes more runners off the road than anything else: running injuries.

How? A major breakthrough in running technology called the Kinetic Wedge.™ A patented feature available only in Brooks running shoes for men and women.

To learn how the Kinetic Wedge can reduce injuries and give you more running comfort, visit your athletic shoe store. Or for a free technical bulletin call 1-800-233-7531.

BROOKS

Triad

■ 63, 64 *Brooks* sports shoes cannot influence the weather, nor the forehand stroke of a tennis player, nor ward off the threat of a snarling dog. But thanks to their special construction, they can at least help to reduce injuries. This is the message of the finely printed text accompanying the black-and-white photographs of tennis and track shoes. From an advertising campaign for *Brooks*. (USA)

■ 65-68 Advertisements from a magazine campaign for *Penn* tennis balls. (USA)

■ 63, 64 Beispiele aus einer Inseratenkampagne mit Schwarzweissphotos für *Brooks* Tennis- und Rennschuhe. *Brooks*-Sportschuhe können zwar das Wetter nicht beeinflussen oder die Vorhand des Tennisspielers und auch keine gefährlichen Hunde aufhalten, aber sie können durch ihre spezielle Konstruktion Sportverletzungen vermindern - dies ist die Werbeaussage des kleingedruckten Textes. (USA)

■ 65-68 Anzeigen aus einer Zeitschriftenkampagne für *Penn* Tennisbälle. (USA)

■ 63, 64 Annonces pour une campagne illustrée en noir et blanc en faveur des chaussures de tennis et à pointes *Brooks*. Si la marque n'a guère de pouvoir sur le temps ni sur le coup droit d'un joueur et encore moins sur un chien méchant, elle excelle cependant à prévenir les mauvaises blessures grâce à des particularités de construction que le texte imprimé en petits caractères met en évidence. (USA)

■ 65-68 Annonces pour une campagne de magazine en faveur des balles de tennis *Penn*. (USA)

ART DIRECTOR:
HOUMAN PIRDAVARI
PHOTOGRAPHER:
DAVE JORDANO
COPYWRITER:
JARL OLSEN
AGENCY:
FALLON MCELLIGOTT
CLIENT:
*PENN ATHLETIC
PRODUCTS DIVISION*
■ 65–68

We admit there are balls which may outlast the new Pro Penn.

Pro Penns are designed to last 30% longer than our regular ball. Which puts them in a league all their own. Available only at selected pro shops.

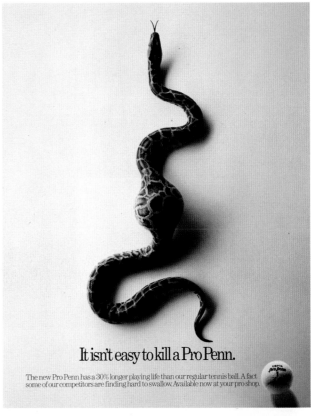

It isn't easy to kill a Pro Penn.

The new Pro Penn has a 30% longer playing life than our regular tennis ball. A fact some of our competitors are finding hard to swallow. Available now at your pro shop.

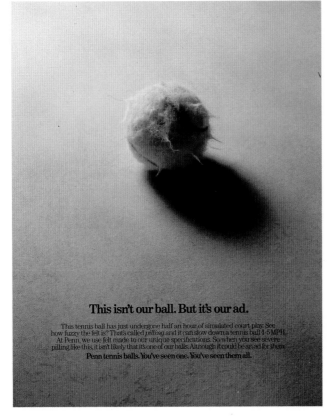

This isn't our ball. But it's our ad.

This tennis ball has just undergone half an hour of simulated court play. See how fuzzy the felt is? That's called *pilling* and it can slow down a tennis ball 4-5 MPH. At Penn, we use felt made to our unique specifications. So when you see severe pilling like this, it isn't likely that it's one of our balls. Although it could be an ad for them.

Penn tennis balls. You've seen one. You've seen them all.

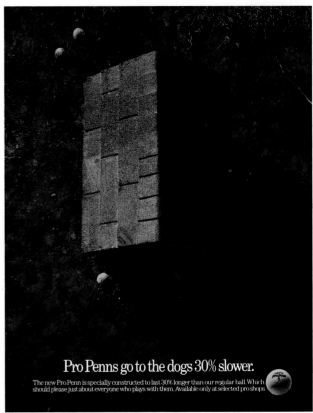

Pro Penns go to the dogs 30% slower.

The new Pro Penn is specially constructed to last 30% longer than our regular ball. Which should please just about everyone who plays with them. Available only at selected pro shops.

Best Performance in a pair of Reeboks April 1, 1987

Best Performance in a pair of Reeboks December 10, 1985

Best Performance in a pair of Reeboks October 6, 1983

ART DIRECTOR:
Cheryl Heller
DESIGNER:
Cheryl Heller
PHOTOGRAPHER:
Herb Ritts
COPYWRITER:
Jerry Cronin
AGENCY:
Heller Breene
CLIENT:
Reebok
■ 69–71

ART DIRECTOR:
Jan van Meel
PHOTOGRAPHER:
Hans Kroeskamp
COPYWRITER:
Fred Hekket
AGENCY:
PPGH/Moussault
CLIENT:
Euro Fashions
▼ ■ 76

CRUYFF VERKOOPT VAN BASTEN.

De zaak is rond: Cruyff gaat Van Basten verkopen. En hij gaat niet naar 't buitenland, zoals velen vreesden.

Dankzij Cruyff Sports kunnen we Van Basten gelukkig in eigen land gaten zien trekken, een-tweetjes zien aangaan en juweeltjes zien scoren.

Cruyff Sports komt namelijk met een Van Basten in supervorm. Een voortreffelijke voetbalschoen die voluit de Van Basten Super heet.

Gemaakt van vederlicht, soepel leer dat de voet bij iedere beweging optimaal steun geeft.

Voorzien van doorgestikte zijkanten die een perfecte kromme bal kunnen afgeven.

Met extra hoge hielstukken, waardoor hij na een paar felle sprints niet gaat slippen.

En met een degelijk uitgekiend noppenprofiel, dat zelfs op de zwaarste velden prima grip geeft.

De Van Basten Super is een eredivisie-schoen met Europacup-aspiraties. En het zou Cruyff Sports niet verbazen als buitenlandse clubs ook voor deze Van Basten grote interesse hebben.

Dan moeten ze wel naar de betere sportzaak. Want daar vind je de Cruyff Sports voetbalschoen, in vele modellen, voor junioren en echte profs, in prijs variërend van f 69,– tot f 279,–.

Vlak naast de Cruyff Sports zaalvoetbalschoenen en trainingspakken. Bel voor het dichtstbijzijnde verkoopadres: 020 - 5112880.

HET RESULTAAT VAN 20 JAAR TOPVOETBAL

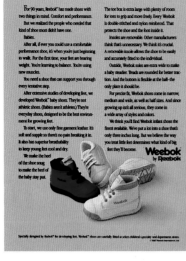

ART DIRECTOR:
CHERYL HELLER
DESIGNER:
CHERYL HELLER
PHOTOGRAPHER:
ANNIE LEIBOVITZ/MYRON
COPYWRITER:
JOE LOVERING 72-74
MARK MYERS 75
AGENCY:
HELLER BREENE
CLIENT:
REEBOK
■ 72-75

■ 69-75 Examples of various advertisements for Reebok's line of sports shoes and *Weebok,* an infant shoe which is also produced by Reebok. The text on the double spreads refers to Reebok's long history as a manufacturer of shoes, and to the importance for babies to wear shoes which are both comfortable and sturdy. (USA)

■ 76 Magazine ad for a Dutch sport shoe proclaiming it "the result of 20 years of superb soccer". (NLD)

■ 69-76 Anzeigen für *Reebok*-Sportschuhe und für Babyschuhe *Weebok*. Im Text auf den Doppelseiten wird erklärt, dass Reebok seit 90 Jahren immer zwei Dinge bei der Produktion ihrer Sportschuhe im Auge hatte: Bequemlichkeit und Leistung. Da dies auch das Wichtigste bei Babyschuhen ist, sei dies die Devise für deren Herstellung. (USA)

■ 76 Zeitschriftenreklame für einen holländischen Fussballschuh. «Das Resultat aus 20 Jahren Spitzenfussball.» (NLD)

■ 69-75 Annonces pour des chaussures de sport *Reebok* et des chaussures pour bébés *Weebok*. Le texte explique que Reebok n'a visé pendant 90 ans qu'au confort et aux performances de ses chaussures de sport, puis que ce chausseur s'est rendu compte que les personnes qui aspiraient le plus à ces qualités ne les trouvaient guère: les bébés. D'où *Weebok*. (USA)

■ 76 Publicité de magazine pour une marque hollandaise de chaussures de foot, «en vedette depuis 20 ans.» (NLD)

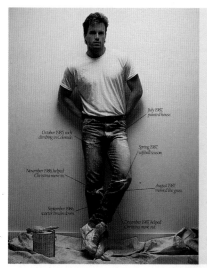

Only jeans that fit this well, get the chance to look this bad.

July 1987 painted house.

October 1985 rock climbing in Colorado.

November 1986 helped Christina move in.

Spring 1987 softball season.

August 1987 mowed the grass.

September 1986 scooter breaks down.

December 1987 helped Christina move out.

Lee® Storm Rider® jeans might just be the best fitting and most comfortable jeans you'll ever wear. And wear. And wear. And wear. And wear. **Storm Riders** **Lee**

You shouldn't have to spend the best years of your life waiting for your jeans to look this good.

In the accepted and time-honored pursuit of worn looking jeans, there is, at last, a genuine alternative to years of hard wear.
New Lee® Frosted Riders®
Lee Frosted Riders give you the same worn look and character you get from jeans that are two or three years old. The difference is you don't have to wait two or three years to get it. Available in relaxed fitting jeans, jackets, skirts and bibs. Grey, black and indigo. **Frosted Riders** **Lee**

Unfortunately, by the time your last pair of jeans looked this good, they were worn out.

It's such a pity. To have gone through so much together, only to part company just when your jeans finally have just the right look.
But that's the whole idea behind new Lee® Frosted Riders®
Lee Frosted Riders give you the same worn look and character you get from jeans that are two or three years old. The difference is you don't have to wait two or three years to get it. Available in relaxed fitting jeans, jackets, skirts and bibs. Grey, black and indigo. **Frosted Riders** **Lee**

Most jeans that look this good have ten times the mileage.

If you don't have time to wait for your jeans to look like they've been around the block a few times, new Lee® Frosted Riders® are for you.
With Lee Frosted Riders, you get the same worn look and distinctive character that normally comes with two or three years of hard living. The difference is you don't have to wait two or three years to get it.
But you better jump into a pair soon. These jeans are going faster than a bored and stroked '57 Chevy on a lonely country road.
Now available in grey, black and indigo. **Frosted Riders** **Lee**

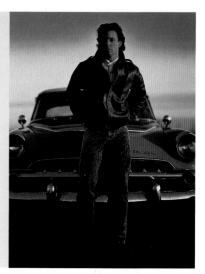

■ 77–83 Examples from an advertising campaign for *Storm Riders* and *Frosted Riders,* two lines of blue jeans from Lee. The headlines give prominence to their durability and worn look. (USA)

■ 77–83 Beispiele aus einer Anzeigenkampagne für die beiden Jeans-Linien *Storm Riders* und *Frosted Riders* von Lee. Die Strapazierfähigkeit und der «getragene Look» werden in den Headlines besonders hervorgehoben. (USA)

■ 77–83 Exemples tirés d'une campagne d'annonces pour les deux gammes de jeans *Storm Riders* et *Frosted Riders* de Lee. La résistance à l'usure du tissu et son aspect délavé sont soulignés dans les slogans employés. (USA)

ART DIRECTOR:
Mark Johnson
PHOTOGRAPHER:
Randy Miller 77
Dennis Manarchy 78-80
COPYWRITER:
Bill Miller 77
Phil Hanft 78-80
AGENCY:
Fallon McElligott
CLIENT:
Lee Jeans
◀■ 77-80

ART DIRECTOR:
Mark Johnson
PHOTOGRAPHER:
Randy Miller
COPYWRITER:
Bill Miller
AGENCY:
Fallon McElligott
CLIENT:
Lee Jeans
■ 81

ART DIRECTOR:
Bob Barrie
DESIGNER:
Bob Barrie
PHOTOGRAPHER:
Rick Dublin
COPYWRITER:
Phil Hanft
AGENCY:
Fallon McElligott
CLIENT:
Lee Jeans
■ 82

ART DIRECTOR:
Tom Lichtenheld
PHOTOGRAPHER:
Jean Moss
COPYWRITER:
George Gier
AGENCY:
Fallon McElligott
CLIENT:
Lee Jeans
■ 83

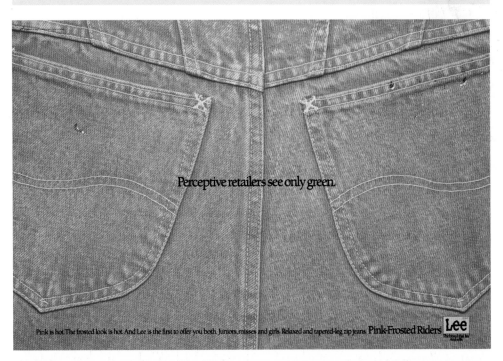

THE MOST EXTRAVAGANT SHOES, BOOTS
AND ACCESSORIES IN MANHATTAN.
440 PARK AVENUE, NEW YORK, N.Y. 10022
1-800-634-9884, N.Y. STATE 212-755-4197
FROM THE WOMEN'S COLLECTION, SECRET GARDEN.
SPRING/SUMMER CATALOG, SIX DOLLARS.

SUSAN **BENNIS**/WARREN **EDWARDS**®

ESPRIT
J E A N S

ART DIRECTOR:
Stan Eisenman
DESIGNER:
Susan Bennis/
Warren Edwards
PHOTOGRAPHER:
Lisa Charles Studio
AGENCY:
Eisenman & Enock
CLIENT:
Susan Bennis/
Warren Edwards
■ 84

ART DIRECTOR:
Tamotsu Yagi
PHOTOGRAPHER:
Roberto Carra
STUDIO:
Esprit Graphic Design
CLIENT:
Esprit De Corp.
■ 85

PHOTOGRAPHER:
Sheila Metzner
CLIENT:
Fendi Profumi S.p.A.
►■ 86

■ 84 Magazine ad for a store selling "Manhattan's most extravagant shoes, boots and accessories". (USA)

■ 85 With a single metal button and a large format, Esprit promotes its jeans. (GER)

■ 86 "Passion of Rome", a phrase used to extol a perfume by Fendi in an advertisement which appeared worldwide in various magazines.

■ 84 Anzeige für ein Geschäft mit den «extravagantesten Schuhen, Stiefeln und Accessoires in Manhattan». (USA)

■ 85 Nur mit dem Metallknopf wirbt Esprit in dieser gross-formatigen Anzeige für seine Jeans. (GER)

■ 86 Das Parfum *Fendi* wird in diesem Inserat, welches weltweit in verschiedenen Zeitschriften erschienen ist, als «Leidenschaft von Rom» angepriesen.

■ 84 Annonce pour une boutique offrant les «chaussures, bottes et accessoires les plus *in* de Manhattan.» (USA)

■ 85 Annonce au grand format pour les jeans *Esprit* en-tièrement centrée sur ce bouton métallique. (GER)

■ 86 Annonce parue simultanément dans les grands maga-zines de monde. On y présente le parfum *Fendi* prisé des connaisseurs comme exhalant les «passions romaines».

la passione di Roma

FENDI

F E N D I   R O M A

EXCLUSIVELY AT

BLOOMINGDALE'S

Order by phone toll-free 1-800-526-5368 N.J. Residents 1-201-342-6707

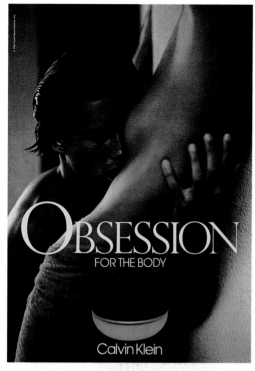

ART DIRECTOR:
Sam Shahid
PHOTOGRAPHER:
Bruce Weber
AGENCY:
CRK Advertising
CLIENT:
Calvin Klein
■ 87–90

■ 87–90 From an advertising campaign for *Obsession*, a line of body care products from Calvin Klein. (USA)

■ 91 Double-spread magazine advertisement for fashions by Carole Little. (USA)

■ 87–90 Beispiele aus einer Anzeigenkampagne für die Körperpflegelinie *Obsession* von Calvin Klein. (USA)

■ 91 Doppelseitige Zeitschriftenanzeige für Mode von Carole Little. (USA)

■ 87–90 Annonces types tirées d'une campagne pour la gamme des soins de beauté *Obsession* de Calvin Klein. (USA)

■ 91 Annonce de magazine double page pour les créations de mode Carole Little. (USA)

ART DIRECTOR:
BILL BERENTER
DESIGNER:
BERENTER, GREENHOUSE & WEBSTER
PHOTOGRAPHER:
DEBORAH TURBEVILLE
COPYWRITER:
BILL BERENTER/ MARTY GREENHOUSE
AGENCY:
BERENTER, GREENHOUSE & WEBSTER
CLIENT:
CAROLE LITTLE
■ 91

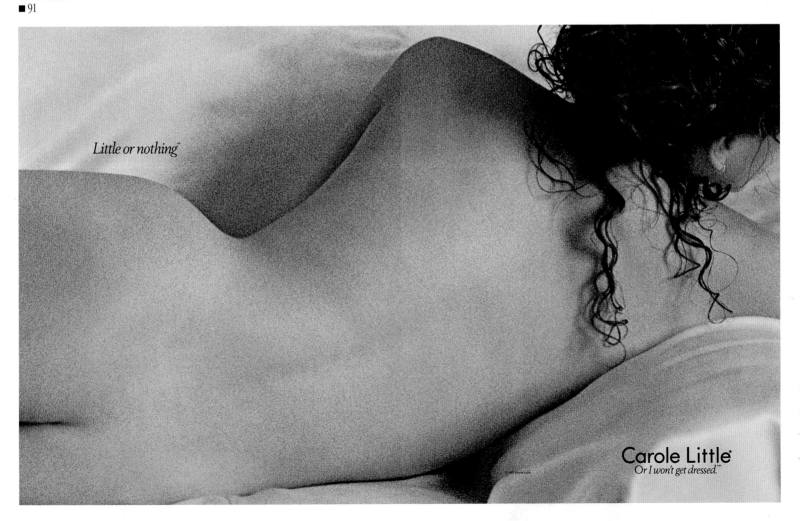

Little or nothing

Carole Little
Or I won't get dressed.

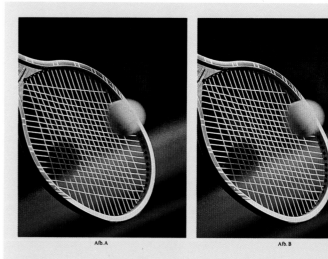

Abb. A   Abb. B   Afb. A   Afb. B

Der Besuch in einem österreichischen Theater (Abb. B) ist deshalb anders, weil Ihnen die Garderobefrau Berta vor dem letzten Vorhang den losen Mantelknopf längst wieder angenäht hat.

Österreich Information:
8037 Zürich, Neue Hard 11,
Telefon 01 /44 33 31/32.
Und Austrian Airlines.

Tennis in Oostenrijk (Afb. B) is daarom zo anders, omdat Annelise Hinterhuber je op de baan evenveel onverwacht tegenspel geeft als na afloop bij een drankje in de tennishal. Oostenrijk. De gezelligheid maakt 't verschil.

Informatie:
Oostenrijks Toeristenverkeers-Bureau,
Singel 464, 1017 AW Amsterdam.
Ook bij uw reisbureau of Austrian Airlines.

ART DIRECTOR:
ERNST BÄCHTOLD
PHOTOGRAPHER:
BERND GRUNDMANN
COPYWRITER:
ROLF PREISIG
AGENCY:
GGK ZÜRICH
CLIENT:
*ÖSTERREICHISCHE
FREMDENVERKEHRS-WERBUNG*
■ 92, 93

■ 92, 93 From a European advertising campaign to promote Austria as a vacation destination. *92:* "Theater in Austria (fig. B) is different because the wardrobe mistress Berta will fix your loose button long before the last curtain." *93:* "Tennis in Austria (fig. B) is different because Annelise Hinterhuber gives such snappy returns on the court as well as at the tennis club bar. Austria. It's the people that make the difference."

■ 94, 95 Double-spread advertisement to introduce the new monthly journal *Discover India.* (IND)

■ 96, 97 Double spreads praising Palm Beach County in Florida both as a vacation paradise and as a place suited to the needs of businessmen. (USA)

■ 92, 93 Beispiele aus einer europäischen Anzeigenkampagne für Österreich als Urlaubsland. Alle Inserate zeigen zwei identische Photographien und im Text wird jeweils erklärt, warum Österreich anders als andere Urlaubsländer ist. *92:* «Tennis in Österreich (Abb. B) ist deshalb anders, weil Annelise Hinterhuber auf dem Tennisplatz genauso schlagfertig ist wie an der Tennisclubbar. Österreich. Der Unterschied liegt in der Geselligkeit.»

■ 94, 95 Doppelseitige Anzeigen zur Einführung der neuen Monatsschrift «Entdecke Indien». (IND)

■ 96, 97 Palm Beach County in Florida wird in diesen doppelseitigen Inseraten als Ferienziel und Ort für Geschäftsreisen angepriesen. (USA)

■ 92, 93 Campagne d'annonces en faveur de la vocation touristique de l'Autriche. *92:* «Le théâtre en Autriche (fig. B) est différent en ce que la garde-robière Berta aura recousu votre bouton de manteau avant le dernier rideau.» *93:* «Le tennis en Autriche (fig. B) est différent en ce qu'Annelise Hinterhuber a la repartie aussi vive sur le court qu'au bar du club de tennis. L'Autriche, le pays où ce sont les gens qui font la différence.»

■ 94, 95 Annonces double page pour le lancement d'un nouveau mensuel, «Découvrez l'Inde». (IND)

■ 96, 97 Le comté de Palm Beach, en Floride, est présenté dans ces annonces sur double page comme une région privilégiée pour les vacances et les voyages d'affaires. (USA)

ART DIRECTOR:
SUNIL MAHADIK
DESIGNER:
SUNIL MAHADIK
PHOTOGRAPHER:
RAFEEQ ELLIAS
COPYWRITER:
RAFEEQ ELLIAS
AGENCY:
NUCLEUS
CLIENT:
*MEDIA TRANSASIA
(INDIA) PVT. LTD.*
■ 94, 95

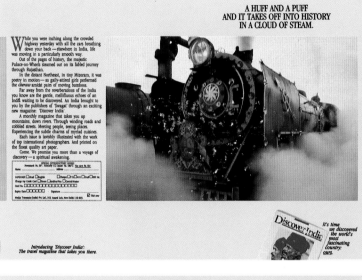

ART DIRECTOR:
HAL TENCH
PHOTOGRAPHER:
JIM ERICKSON
COPYWRITER:
JOHN MAHONEY
AGENCY:
THE MARTIN AGENCY
CLIENT:
PALM BEACH COUNTY
■ 96, 97

ART DIRECTOR:
JOHN MULLER/PATT WILLIAMS
DESIGNER:
JOHN MULLER
COPYWRITER:
ROB PRICE
AGENCY:
MULLER + CO.
CLIENT:
JAZZ COMMISSION KANSAS CITY
■ 98-101

ART DIRECTOR:
MIKE ROSEN
DESIGNER:
MIKE ROSEN
COPYWRITER:
MIKE ROSEN
AGENCY:
GOLDSMITH/JEFFREY
CLIENT:
*CITIZENS AGAINST
COCAINE ABUSE*
►■ 102

ART DIRECTOR:
GARY GOLDSMITH
DESIGNER:
GARY GOLDSMITH
COPYWRITER:
NEAL GOMBERG
AGENCY:
GOLDSMITH/JEFFREY
CLIENT:
*CITIZENS AGAINST
COCAINE ABUSE*
►■ 103

Don't let the good die young.

This may be her swan song.

They're in a jam.

Save the Wails.

■ 98-101 From a campaign which seeks to raise money for the preservation of documentary material relating to the history of jazz. The use, in part, of strongly damaged black-and-white photographs underlines the urgency. (USA)

■ 102, 103 Black-and-white advertisements sponsored by Citizens Against Cocaine Abuse. They call attention to the dangers of addiction, the damage to physical health, and the consequences of legal punishment. (USA)

■ 98-101 Inserate mit teilweise stark beschädigten Schwarzweissaufnahmen aus der Kampagne einer Kommission, die sich um die Erhaltung von Photos, Filmen und Aufnahmen grosser Jazz-Musiker der Vergangenheit bemüht. (USA)

■ 102, 103 Schwarzweiss-Anzeigen für eine Bürgerinitiative gegen Missbrauch von Kokain. Es wird auf die Gefahr der Abhängigkeit, die körperlichen Schäden und auf die gesetzliche Bestrafung aufmerksam gemacht. (USA)

■ 98-101 Annonces illustrées de photos noir et blanc souvent en mauvais état de conservation, pour la campagne d'un comité pour la préservation des photos, films et enregistrements des grands musiciens de jazz au passé. (USA)

■ 102, 103 Annonces noir et blanc pour une initiative contre l'abus de cocaïne lancée par un groupe de citoyens. On y souligne le danger de la dépendance, les effets néfastes pour la santé et la législation pénale en la matière. (USA)

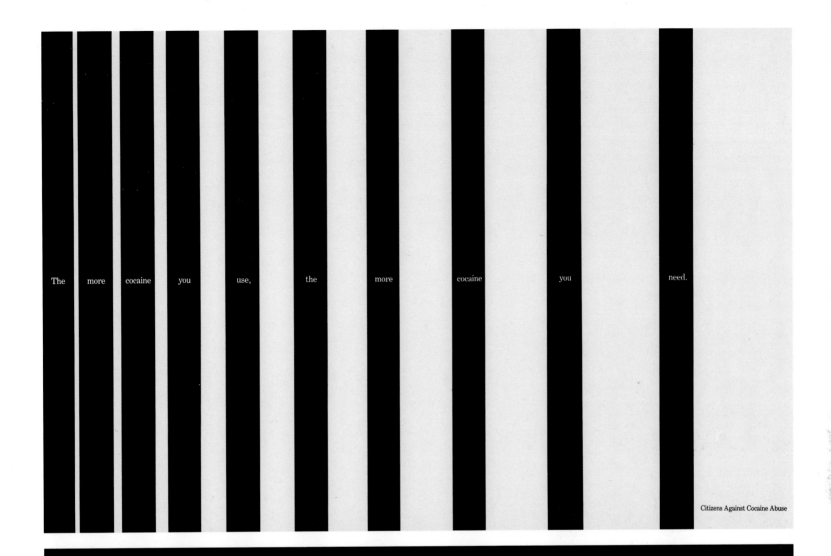

The   more   cocaine   you   use,   the   more   cocaine   you   need.

Citizens Against Cocaine Abuse

Doing cocaine can interfere with the electrical system of the brain and heart causing spasms of the heart muscle, it can constrict the arteries leading to cardiac arrest and death, and even if you are lucky enough to live and get caught the sentence you'll receive will make this one seem short.

Citizens Against Cocaine Abuse

■104 The fateful story of the American General George A. Custer provides the background for this advertisement of the US West Telephone Company. Without further consideration, Custer accepted a report which predicted success for a planned attack on the Sioux Indians. Instead, in 1876, the superiority of the Sioux under their Chief Sitting Bull led to the defeat of General Custer and all of his 250 troops at Little Bighorn River in the State of Montana. (USA)

■105-115 Publicity campaign for American Express Credit Cards. Well-known personalities, as photographed by Annie Leibovitz, are featured in these advertisements. The name of the person portrayed and the year in which his card was issued appears on the right sides of the double spreads. (USA)

■104 Das Schicksal des amerikanischen Generals George A. Custer wird als Aufhänger dieses Inserates der Telephongesellschaft US West benutzt. General Custer vertraute der Nachricht seines Informanten, der Angriff auf die Sioux-Indianer sei problemlos, ohne diese zu überprüfen. Durch die Übermacht der Indianer unter Häuptling Sitting Bull fiel Custer 1876 mit seiner gesamten Truppe von 250 Mann am Little Bighorn River im Staate Montana. (USA)

■105-115 Inseratenkampagne für die American-Express-Kreditkarte, für welche bekannte Persönlichkeiten von der Photographin Annie Leibovitz aufgenommen wurden. Rechts auf den Doppelseiten steht jeweils der Name des Abgebildeten und das Jahr, in dem er Karteninhaber wurde. (USA)

■104 Le sort tragique du général américain George A. Custer est le thème accrocheur de cette annonce de la société des téléphones US West. Faisant confiance à ses informateurs qui l'assuraient d'une victoire facile sur les Sioux, Custer fut cerné par les Indiens commandés par Sitting Bull. Après une défense héroïque, le général imprudent se fit massacrer en 1876 avec 250 hommes au bord du Little Bighorn River, dans le Montana. (USA)

■105-115 Campagne d'annonces pour la carte de crédit American Express. La photographe Annie Leibovitz a illustré cette publicité de portraits de personnalités dont le nom figure à droite sur la photo en même temps que l'année de l'obtention de la carte. (USA)

ART DIRECTOR:
DEAN HANSON
PHOTOGRAPHER:
NICHOLAS DEVORE
COPYWRITER:
ROD KILPATRICK/BILL MILLER
AGENCY:
FALLON MCELLIGOTT
CLIENT:
US WEST
■104

ART DIRECTOR:
PARRY MERKLEY
PHOTOGRAPHER:
ANNIE LEIBOVITZ
COPYWRITER:
GORDON BOWEN
AGENCY:
OGILVY & MATHER
CLIENT:
AMERICAN EXPRESS
TRAVEL RELATED SERVICES
►■105-115

A brief history lesson for companies that take their communications for granted.

GEORGE A. CUSTER
LIEUT. COLONEL
BVT. MAJOR GENERAL
7 U.S. CAV
FELL HERE
JUNE 25 1876

Your company's place in history will be determined by how well you send and receive information.
Managing that information is essential to your company's ability to compete.
That's why choosing the right communications system and the right supplier is so very important.
We are U S WEST. And, when it comes to meeting the telecommunications needs of business customers, no one has a longer history than we do.
For over a hundred years, our three Bell companies have provided telecommunications products and services for thousands of successful companies.
What we've done for them, we can do for you.
We can help you meet today's telecommunications needs while preparing for tomorrow's.
We can help your company make history, not be history. Nobody knows the trails better.

USWEST

MOUNTAIN BELL. NORTHWESTERN BELL. PACIFIC NORTHWEST BELL.

"WE'RE THE NEW STANDARD FOR BANKING SERVICES IN ATLANTA. THAT'S A PROMISE."

We know you've heard all of this before. We know you have a hard time believing any of it, or even understanding why a bank would bother saying it.

So many banks make monumental, chest-beating claims, then turn out to be just like all the other banks.

So when we make a claim, we're going to give you a reason to believe it. First things first. First National Bank of Cobb County is now Barnett Bank. It's the same people, with a new name.

Okay, here's the first promise. Barnett will offer you a unique range of products. Here's your reason to believe it. Premier Account. You get your own Personal Banker: one individual who will handle all your banking needs. A CreditLine account from $5,000 to $90,000 accessible simply by writing a check. And you get our Premier VISA® with a minimum credit line of $5,000. All for less than you'd normally pay for a gold card alone.

You can give our Customer Service Center a call at (404) 429-3802 if you have questions about the merger or the new services you'll receive as a customer of Barnett.

We want to be your bank in a big way. But we know you're skeptical. So for now we'll keep the promise we've made and earn your trust. And one day, we'll earn your business.

Barnett Bank

We'll Keep Our Promises.

All Barnett Banks are members of FDIC. © 1987 Barnett Banks, Inc.

"WE AT BLAH, BLAH, BLAH NATIONAL BANK PROMISE YOU BLAH, BLAH, BLAH, BLAH AND BLAH."

It's hard to distinguish the claims made by one bank from the claims made by another.

So when we make a promise to you, we realize we're going to have to give you some very good reasons to believe it.

Who are we? Until recently, we were the people of First National Bank of Cobb County. But now we're proud to announce that we're part of Barnett Bank.

We're still the same people, of course, but we're now in a better position to make you promises others can't make, and to back all those promises with services that others don't offer.

Take Senior Partners.® It's one of the most successful programs in the country for people 55 or over, and we're now offering it here for the first time.

It gives you a package of financial services, including free checking, free checks, free travelers and cashier's checks, a combined monthly statement, a great deal on our brokerage services and more.

We have other new services that are equally impressive even if you aren't 55. But if that sounds like a lot of blah, blah, blah, then give our Customer Service Center a call at (404) 429-3802 and let us give you all of the facts.

You see, we're replacing promises, promises with something a lot more impressive.

Actions, actions.

Barnett Bank

We'll Keep Our Promises.

"WE PROMISE TO BRING YOU BANKING SERVICES YOU'VE NEVER HAD, AND WE MEAN BUSINESS."

Oh come on now. Who are you kidding? Ha ha ha ha ha ha ha. Oh gosh, that's a new one. Gosh, I've never heard that promise before. Stop it already, you're killing me. You are the funniest banker. Oh gosh, I can't take this anymore. Tee he hee HA HA HA Hoo hoo hoo hoo hoo hee hee HA hee chuckle chuckle

Gfaw Gosh this hurts. Man oh man, you are the funniest banker I have ever heard. I think you should be on television. HA HA HA HA HA HA HA HA HA HA

HA HA HA HA HA HA HA ha ha ho ha ha ha ha ha hoo hoo hoo hee hee hee hee hee hee Giggle giggle chuckle. Oh I can't stop laughing Yeah, that joke is an oldie but

goody. It gets a laugh everytime a banker tells it. HA HA HA HA HA HA HA ha ha ha ha ha ha ha hoo hoo hee hee hee. when will this ever end?

If only bankers knew exactly how you feel when they make big promises. The exact same promises that every other bank makes. The exact same promises that they never really keep.

We're going to have to make some promises too. But this time, we'll give you a reason to believe them.

First things first, though. First National Bank of Cobb County is now Barnett Bank. We're the same people, but our bank now has a new name.

Here's the promise. We're going to offer you some unique products. Like the Premier Account which gives you a Personal Banker and a line of credit of at least $10,000. And Senior Partners,® a financial package that gives free checking and other special banking privileges if you're 55 or over.

There's a lot more you can expect from Barnett Bank as well. Like our Customer Service Center you can call at (404) 429-3802 if you have any questions about the merger or about the services we offer.

We want to be your bank in a big way. But we know you're probably very skeptical about it.

That's understandable. So for now we'll keep the promises that we've made and earn your trust. One day we'll earn your business.

Barnett Bank

We'll Keep Our Promises.

ART DIRECTOR:
CABELL HARRIS
PHOTOGRAPHER:
JIM ERICKSON
COPYWRITER:
DANIEL RUSS
AGENCY:
THE MARTIN AGENCY
CLIENT:
BARNETT BANKS, INC.
◀ ■ 116-118

It's Too Bad Buildings Can't
Be Put Up As Fast As We Can
Put Up The Financing.

Nobody makes quicker work of construction, acquisition, and development
loans than we do. A promise which we think you'll agree is, well, dynamite.
Barnett Is Florida's Largest Commercial Real Estate Lender.

Barnett
Bank

All Barnett Banks are members of FDIC. © 1987 Barnett Banks, Inc.

ART DIRECTOR:
DIANE COOK TENCH
COPYWRITER:
LUKE SULLIVAN
AGENCY:
THE MARTIN AGENCY
CLIENT:
BARNETT BANKS, INC.
■ 119-122

■ 116-118 In a series of advertisements, the Barnett Bank seeks to define the image for itself of being different from other banks. "We'll keep our promises" is the common slogan used to exemplify the image. (USA)

■ 119-122 From another series of advertisements for the Barnett Bank in Florida. Various aspects of the bank's services are described and illustrated. (USA)

■ 116-118 Aus einer Werbekampagne für die Barnett Bank, die in diesen Anzeigen behauptet, anders als andere Banken zu sein und dies mit dem einheitlichen Slogan «Wir halten unsere Versprechen» bekräftigt. (USA)

■ 119-122 «Zu schade, dass Gebäude nicht so schnell errichtet werden können, wie wir den Finanzierungsplan aufstellen.» Aus einer weiteren Kampagne der Barnett Bank. (USA)

■ 116-118 Campagne publicitaire pour la Barnett Bank qui affirme son originalité par rapport à d'autres établissements bancaires. Toutes ces annonces débouchent sur une déclaration solennelle: «Nous tenons nos promesses». (USA)

■ 119-122 «C'est bien dommage que les immeubles ne puissent pas sortir de terre aussi vite que nous accordons le prêt financier pour les construire.» Pour la Barnett Bank. (USA)

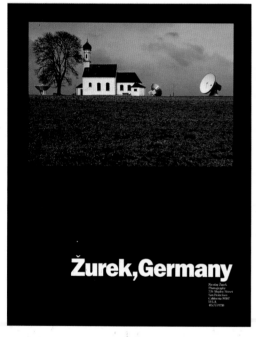

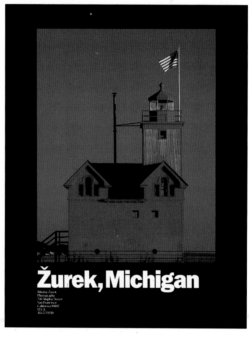

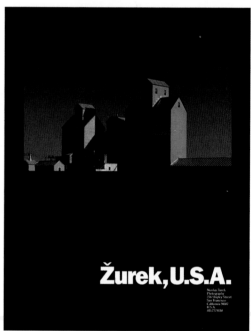

■ 123–125 Advertisements intended primarily for graphic artists, designers and typographers publicizing a sample book of Linotype. It can also be ordered in the form of a poster. (GBR)

■ 126–128 Advertisements of Nicolay Zurek, the American photographer, for his own promotion. (USA)

■ 129–131 Double spreads for printing colors. (USA)

■ 123–125 Anzeigen für ein Schriftmusterbuch von Linotype. Die Inserate, die sich hauptsächlich an Graphiker, Designer und Typographen richteten, konnten auch als Poster bezogen werden. (GBR)

■ 126–128 Inserate zur Eigenwerbung des amerikanischen Photographen Nicolay Zurek. (USA)

■ 129–131 Doppelseitige Anzeigen für Druckfarben. (USA)

■ 123–125 Annonces pour un catalogue de caractères Linotype. Destinées principalement aux graphistes, aux designers et aux typographes, elles étaient également proposées sous forme d'affiches décoratives. (GBR)

■ 126–128 Annonces autopromotionnelles du photographe américain Nicolay Zurek. (USA)

■ 129–131 Annonces pour encres d'imprimerie. (USA)

ART DIRECTOR:
BRIAN SIMMONS
DESIGNER:
GEOFF FRY
AGENCY:
NICKLIN ADVERTISING
CLIENT:
LINOTYPE LTD.
◀■ 123–125

TRUE COLOR DOES NOT MATCH A CHART, BUT A MIND.

"Close enough," you may have told the printer.

But close enough to what? The limited color chart you worked from? Or the unlimited spectrum in your mind?

Since 1907, Toyo ink has been reproducing the colors of the mind for the finest art books and folios around the world.

The world's most demanding designers insist on Toyo for its purity and brilliance of color.

Art directors with a penchant for perfection rely on Toyo ink for its vast selection of colors: over 700 to date.

Printers, anxious to provide their clients with the best, are using Toyo ink and finding it prints beautifully and easily on virtually any type of press.

Even other ink companies marvel at the Toyo Ink System: Over 90% of the available colors can be created from just 14 base inks, including the four process colors.

With its introduction into the United States, Americans are now learning what Japanese have known for so long. What good is putting ink to paper if the color you see is not the color you first saw in your mind?

PIGMENTS OF THE MIND NATION.

CCS:TOYO

ART DIRECTOR:
TYLER SMITH
DESIGNER:
TYLER SMITH
ILLUSTRATOR:
ANTHONY RUSSO
COPYWRITER:
LEE NASH
AGENCY:
TYLER SMITH
CLIENT:
CCS/TOYO
■ 129

ART DIRECTOR:
NICOLAY ZUREK
DESIGNER:
JERRY BERMAN
PHOTOGRAPHER:
NICOLAY ZUREK
AGENCY:
SIDJAKOV BERMAN GOMEZ & PARTNERS
CLIENT:
NICOLAY ZUREK
◀■ 126–128

NOW AVAILABLE, THE COLORS OF YOUR MIND.

Imagine.

Suddenly before you is a color you had dreamed of, but never knew existed.

Not a halfhearted hybrid, but a living, vibrant color.

Imagine, furthermore, gazing at a profusion of newly discovered, totally fresh reds, blues, browns and yellows. In all, 700 of the purest, most brilliant colors ever seen outside of your own head.

These are the colors of Toyo ink, part of a total color system so remarkable, over 90% of its available colors can be created from just 14 base inks, including the four process colors.

Every day, more printers discover it.

Every day, more art directors and designers insist on it.

They've learned what the Japanese have known for so long: What good is putting ink to paper if the color you see is not the color you first saw in your mind?

PIGMENTS OF THE IMAGINATION.

CCS:TOYO

ART DIRECTOR:
TYLER SMITH
DESIGNER:
TYLER SMITH
PHOTOGRAPHER:
CLINT CLEMENS
COPYWRITER:
LEE NASH
AGENCY:
TYLER SMITH
CLIENT:
CCS/TOYO
■ 130

PIGMENTS OF THE IMAGINATION.

One shade of blue means sadness. Another is coolness. Another vastness. Another emptiness.

How you see color in your mind is how Toyo ink has been reproducing color since 1907.

Toyo's international success is not due entirely to its quality of color.

Nor is it a matter of Toyo's outstanding selection of colors, over 700 to date.

It is not even because Toyo ink prints so beautifully and easily on virtually any type of press.

It is the intelligence of the Toyo ink System. Over 90% of the available colors can be created from just 14 base inks, including the 4 process colors.

All over the world, people insist on Toyo ink and accept no substitutes.

After all, what good is putting ink to paper if the color you see is not the color you first saw in your mind?

CCS:TOYO

ART DIRECTOR:
TYLER SMITH
DESIGNER:
TYLER SMITH
ILLUSTRATOR:
TYLER SMITH
PHOTOGRAPHER:
MYRON
COPYWRITER:
LEE NASH
AGENCY:
TYLER SMITH
CLIENT:
CCS/TOYO
■ 131

IF YOU THINK SMOKING POT IS BAD FOR YOU, TRY INHALING GARBAGE.

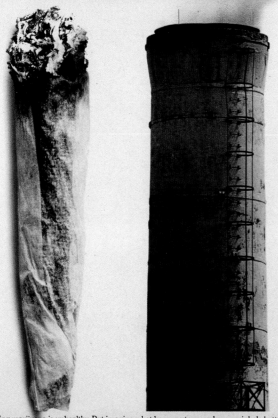

Sure, smoking marijuana is unhealthy. But imagine what happens to you when you inhale batteries, hospital waste, plastics, and oil filters. That's the kind of trash Hennepin County's new garbage burning plant will burn. Sending cancer causing dioxins and lead compounds into the air. Please help stop the incinerator by calling or writing Earth Protector. 1138 Plymouth Bldg., Mpls., MN 55402. (612) 375-0202. Donations are welcome. It's the least you can do to stop the air from going to pot.

MINNESOTANS AGAINST THE GARBAGE BURNING PLANT

If you like our products, please buy them. If you need our products, please don't.

Naturally, we at Phillips are delighted when we hear that people enjoy our products.

But some people enjoy them a bit too much. And that's something we don't like to hear.

After all, there's a fine line between having a drink because

you'd like to and having a drink because you need to.

And once you've crossed that line, there's no crossing back. No matter what anyone tells you.

So if you choose to drink, make sure it's for the right reasons. If it isn't, then stop.

Now, don't get us wrong. Like any company, we hope to put our products before a wide audience.

But we'd prefer that it not be a captive audience.

Phillips Beverage Company
Fine wines and spirits for four generations.

ART DIRECTOR:
Jac Coverdale

PHOTOGRAPHER:
Steve Umland/Jim Arndt

COPYWRITER:
Joe Alexander

AGENCY:
Clarity Coverdale Rueff

■ 132

ART DIRECTOR:
Ricardo Nicolay

AGENCY:
CLIPS Propaganda

CLIENT:
PHB Electrônica Ltda.

▼ ■ 134

ART DIRECTOR:
Tom Lichtenheld

PHOTOGRAPHER:
Mark LaFavor

COPYWRITER:
Rod Kilpatrick

AGENCY:
Fallon McElligott

■ 133

ART DIRECTOR:
Michael Fazende

COPYWRITER:
John Stingley

AGENCY:
Fallon McElligott

CLIENT:
Marine Midland

▼ ■ 135

On·Off   On

UPS 250. Este é o no break de bateria selada que dispensa manutenção, não exala gases e tem vida longa.

Resultado de um trabalho de pesquisa, muita tecnologia e rígido controle de qualidade no laboratório de testes da PHB, o UPS 250 não deixa o seu computador perder programas. Nem você perder o sono.

Indispensável para os micros (PC, XT, AT), sistemas telefônicos (KS, PBX, PABX), máquinas de telex, o UPS 250 também é a caixa de luz de inúmeros

outros equipamentos eletrônicos sensíveis às variações da rede elétrica.

Com garantia de 6 meses e assistência técnica permanente.

Acende, apaga. Liga, desliga. Não importa o que acontece ao redor. Com o UPS 250, o seu computador está sempre ligado. Você sabe o que isso significa.

phb
eletrônica ltda.

R. Camburiú 255 · CEP 05058 São Paulo. SP · Fones: (011) 831·8046/831·8019 · Telex(11)180490

If it runs, we'll finance it.

Before you ask what it is, let us save you the trouble. We don't know.

That's the point. At Marine Midland Automotive Financial, we don't care what new car line you sell. Or who the manufac-

turer is. Or where a car comes from. If it runs, we'll most likely finance it.

So rather than dealing with a lot of financial sources who only handle one line, you can deal with one source for everything. That means you know what to expect.

With consistent deals and service. So it's easier to work with your customers.

What's more, we'll also finance your inventory. Your leasing program. Your build-ings. Even acquisitions of other dealerships. Call 800-448-3400, ext. 334, for the

name and number of your local representative.

We can't think of an easier way to move cars. Unless, of course, they grew legs and walked off the lot themselves.

MARINE MIDLAND AUTOMOTIVE FINANCIAL CORPORATION

For people with lots of equity in their homes.

For a limited time, you can choose one of two home equity credit options at Continental and save $200 on your application and closing costs.

Tapping your home equity for home improvement, medical, education or other expenses can have big tax benefits, and Continental makes it easy to apply.

To borrow up to 80% of the appraised value of your home, less your first mortgage balance, choose our Home Equity Loan.

It currently gives you a low 11.75% fixed Annual Percentage Rate and a fixed repayment schedule.

For a more flexible arrangement, use our Home Equity Line of Credit to get a revolving line of up to 75% of your home's appraised value, less your first mortgage balance. Then take out loans as you need them (just by making a phone call or by writing a check if your line is over $25,000) and make interest-only monthly payments for up to seven years. Naturally, you can make payments on the principal at any time.

Depending on your daily principal balance, the APR on the line is only ½ to 1½% above the designated prime, which can change monthly.

When your line matures you can pay it off, or apply to either renew it for another seven years, or convert to a fixed rate installment loan.

Whichever plan you choose, it's easy to apply.

Just call (312) 828-LOAN to apply or to get more information.

Home Equity Loans. ⬥ Continental Illinois
We make money work.

For people who feel left out of that ad over there.

We have an exclusive new credit line designed just for people with good incomes, but not much equity in their homes. People who until now couldn't qualify for traditional home equity loans or lines of credit.

It's called the Equity Alternative line of credit. You qualify for the Equity Alternative based on your total ability to repay—which includes your income, net worth and credit worthiness. Your line could be approved for up to 100% of your home's value, less your mortgage balance. And because the loan is secured by your home, a portion of the interest you pay may be tax deductible.

The Equity Alternative account is a revolving line of credit for anywhere from $5,000 to $20,000 (maybe even more) accessed through a Continental Illinois Market Rate checking account. The Annual Percentage Rate is set at 3% above the designated prime rate, and may change monthly.

After making monthly payments for up to ten years, you'll have several options. You can pay back the loan, or apply to renew it for another ten years. And, of course, you can apply to convert to a fixed-rate installment loan whenever your wish.

With the Equity Alternative, you don't have to pay points or appraisal fees. Just initial fees of $100 the first year and $20 a year after that.

What's more, there's no lengthy approval process. In fact, you can even apply over the phone. And you could have money in as soon as ten days. Just call (312) 828-LOAN. And do it today.

After all, you own a home. Why be left out in the cold?

The Equity Alternative. ⬥ Continental Illinois
We make money work.

ART DIRECTOR:
BOB BARRIE

DESIGNER:
BOB BARRIE

PHOTOGRAPHER:
RICK DUBLIN

COPYWRITER:
MIKE LESCARBEAU

AGENCY:
FALLON McELLIGOTT

CLIENT:
CONTINENTAL ILLINOIS BANK

■ 136

■ 132 The opponents to an incineration plant in Minnesota compare the harmful effects of inhaling the fumes of burning rubbish to those of inhaling marijuana. They contend that the former can be even worse. (USA)

■ 133 A firm producing alcoholic beverages clearly indicates that it would prefer not to sell its products to those who are dependent upon them. (USA)

■ 134 The characteristics of electronic systems are compared to the properties of a match. (BRA)

■ 135 In this advertisement, the Marine Midland Automotive Corp. describes its financing programs. (USA)

■ 136 Newspaper advertisements for two different forms of credit available to home owners. (USA)

■ 132 Gegen das Einatmen der Abgase einer Müllverbrennungsanlage ist das Rauchen von Marijuana gar nichts – dies ist die Argumentation einer Kampagne gegen eine Verbrennungsanlage in Minnesota. (USA)

■ 133 «Wenn Sie unsere Produkte mögen, kaufen Sie sie bitte. Wenn Sie sie brauchen, tun Sie es bitte nicht.» Anzeige für alkoholische Getränke. (USA)

■ 134 Die Eigenschaften elektronischer Anlagen werden mit denen eines Streichholzes verglichen. (BRA)

■ 135 «Wenn es läuft, finanzieren wir es.» Anzeige für Autofinanzierungen. (USA)

■ 136 Zeitungsanzeigen für zwei verschiedene Arten von Krediten für Hausbesitzer. (USA)

■ 132 «Si vous croyez que fumer un joint, c'est mauvais pour la santé, essayez donc les fumées d'incinération des ordures» – d'une campagne visant à interdire la construction d'une usine d'incinération au Minnesota. (USA)

■ 133 «Si vous aimez nos produits, achetez-les. Si vous en avez besoin, ne les faites pas.» Annonce pour un distributeur de boissons alcoolisées. (USA)

■ 134 Annonce où les caractéristiques d'une installation électronique sont comparées à celles d'une allumette. (BRA)

■ 135 «Si ça roule, on vous le financera.» Annonce pour le crédit automobile. (USA)

■ 136 Annonces de journaux pour deux types de crédit mis à la disposition des propriétaires d'immeubles. (USA)

71 Jahre nach «Piggly Wiggly».

Einladende Beleuchtung, freundliche Farben, eine theatralische Warenpräsentation, vor allem aber Dienst am Kunden – das gilt für Amerikas Supermärkte der Zukunft, wie zum Beispiel für den «Von's Pavillon» in Garden Grove bei Los Angeles. Dort werden Konsumenten von einem sprechenden Computer zu den gewünschten Abteilungen geleitet, wo sie u. a. aus drei Dutzend Ice-Cream-Aromen oder 26 Wurstsorten wählen können. (Notabene 71 Jahre nach dem ersten US-Supermarkt, dem «Piggly Wiggly» in Memphis, Tennessee.)

Neue Zürcher Zeitung

Toter Buchstabe.

Am 1. Januar 1987 hat das Bundesgesetz über den Natur- und Heimatschutz (NHG) den 20. Jahrestag seiner Inkraftsetzung erlebt. Damals, 1967, galt es als fortschrittlich. Doch auch dieses Gesetz hat erfahren müssen, dass es gerade so gut ist wie sein Vollzug. Wer nachliest, was das NHG u. a. postuliert, nämlich «Bei der Schädlingsbekämpfung, insbesondere mit Giftstoffen, ist darauf zu achten, dass schützenswerte Tier- und Pflanzenarten nicht gefährdet werden», kommt nicht um die bittere Feststellung herum, dass bis heute manches toter Buchstabe geblieben ist.

Neue Zürcher Zeitung

ELEFANTENHOCHZEIT WECKT UNBEHAGEN.

Meldungen, vor allem aus Amerika, wonach sich «Multi X» und «Multi Y» zum «Multi XY» zusammengeschlossen haben, sind schon fast an der Tagesordnung. Und neue Spekulationen über «wer mit wem» werden aus sogenannt gut informierten Quellen auch regelmässig in Umlauf gebracht. Bei den Gesetzgebern vieler Länder herrscht über diesen «Wirtschafts-Gigantismus» allerdings nicht eitel Freude: So werden u. a. auch in der Bundesrepublik Deutschland Verschär-

fungen in der Kontrolle von «Heiratswilligen» gefordert. Auf der andern Seite aber gibt es Spitzenverbände in der Wirtschaft, die in einem Verbot von Grossfusionen zwischen diversifizierten Unternehmen einen krassen Widerspruch zu den Vorstellungen der grossen westlichen Industrieländer sehen würden.

Neue Zürcher Zeitung

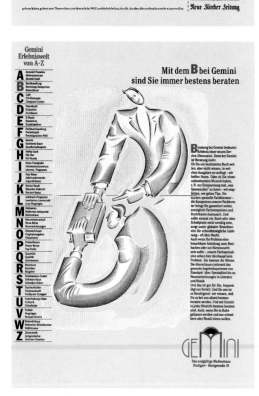

Mit dem **B** bei Gemini sind Sie immer bestens beraten

Das **A** für Auswahl ist bei Gemini das grösste Erlebnis

Das **S** von Gemini steht für Stuttgarts sensationelles Schallplatten Sortiment

---

■ 137–139 The *Neue Zürcher Zeitung* uses various topics of current affairs to solicit new subscriptions. *137* "Piggly Wiggly" refers to the opening of the first American supermarket; *138* refers to environmental protection legislation; and *139* "Elephant wedding is cause for concern" alludes to the recent merger of two industrial firms. (SWI)

■ 140–142 From a newspaper campaign for Gemini, the German media firm. The letter "B" signifies its advisory service, "A" its scope, and "S" its record department. (GER)

■ 143 From an advertising campaign for the Swiss Sunday Paper *Sonntagszeitung*. All double-spread ads refer to two different subjects that are under the same term. (SWI)

■ 144 Advertisement soliciting subscriptions to *The Wall Street Journal*. Delivery of a daily newspaper assures the most current information from the world of finance. (USA)

■ 137–139 Inserate aus einer Abonnenten-Kampagne der *Neuen Zürcher Zeitung*. Es werden verschiedene Themenkreise der Zeitung behandelt: «Piggly Wiggly» war der erste Supermarkt in den USA; bei *138* geht es um das Natur- und Heimatschutzgesetz; mit der Elefantenhochzeit wird auf Grossfusionen in der Wirtschaft angespielt. (SWI)

■ 140–142 Aus einer Pressekampagne des Medienhauses Gemini. Das B steht hier für «Bearbeitung», A für «Auswahl» und «S» für die Schallplattenabteilung. (GER)

■ 143 Aus einer Anzeigenkampagne für die *Sonntagszeitung*. Die Inserate beziehen sich jeweils auf zwei verschiedene Dinge, die unter dem selben Begriff laufen. (SWI)

■ 144 «Ist es das Licht am Ende des Tunnels oder ist es ein anderer Zug?» Anzeige des *Wall Street Journals*, das den Lesern klare Informationen verspricht. (USA)

■ 137–139 Annonces de la *Neue Zürcher Zeitung* pour le recrutement d'abonnés, avec référence à divers sujets abordés dans ce quotidien: *137* «Piggly Wiggly», le premier supermarché américain; *138* la loi sur la protection de la nature et du patrimoine national; *139* le mariage entre deux éléphants, symbole de la fusion de groupes industriels. (SWI)

■ 140–142 Campagne de presse du spécialiste des medias Gemini. Le B représente l'aspect conseils, le A la sélection, le S la production de disques. (GER)

■ 143 D'une campagne d'annonces pour le journal du dimanche *Sonntagszeitung*. Les annonces double page se rapportent à deux choses classées sous le même concept. (SWI)

■ 144 «Est-ce la lumière annonçant la fin du tunnel ou seulement les feux d'un train que croise?» Annonce du *Wall Street Journal* promettant des informations claires. (USA)

ART DIRECTOR:
URS FÜRER
DESIGNER:
DANIEL BEURET
ILLUSTRATOR:
KARIN SCHIESSER/
DANIEL BEURET
PHOTOGRAPHER:
CHRISTIAN KÜENZI
COPYWRITER:
PETER F. KELLER
AGENCY:
ADOLF WIRZ AG
CLIENT:
NEUE ZÜRCHER ZEITUNG
◀■ 137-139

ART DIRECTOR:
MAX WEBER
DESIGNER:
MAX WEBER
COPYWRITER:
RENÉ FISCH
AGENCY:
AEBI, SUTER, GISLER
& STUDER/BBDO
CLIENT:
TAGES-ANZEIGER VERLAG
■ 143

ART DIRECTOR:
PETER ZEPP
ILLUSTRATOR:
BUSH HOLLYHEAD 140
HEINZ EDELMANN 141
GEORGE HARDIE 142
COPYWRITER:
MONIKA KNUTH
AGENCY:
ROBERT PÜTZ GMBH
CLIENT:
GEMINI MEDIENCENTER
◀■ 140-142

ART DIRECTOR:
DEAN HANSON
PHOTOGRAPHER:
RICK DUBLIN
COPYWRITER:
BRUCE BILDSTEIN
AGENCY:
FALLON McELLIGOTT
CLIENT:
WALL STREET JOURNAL
■ 144

ST. MARY'S STAFF WOULD LIKE TO THANK ALL OF THE PEOPLE THAT RUN RED LIGHTS, BREAK THE SPEED LIMIT AND MAKE LOUD NOISES ALL HOURS OF THE DAY & NIGHT.

We salute central Virginia's rescue squad workers during Emergency Medical Services Week. We think you're real lifesavers.

ST. MARY'S HOSPITAL
A Bon Secours Health Care Facility

ON MAY 15TH, WE WILL BE REMINDED THAT THIS SHIELD PROTECTS ALL BUT THE ONES WHO WEAR IT.

The unfortunate thing is that this shield is only a symbol. And in the last century 26 Richmond Police Officers gave their lives while carrying it.

So at 2 pm on May 15th, the Richmond Police Memorial Foundation will unveil a monument dedicated to these brave souls.

While it is a memorial to the Police Officers who died while on duty, it also recognizes the many individuals and corporations who contributed directly or indirectly to the creation of this tribute.

Please don't miss this event at Festival Park (in between Richmond Coliseum and Sixth Street Marketplace). The distinguished speakers have something important to say. And it's something we all need to remember.

This message is proudly brought to you by Virginia Power.

ART DIRECTOR:
Cabell Harris
PHOTOGRAPHER:
Dean Hawthorne
COPYWRITER:
Mike Hughes
AGENCY:
The Martin Agency
CLIENT:
St. Mary's Hospital
■ 145

ART DIRECTOR:
Cabell Harris
PHOTOGRAPHER:
Dean Hawthorne
COPYWRITER:
Daniel Russ
AGENCY:
The Martin Agency
CLIENT:
Richmond Police Memorial Foundation
■ 146

Save Our Schools.

This year, 27,000 students from some 240 schools, many right here in this area, will attend class on the Chesapeake Bay.

They will learn what scientists have learned. That the nation's largest estuary has the potential to support the greatest mixture of wildlife and aquatic resources on this planet. That toxic chemicals, sewage and sediment are literally killing this potential. And that they have the ability to sustain the efforts now underway to restore and preserve the Bay for future generations.

Which is why the Chesapeake Bay Foundation refers to this environmental education program as "a long term investment."

And as a major financial institution serving this region, Signet Bank understands the value of a smart investment. So, we recently made a considerable contribution to CBF's educational fund. In fact, the largest single contribution they've ever received.

But that's just for starters. Because Signet Bank has come up with an additional way to show their commitment to both this cause and the people of the Northern Neck. For every new checking or savings account opened before June 30th at any Signet branch listed below, another $5 will be given to the Foundation.

To open an account or to pick up additional information on how you can get involved in the Chesapeake Bay Foundation, we encourage you to stop by today.

SIGNET BANK
Remember This Name. One Day We'll Be Your Bank.
Signet Bank/Virginia, Member FDIC. Burgess, Colonial Beach, Montross, Reedville, Warsaw, White Stone offices.

ART DIRECTOR:
JERRY TORCHIA

PHOTOGRAPHER:
NICK COLYANIS

COPYWRITER:
ANDY ELLIS

AGENCY:
THE MARTIN AGENCY

CLIENT:
SIGNET BANKING CORPORATION

■ 147

■ 145 Announcement sponsored by a hospital staff. The finely printed text adds a note of explanation. "We salute central Virginia's rescue squad workers during Emergency Medical Services Week. We think you're real lifesavers." (USA)

■ 146 Public service announcement inviting attendance at the public dedication of a monument commemorating policeman who died while on duty. (USA)

■ 147 The Signet Bank announces that it has already given substantial support to an environmental education program, and that it will contribute an additional $5 for every checking account which is opened in the near future. (USA)

■ 145 «Die Belegschaft des St.-Mary's-Spitals dankt allen, die Rotlicht überfahren, die Höchstgeschwindigkeit überschreiten und Tag und Nacht grossen Lärm machen» – gemeint sind die Rettungswagen. (USA)

■ 146 Inserat im Gedenken an Polizisten, die im Dienst ihr Leben liessen: «Am 15. Mai werden wir daran erinnert, dass diese Marke alle schützt, nur nicht jene, die sie tragen.» (USA)

■ 147 «Rettet unsere Schulen» – mit diesem Inserat spielt die Signet Bank auf ihre Unterstützung eines Umweltprogramms an. Bei Eröffnung neuer Konten verspricht die Bank weitere Zuwendungen an den Umweltfond. (USA)

■ 145 «Le personnel de l'Hôpital St. Mary's remercie tous ceux qui passent au rouge, font des dépassements de vitesse et font un tas de bruit jour et nuit» – il s'agit bien entendu des chauffeurs d'ambulances. (USA)

■ 146 Annonce pour la journée du souvenir des policiers abattus dans l'exercice de leurs fonctions: «leur emblème qui nous protège ne les a pas protégés du sacrifice.» (USA)

■ 147 «Sauvez nos écoles» – la Signet Bank se réfère dans cette annonce au soutien qu'elle accorde à un programme environnemental. A chaque ouverture de compte, la banque s'engage à verser un don supplémentaire. (USA)

FEDERAL EXPRESS DELIVERS COAST TO COAST.

When you have an important package to be sent out of the country, don't trust it to just any air express company. Choose the one that invented the business—Federal Express.

Federal Express can ship packages up to 150 pounds to thousands of cities in over 85 countries. And only Federal has the COSMOS™ tracking system, that can trace international shipments within hours.

We also have one of the best reliability rates in the business. A fact we stand behind with this guarantee—if we deliver a shipment late (even just 60 seconds late), you can request your money back.

So next time, call Federal Express. And expand your horizons. For a free international starter kit, call Federal at 1-800-238-5355.

WORLDWIDE SERVICE FROM FEDERAL EXPRESS.

ART DIRECTOR:
BOB BRIHN
ILLUSTRATOR:
BOB BLEWETT
COPYWRITER:
GEORGE GIER
AGENCY:
FALLON McELLIGOTT
CLIENT:
FEDERAL EXPRESS
■148

format '87

Internationale Fachmesse für Bodendesign. Frankfurt, 6.–10. Mai 1987.

Messe Frankfurt

ART DIRECTOR:
PETER HESSLER
DESIGNER:
PETER HESSLER
ILLUSTRATOR:
JOACHIM BEHRENDT
COPYWRITER:
*JOCHEN BEITHAN/
ANDREA SCHWAB*
AGENCY:
BEITHAN, HESSLER, LUTZ
CLIENT:
MESSE FRANKFURT GMBH
■149

■148 Advertisement for the courier service of Federal Express which offers a new service between the United States and the European continent – two different "coasts" from the ones usually associated with this phrase. (USA)

■149 Advertisement which appeared in daily newspapers to publicize "format 87", a trade fair for floor coverings. Various points of view are expressed in texts. (GER)

■150-153 Advertisements sponsored by the Association of Swiss Carpet Manufacturers. The slogans are based on a play on words which connote the relationship between the German expressions for flooring and ground. *151* "It's clear that more and more foreigners want to live on Swiss ground" is one example. (SWI)

■148 «Federal Express liefert von Küste zu Küste». Diese Wendung wird normalerweise für den inneramerikanischen Transport zwischen Ost- und Westküste verwendet. Anzeige für den Courier-Service von Federal Express. (USA)

■149 In Tageszeitungen veröffentlichtes Inserat als Werbung für die Bodenbelagsmesse «format 87». In den Feldern werden verschiedene Gesichtspunkte aufgeführt. (GER)

■150-153 Beispiele aus einer Image-Kampagne mit einheitlich gestalteten Anzeigen des Verbandes schweizerischer Teppichfabrikanten für Schweizer Teppiche, mit einem einheitlichen Gütesiegel versehen sind. Die Slogans spielen alle mit der Mehrdeutigkeit des Ausdrucks «Schweizer Boden». (SWI)

■148 «Le Federal Express livre d'une côte à l'autre.» Il est bien entendu question ici des transports américains de la côte américaine à la côte européenne et vice-versa. Annonce pour le service de courrier du Federal Express. (USA)

■149 Annonce de journal pour la foire «format 87» (revêtements de sol). Les différentes cases servent à exprimer différents points de vue d'intérêt pour les visiteurs. (GER)

■150-153 Annonces homogènes pour une campagne de prestige de l'Association suisse des fabricants de tapis destinée à développer les ventes de tapis suisses pourvus d'un label de qualité. Les slogans amusants se réfèrent au «sol suisse», par exemple *fig. 150* «fameux, les loisirs sur sol suisse!» (SWI)

DIE FREIZEIT MACHT AUF

System: 100% Grobfaser Polypropylen, 2 Farben, Polster: 285 x 285 cm, mit Verschlüsslungen. Rückenmaterial: Drainage aus verfestertem Kunststoff. Hersteller: **Ruco** Farben, 8852 Lachen.

SCHWEIZER BODEN EINFACH SPASS.

Spass macht, dass der Schweizerteppich für jedes Freizeitvergnügen zu haben ist. Viele verschiedene Modelle sind und viele unterschiedliche Bedürfnisse zugeschnitten. So auch auf diejenigen von Menschen, die ihre Mussestunden im Hobby-, Bastel oder Spielzimmer und auf dem Balkon oder der Gartenterrasse verbringen. Zugeschnitten sind sie aber auch auf jeden Geschmack. Und den kann man sowohl durch grosser Auswahl leicht verwirklichen, als auch dank dont guter Qualität lange geniessen. Dafür bürgt das Swiss Fabric Signet. Mit Garantie. Alpina Teppichwerke Wetzikon, Teppichfabrik Bachs, Fisco Enggistein, Forbo-Ennenda, Forbo-Lachen, Kisler-Zingg Reichenburg, Teppichfabrik Malans, Teppichfabrik Mekhnes, Ruckstuhl Langenthal, Stamfler Eglisau, Tisca Umäsch, Tisca Bühler, Teppichfabrik Waren Sennwald.

DER SCHWEIZERTEPPICH
Der Schweizer Boden

VERSTÄNDLICH, DASS IMMER MEHR AUSLÄNDER AUF

Grisom-Stabilo: 100% reine Schurwolle, Polyurethanschaum-Rücken, 7 Farben, 415 cm breit. Hersteller: **MABANA** Teppichfabrik Malans AG, 7208 Malans.

SCHWEIZER BODEN LEBEN WOLLEN.

Verständlich, dass immer mehr Menschen in aller Welt das Bessere lieben. Und deshalb den Schweizerteppich bevorzugen. Der zieht gut aus und ist es auch. Und das aus Faszinierend viele Arten. Machen Sie es wie qualitätsbewusste Leute ausserhalb der Schweiz: Achten Sie beim Auswählen nicht nur auf Muster und Farben. Sondern auch auf das Swiss Fabric Signet. Denn immer Sie zu einem attraktiven Teppich, der auch nach Jahren hält, was andere sich mehr nur versprechen. Mit Garantie. Alpina Teppichwerke Wetzikon, Teppichfabrik Bachs, Fisco Enggistein, Forbo-Ennenda, Forbo-Lachen, Kisler-Zingg Reichenburg, Teppichfabrik Malans, Teppichfabrik Mekhnes, Ruckstuhl Langenthal, Stamfler Eglisau, Tisca Umäsch, Tisca Bühler, Teppichfabrik Waren Sennwald.

DER SCHWEIZERTEPPICH
Der Schweizer Boden

GUT MÖGLICH, DASS SICH REAGAN ZUR ZEIT AUF

Spectra-C CVK: Polyamid, 25 Farben, 400 cm breit. Hersteller: ▪️ Alpina Teppichwerke AG, 8623 Wetzikon.

SCHWEIZER BODEN AUFHÄLT.

Reagan ist ein Mann der Macht. Männer der Macht schützen Hände und Köpfe in repräsentativen Räumen. Repräsentative Räume befinden sich in renommierten Häusern. Und renommierte Häuser entscheiden sich beim Einrichten stets für das Beste. Also zum Beispiel für den Schweizerteppich. Entscheiden auch Sie sich für raffiniertes Design und vorzügliche Verarbeitung. Achten Sie auf das Swiss Fabric Signet. Dann werden Sie an Ihrem Teppich länger Freude haben. Mit Garantie. Alpina Teppichwerke AG, Teppichfabrik Bachs, Fisco AG, Forbo-Ennenda AG, Forbo-Teppichfabrik AG, E. Kisler-Zingg AG, Teppichfabrik Malans AG, Ruckstuhl Mekhnes AG, Ruckstuhl AG, Stamfler AG, Tisca Teppichboden AG, Tisca Teichhäuser + Co. AG, Teppichfabrik Waren AG.

DER SCHWEIZERTEPPICH
Der Schweizer Boden

ART DIRECTOR:
Silvio Galbucci
DESIGNER:
Charlie H. Hofer
PHOTOGRAPHER:
Patrick Rohner
COPYWRITER:
Daniel Matter
AGENCY:
Adolf Wirz AG
CLIENT:
Verband Schweiz.
Teppichfabrikanten
■ 150–153

AUF

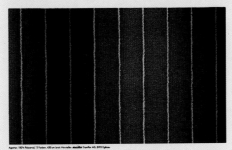

Agartex: 100% Polyamid, 12 Farben, 420 cm breit. Hersteller: **maxfer** Stamfler AG, 8193 Eglisau.

SCHWEIZER BODEN KANN MAN SEHR BEQUEM VORWÄRTS- KOMMEN.

Wo ein Schweizerteppich den geschäftlichen Alltag eine nicht alltägliche Basis gibt, ein fühlen sich Kunden wohl wie Mitarbeiter und Chefs. Der Kunden imponiert das gediegene Design, den Mitarbeitern das gediegene Design und das angenehme Material. Und den Chefs das gediegene Design, das angenehme Material und die sorgfältige Verarbeitung. Und allen zusammen imponiert, wie lange es ein Schweizerteppich trotz grösster Belastung imponiert kann. Dafür bürgt das Swiss Fabric Signet. Mit Garantie. Alpina Teppichwerke Wetzikon, Teppichfabrik Bachs, Fisco Enggistein, Forbo-Ennenda, Forbo-Lachen, Kisler-Zingg Reichenburg, Teppichfabrik Malans, Teppichfabrik Mekhnes, Ruckstuhl Langenthal, Stamfler Eglisau, Tisca Umäsch, Tisca Bühler, Teppichfabrik Waren Sennwald.

DER SCHWEIZERTEPPICH
Der Schweizer Boden

When An Agency In Virginia Was Named The Hottest Agency In America, The News Echoed Through Manhattan.

This year both *Advertising Age* and *Adweek* named The Martin Agency in Richmond the hottest agency in America.

ART DIRECTOR:
WAYNE GIBSON
COPYWRITER:
DANIEL RUSS
AGENCY:
THE MARTIN AGENCY
CLIENT:
THE MARTIN AGENCY
■ 154

■ 154 The Manhattan skyline, filled with countless expressions of "Damn," reflects a certain envy of its competitor! For The Martin Agency's own promotion. (USA)

■ 154 «Als eine Agentur in Virginia zur heissesten Agentur Amerikas ernannt wurde, ging die Nachricht wie ein Echo durch Manhattan.» Eigenwerbung der Martin Agency. (USA)

■ 154 «Lorsqu'une agence de Virginie fut élue l'agence la plus *in* d'Amérique, l'écho s'en fit entendre dans tout Manhattan.» Autopromotion de la Martin Agency. (USA)

BROCHURES

BROCHURES

BROSCHÜREN

BROCHURES

ART DIRECTOR:
WOODY PIRTLE
DESIGNER:
JEFF WEITHMAN/WOODY PIRTLE
PHOTOGRAPHER:
VARIOUS
STUDIO:
PIRTLE DESIGN
CLIENT:
COLORDYNAMICS
■ 155–162

■155-162 Cover and double spreads promoting Color Dynamics, a printing company. (USA)

■155-162 Umschlag und Doppelseiten einer Werbebroschüre der Druckerei ColorDynamics. (USA)

■155-162 Couverture et doubles pages d'une brochure publicitaire de l'imprimerie ColorDynamics. (USA)

■ 163-165 The cover pages for various circular letters as used by the International Design Center in New York. (USA)

■ 166-168 By means of note pads upon whose covers exacting color photographs are reproduced, Bradley offers proof of its printing expertise. (USA)

■ 169-174 Cover and double spreads from a brochure illustrating award-winning annual reports from the 1987 Mead Annual Report show. (USA)

■ 163-165 Umschlagseiten verschiedener Rundschreiben des International Design Centers, New York. (USA)

■ 166-168 Mit Notizblöcken, auf deren Umschlagseiten farblich anspruchsvolle Photos abgebildet sind, stellt die Druckerei Bradley ihr Können unter Beweis. (USA)

■ 169-174 Umschlag und Doppelseiten einer Broschüre, in der Jahresberichte abgebildet sind, die 1987 bei der Mead Annual Report Show Preise gewonnen haben. (USA)

■ 163-165 Pages de couverture de diverses circulaires de l'International Design Center de New York. (USA)

■ 166-168 Ces blocs-notes illustrés en couverture de photos de grande qualité chromatique servent à démontrer le savoir-faire technique de l'imprimerie Bradley. (USA)

■ 169-174 Couverture et doubles pages d'une brochure reproduisant les rapports annuels primés lors de la Mead Annual Report Show de 1987. (USA)

ART DIRECTOR:
MASSIMO VIGNELLI/MICHAEL BIERUT

DESIGNER:
MICHAEL BIERUT/
ALAN HOPFENSPERGER 163
LUCY COSSENTINO FRUEH 164, 165

PHOTOGRAPHER:
LORI SCHULWEIS

COPYWRITER:
FERN MALLIS/ANN DERMANSKY

AGENCY:
VIGNELLI ASSOCIATES

CLIENT:
INTERNATIONAL DESIGN CENTER,
NEW YORK

◀■ 163-165

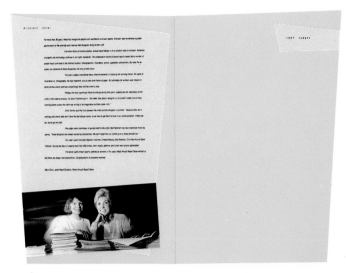

DESIGNER:
STEVE BAGBY

PHOTOGRAPHER:
PENINA MEISELS 166
HANK BENSON 167
TOKUNO 168

COPYWRITER:
KEITH CAHELA

AGENCY:
BAGBY DESIGN INC.

CLIENT:
BRADLEY PRINTING CO.

◀■ 166-168

ART DIRECTOR:
MIKE WEYMOUTH

DESIGNER:
TOM LAIDLAW

PHOTOGRAPHER:
MIKE WEYMOUTH/LARRY LONG

STUDIO:
WEYMOUTH DESIGN, INC.

CLIENT:
MEAD LIBRARY OF IDEAS

▲■ 169-174

ART DIRECTOR:
BRAD COPELAND
DESIGNER:
KEVIN IRBY
ILLUSTRATOR:
KEVIN IRBY
AGENCY:
COPELAND DESIGN
CLIENT:
*ART DIRECTORS CLUB
OF ATLANTA*
■ 175-177

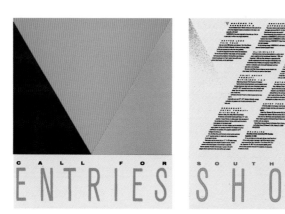

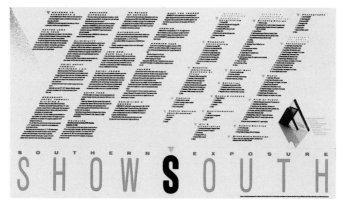

Art Director:
Gil Schaefer/Peter Pigott
Designer:
Judy Sevebrin/Gil Schaefer
Illustrator:
Judy Sevebrin
Photographer:
John Schaefer
Agency:
Innovation
Client:
Innovation
◀ ■ 178

Art Director:
John Bacon
Designer:
John Bacon
Illustrator:
John Bacon
Copywriter:
John Brown
Agency:
Lida Advertising Co.
Client:
*American Institute of
Graphic Arts, Wichita*
▶ ■ 179

■ 175-177 Call for Entry to the annual competition of the Art Directors Club of Atlanta. (USA)

■ 178 Envelope and invitation to celebrate the completion of the agency Innovation's newly renovated offices. The letters on the envelope can be vertically read as "innovation" and horizontally read as "invitation". (USA)

■ 179 Invitation of the Wichita (Kansas) AIGA chapter to a show of suggestions for one and two color designs. (USA)

■ 175-177 Einladung zur Teilnahme am jährlichen Wettbewerb des Art Directors Club von Atlanta. (USA)

■ 178 Couvert und Einladung der Agentur Innovation zur Feier der vollendeten Renovation ihrer Büros. Die Buchstaben auf dem Couvert bilden senkrecht gelesen immer das Wort «Innovation» und waagerecht «Invitation». (USA)

■ 179 Einladung der AIGA Wichita, Kansas, zu einer Ausstellung von ein- und zweifarbigen Designlösungen. (USA)

■ 175-177 Invitation à participer au concours annuel de l'Art Directors Club d'Atlanta. (USA)

■ 178 Enveloppe et invitation de l'agence Innovation à venir fêter l'achèvement des travaux de rénovation entrepris dans ses bureaux. Sur l'enveloppe, on lit partout à la verticale «Innovation», à l'horizontale «Invitation». (USA)

■ 179 Invitation de l'AIGA de Wichita (Kansas) à une exposition de travaux de design mono- et bichromes. (USA)

ART DIRECTOR:
BENITA RAPHAN
DESIGNER:
BENITA RAPHAN
PHOTOGRAPHER:
KOTO BOLOFO
AGENCY:
BENITA RAPHAN DESIGN
CLIENT:
AGENCE FAM, FABIENNE MARTIN
■ 180-183

■ 180-183 Cover and double
spreads from the catalog of
the FAM Modeling Agency
based in Paris. (FRA)

■ 180-183 Umschlag und
Doppelseiten eines Kataloges
der französischen Modell-
Agentur FAM. (FRA)

■ 180-183 Couverture et
pages doubles d'un catalogue de l'agence de manne-
quins FAM. (FRA)

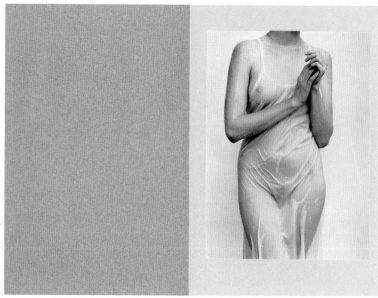

ART DIRECTOR:
WOODY PIRTLE
DESIGNER:
WOODY PIRTLE/JEFF WEITHMAN
ILLUSTRATOR:
WOODY PIRTLE
COPYWRITER:
WOODY PIRTLE/JOE RATTAN
STUDIO:
PIRTLE DESIGN
CLIENT:
PIRTLE DESIGN
■ 184-187

■ 184-187 In this brochure,
imaginatively painted
brooms allude to the skilled
creativity of the Pirtle
Design Group. (USA)

■ 184-187 Phantasievoll
angemalte Besen werben in
dieser Broschüre für das
Können der Agentur Pirtle
Design. (USA)

■ 184-187 Dans cette bro-
chure, des balais artistement
décorés démontrent le
savoir-faire de l'agence Pirtle
Design. (USA)

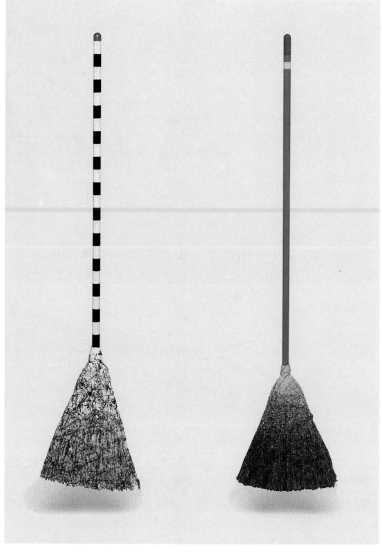

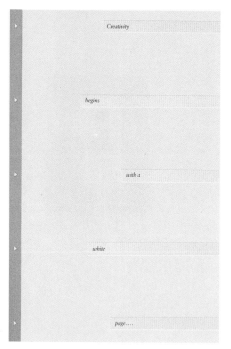

Creativity

begins

with a

white

page....

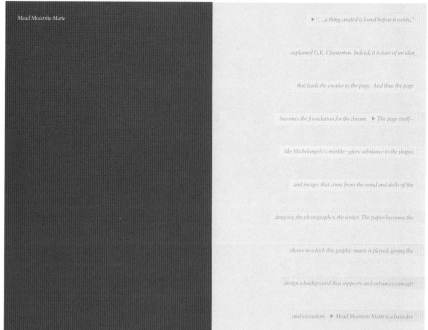

Mead Moistrite Matte

►"...a thing created is loved before it exists,"

explained G.K. Chesterton. Indeed, it is love of an idea

that leads the creator to the page. And thus the page

becomes the foundation for the dream. ►The page itself—

like Michelangelo's marble—gives substance to the shapes

and images that come from the mind and skills of the

designer, the photographer, the writer. The paper becomes the

silence in which this graphic music is played, giving the

design a background that supports and enhances concept

and execution. ►Mead Moistrite Matte is a basis for

ART DIRECTOR:
ROGER COOK/DON SHANOSKY
DESIGNER:
ROBERT FRANKLE
PHOTOGRAPHER:
ROBERT LLEWELLYN
COPYWRITER:
DAVE EYNAN
AGENCY:
COOK & SHANOSKY ASSOCIATES
CLIENT:
MEAD PAPER
■ 188–191

►Light

as a

straw

hat on

a spring

day—

worn

above a

student's

smile...

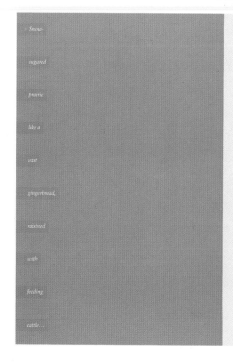

Snow-

sugared

prairie

like a

vast

gingerbread,

raisined

with

feeding

cattle...

ART DIRECTOR:
DANIEL FELDER/
PETER CHRISTENSEN
DESIGNER:
DANIEL FELDER/
PETER CHRISTENSEN
COPYWRITER:
MARK VOGEL
AGENCY:
SEC WERBEAGENTUR
CLIENT:
SEC WERBEAGENTUR
■ 192

We'd like to leave you with one last thought on choosing a giant New York agency.

ART DIRECTOR:
KEVIN GRIMSDALE
COPYWRITER:
JOHN MAHONEY
AGENCY:
THE MARTIN AGENCY
CLIENT:
THE MARTIN AGENCY
■ 193

Large, lumbering New York agencies once ruled the earth. But times have changed. The present and the future belong to advertising agencies that can not only react fast to fast-changing markets, but more importantly, anticipate them. An agency like us. To our mind, we think choosing The Martin Agency is just another case of natural selection.

■ 188-191 "Creativity begins with a white page". Cover and double spreads from a promotional brochure to introduce a new quality paper by Mead Paper. (USA)

■ 192 Folder for the announcement of a new telephone number and address of the SEC advertising agency. (SWI)

■ 193 "Large, lumbering New York agencies once ruled the earth. But times have changed." The Martin Agency uses a rubber dinosaur to illustrate the thought, and to demonstrate its own flexibility. (USA)

■ 188-191 «Kreativität beginnt mit einer weissen Seite» – Umschlag und Doppelseiten einer Werbebroschüre für eine neue Papiersorte von Mead Paper. (USA)

■ 192 Faltprospekt, mit dem die neue Telephonnummer und Adresse der SEC Werbeagentur angekündigt wird. (SWI)

■ 193 Mit einem Hartgummi-Dinosaurier wirbt die Martin Agency für ihre Flexibilität. «Grosse, schwerfällige New Yorker Agenturen regierten einst die Welt. Doch die Zeiten haben sich geändert.» (USA)

■ 188-191 «La créativité commence par une page blanche» – couverture et doubles pages d'une brochure publicitaire vantant les mérites d'un nouveau papier Mead. (USA)

■ 192 Dépliant indiquant le changement d'adresse et de numéro de téléphone de l'agence de publicité SEC. (SWI)

■ 193 Ce dinosaure en ébonite sert à mettre en évidence la souplesse et la capacité d'adaptation de l'agence Martin. «Les grandes agences new-yorkaises à la démarche pesante ont jadis régné sur le monde. Mais les temps ont changé.» (USA)

CHANGING LIGHT

ART DIRECTOR:
CHERYL HELLER
DESIGNER:
CHERYL HELLER
PHOTOGRAPHER:
HERB RITTS/MYRON
COPYWRITER:
PETER CAROLINE
AGENCY:
HELLER BREENE
CLIENT:
S.D. WARREN CO.
► ■ 197–202

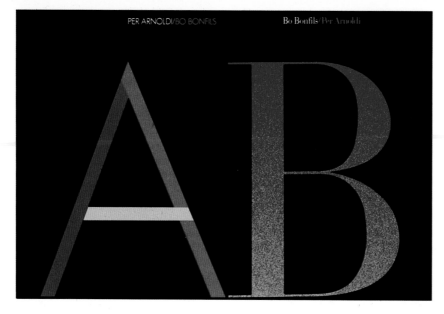

DESIGNER:
PAUL HAUGE
STUDIO:
ACCD DESIGN OFFICE
CLIENT:
ART CENTER COLLEGE
OF DESIGN, PASADENA
▲ ■ 194, 195

PER ARNOLDI/BO BONFILS   Bo Bonfils/Per Arnoldi

DESIGNER:
PER ARNOLDI/BO BONFILS
◄ ■ 196

■194, 195 Front page and inner page from an invitation to an exhibition of lamps and lighting systems sponsored by the Pasadena (California) Art Center College of Design. (USA)

■196 Invitation to an exhibition of works by the Danish poster designers Per Arnoldi and Bo Bonfils at the Musée de la Publicité in Paris. (FRA)

■197–202 Envelope, embossed cover and double spreads from the brochure of a paper manufacturer. (USA)

■194, 195 Einladung – Vorder- und Innenseite – des Art Center College of Design, Pasadena, Kalifornien, zu einer Ausstellung über Lampen und Lichtsysteme. (USA)

■196 Einladung für eine Ausstellung im Musée de la Publicité in Paris mit Werken der beiden dänischen Plakatkünstler Per Arnoldi und Bo Bonfils. (FRA)

■197–202 Couvert, Umschlag mit Reliefprägung und Doppelseiten der Werbebroschüre eines Papierherstellers. (USA)

■194, 195 Recto et verso de l'invitation de l'Art Center College of Design de Pasadena, en Californie, à une exposition de lampes et systèmes d'éclairage. (USA)

■196 Invitation du Musée de la Publicité de Paris à une exposition de l'œuvre des deux affichistes danois Per Arnoldi et Bo Bonfils. (FRA)

■197–202 Enveloppe d'expédition, couverture gaufrée et doubles pages de la brochure publicitaire d'un papetier. (USA)

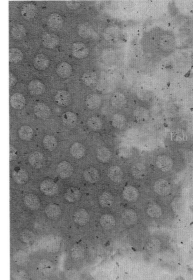

Immediately you expect to begin reading about cunning trout, powerful salmon, and other aquatic wonders that forever evade the fisherman's grasp. Well, not this time. This piece, you see, is not about the fish that got away, but about the men who got away. Mike, Charley, and Dick. Three men who answered the siren call and never turned back. What would make one forsake the chance to live a "normal life" and instead spend his days fishing? It's something that can only be known to someone who has spent long days fishing on a river. It's the beckoning beauty of the craft, and of the land itself. And the only way we could possibly capture that elusive beauty, was to use a special paper that was up to the task—our Warren Lustro Dull. Lustro Dull is a paper that can help elicit the beauty in any subject. Portraits, landscapes, still lifes, product shots. There are many reasons why, the foremost being the smooth uniform surface that provides for an unbroken film of ink. Thus your work reproduces the way you intended it to, with warm tones, and rich details.

How to best prepare a fresh trout dinner? The purist will say, a cast-iron pan, a little cornmeal, and some lemon if you have it. Others, who have been exposed to nouvelle ways, may expound about the wonders of pepper, and the importance of using a red-hot skillet. But, on the other hand, talk to anyone involved with the graphic arts about how to best present an idea, and no one will disagree about the importance of using the right paper, such as Warren Lustro Dull. The dull quality of Lustro offers a glare-free, smooth surface that reproduces a high-gloss, mottle-free ink film with maximum contrast.

ART DIRECTOR:
CHARLES S. ANDERSON
DESIGNER:
CHARLES S. ANDERSON/
JOE DUFFY
ILLUSTRATOR:
JOE DUFFY/S. WERNER/
C. ANDERSON/L. SCHULTE
COPYWRITER:
CHUCK CARLSON
AGENCY:
THE DUFFY DESIGN GROUP
CLIENT:
FRENCH PAPER CO.
■ 203–206

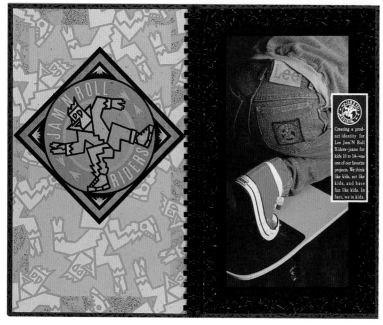

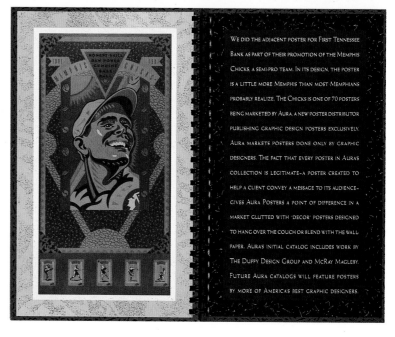

ART DIRECTOR:
JOE DUFFY/
CHARLES S. ANDERSON
DESIGNER:
JOE DUFFY/C. ANDERSON/
S. WERNER
ILLUSTRATOR:
J. DUFFY/C. ANDERSON/
LYNN SCHULTE/S. WERNER
COPYWRITER:
CHUCK CARLSON
AGENCY:
THE DUFFY DESIGN GROUP
►►■ 207–213

■ 203–206 Cover and double spreads of a spirally-bound brochure with which the French Paper Co. publicizes its new *Speckletone* colors. Several of the advertising assignments carried out by the Duffy Design Group are illustrated. This agency was also responsible for the design of the brochure. (USA)

■ 207–213 With mountings characteristic of those used for postage stamps, a process which necessitates an exacting technical know-how, Dickson's proves the guaranteed high quality of its work as a printer. (USA)

■ 203–206 Umschlag und Doppelseiten einer spiralgebundenen Broschüre, mit der der Papierhersteller French Paper Co. für die neuen *Speckletone*-Farben wirbt. Darin abgebildet sind verschiedene Werbeaufträge, die von der Duffy Design Group ausgeführt wurden. Diese Agentur war auch verantwortlich für die Gestaltung der Broschüre. (USA)

■ 207–213 Mit Briefmarken-ähnlichen Aufklebern, deren Herstellung ein hohes technisches Können voraussetzt, stellt die Druckerei Dickson's in diesem Buch die von ihr garantierte Qualität unter Beweis. (USA)

■ 203–206 Couverture et exemples des doubles pages d'une brochure publicitaire à reliure spirale où le papetier French Paper Co. présente les nouveaux coloris *Speckletone*. On y trouve diverses commandes publicitaires exécutées par l'agence américaine The Duffy Design Group, qui a aussi réalisé cette brochure. (USA)

■ 207–213 Des autocollants ressemblant à des timbres-poste et dont la fabrication requiert un savoir-faire technique poussé permettent à l'imprimerie Dickson's de se positionner dans le faveur de ses clients prospectifs. (USA)

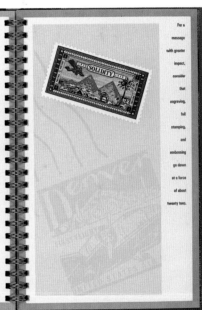

FS-Six passes: 4 tint foils, 1 pigmented, 1 metallic. EN-1 pass: dark lavender. EM-One pass: Single-level emboss of stamp. NOTE: Zero registration tolerance allowed in four press runs for tint foils.

For companies that need to communicate their solid foundations, foil stamping and engraving say it best. For example, in our Solidity stamp, the copper metallic foil stamping reinforces the stateliness and permanence of the pyramids. The reflective copper combines with the dark lavender engraving ink to create a tremendous contrast of textures. Engraving inks have greater opacity and intensity than other inks. Plus, the engraving press forces the ink into the paper fibers for greater image integrity and printing durability. When you need high-gloss engraving, we can use varnish-based engraving inks. While they are impressive in their brilliance, gloss engraving inks add extra drying time and expense. In some cases, foil stamping can achieve a similar effect at a lower cost. Both foil stamping and embossing combine well with engraving. On the adjacent stamp, the tint foils abutting the dark lavender engraving help create greater contrast and definition. For a good example of how well embossing, engraving, and foil stamping work together, see Stamp 5. A fine engraver has the skills of both artist and artisan. Those at Dickson's are masters at free-hand engraving and always touch up photo-engraved dies with hand-tooling to regain detail lost in the etching process. The ability of an engraved image to hold detail allows you to build a monument to corporate strength, all in the space of a postage stamp.

For a message with greater impact, consider that engraving, foil stamping, and embossing go down at a force of about twenty tons.

Any letterhead design tells your readers who you are. A superior letterhead design tells them why you are who you are.

Prestige cannot be spelled out in so many words. But with engraving, you can put it on paper for everyone to see. Engraved lines have opacity and detail not possible in other forms of printing. The reason for that is the process itself. An engraving die holds a negative image photo-etched or hand-tooled into metal—usually copper or steel. The entire plate is inked and then wiped clean, leaving ink only in the negative, or intaglio, areas of the die. When paper and die are brought together on press, the paper is forced into the intaglio areas by a counter—a male match to the female die. This adds a small measure of embossing to engraved images. In fact, embossing is much like engraving, but without the use of ink. Because the counter effectively seals the edges of the areas being printed, it keeps the ink from spitting—feathering into the surrounding paper. That's why 4-point engraved type comes out crisp enough to read easily and hairline detail refuses to muddy. Metallic inks bring yet another option to engraving. The silver metallic ink on the adjacent stamp has an antique finish because it's not burnished. Burnishing adds gloss or polish to engraved metallic inks with a second pass through the press using the same die, not inked. Like prestige, engraving has no substitute. No other form of printing offers more elegance, more dignity, more opportunity to impress.

FS-Three passes: 1 tint, 2 metallic. EN-2 passes: Line-work, black and silver. EM-1 pass: Stamp single-level embossed. NOTE: Silver engraving ink is not burnished to contrast with the metallic foils.

The question isn't how much humor should you put into a letterhead design, but how much do you dare leave out.

How to show a corporation's sense of humor in a letterhead design is serious business. Although people who work in corporations laugh easily, making a whole company smile is hard work. But the work is worth it. American consumers reward a play of wit—if it's not forced. The world soon tires of a joker. On a laughter line that runs from warm chuckles to screaming whoops, it's best to shoot for the chuckle end. The pearl foils in this stamp soften the zaniness of our clown by adding an air of artistry. Pearl foils have an intriguing finish, with illusory depth that invites people to look into them, not just at them. Like all good clowns, this one shows impeccable attention to detail in his make-up and costume. It's there because the line-work photo-etched into the copper engraving die that makes the image was touched up with hand-tooling to add crispness. And the separations for the foils required tolerances measured to within one thousandth of an inch. The engraving die used for this stamp was chrome-plated to extend its life. Copper dies can be chromed, stripped, and re-chromed to last nearly indefinitely. That means an engraving die, like a good sense of humor, can be pulled off the shelf and used whenever the need arises. The economics of that fact have been known to put big smiles on the faces of chief financial officers. Considering most CFO's ability to scowl, that takes some magic.

LI-One pass: flesh tone. FS-Seven passes: 5 pearl, 1 metallic, 1 pigmented. EN-3 passes: all line-work. EM-Stamp single-level embossed. NOTE: Abutting pearl foils requires a perfect register each time.

ART DIRECTOR:
Cheryl Heller
DESIGNER:
Cheryl Heller/David Lopes
PHOTOGRAPHER:
Clint Clemens
COPYWRITER:
Peter Caroline
AGENCY:
Heller Breene
CLIENT:
S.D. Warren Co.
■ 214–219

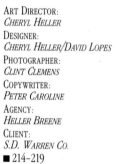

Coke was a nickel, Eisenhower was President, and a car was a creative medium. This was the Fifties, when America's youth took the raw material Detroit provided, and created a new art form...rolling, roaring, glistening beasties...custom-crafted conveyances that shattered the peace of the neighborhood and blew the minds of solid citizens. Drawn to the fabled exploits of shadetree mechanics and acetylene artists, we learned a new vocabulary: bored and stroked, tucked and rolled, chopped and channeled, dechromed and frenched. Our dreams were metalflake, candy-apple, pearlescent, pin-striped, and flamed. And we gauged performance not by figures on paper, but by rubber on blacktop. That was then and this is now. Figures on paper have now assumed more relevance to our lives. And images on paper

can now deliver more impact, excite and inspire us, particularly when they're printed on the paper you're looking at now, Warren Lustro Gloss. Its smooth, level surface allows an outstanding continuity of ink film, with consequently higher printed gloss. Because this flat surface reflects light in a highly directional and uniform manner, dark areas are deep and rich, highlights sparkle with gem-like detail, colors glow from within, and gloss takes on new meaning. Don't overlook the consistency of Lustro Gloss...you'll find the surface is remarkably uniform both from side to side and from run to run. Take a close look at Lustro. It's an impressive vehicle... one to take us back to a special time, when gas was 23 cents a gallon and mythic monsters cruised the boulevards.

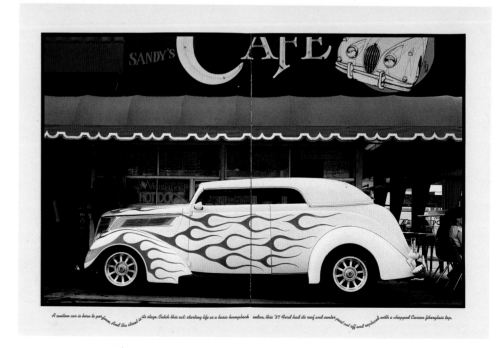

A custom car is born to perform. And the street is its stage. Catch this act: starting life as a basic humpback sedan, this '37 Ford had its roof and center posts cut off and replaced with a chopped Carson fiberglass top.

■ 214–219 Automobiles in the form of "Street Dreams" is the theme of this brochure for S.D. Warren, a manufacturer of paper products. The unfolding double spread *(218)* shows a 1948 *Plymouth Special Deluxe* and its partly wooden framework. (USA)

■ 214–219 «Strassenträume» – Autos sind das Thema dieser Werbebroschüre für den Papierhersteller S.D. Warren. Die beidseitig ausklappbare Doppelseite *(218)* zeigt einen *Plymouth Special Deluxe* mit Holzteilen aus dem Jahr 1948. (USA)

■ 214–219 «Rêves sur roues»: les automobiles constituent le sujet de cette brochure réalisée pour le papetier S.D. Warren. La double page qui se déplie sur les deux côtés *(fig. 218)* montre une *Plymouth Special Deluxe* 1948 carrossée en bois. (USA)

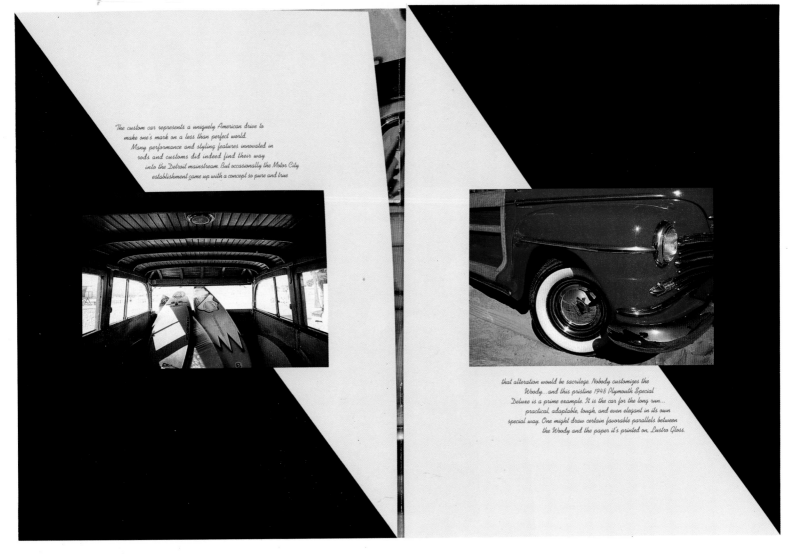

The custom car represents a uniquely American drive to make one's mark on a less than perfect world. Many performance and styling features innovated in rods and customs did indeed find their way into the Detroit mainstream. But occasionally the Motor City establishment came up with a concept so pure and true

that alteration would be sacrilege. Nobody customizes the Woody...and this pristine 1948 Plymouth Special Deluxe is a prime example. It is the car for the long run... practical, adaptable, tough, and even elegant in its own special way. One might draw certain favorable parallels between the Woody and the paper it's printed on, Lustro Gloss.

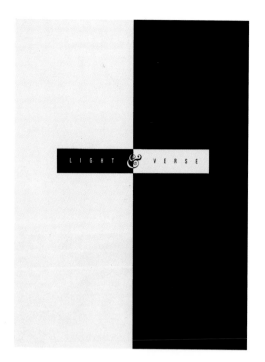

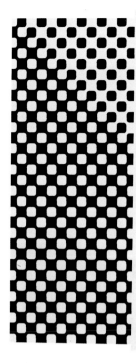

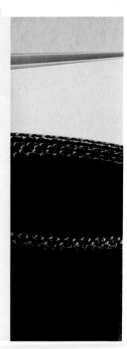

ART DIRECTOR:
JOHN VAN DYKE
DESIGNER:
JOHN VAN DYKE
PHOTOGRAPHER:
TERRY HEFFERNAN
COPYWRITER:
JOHN BELL
AGENCY:
VAN DYKE COMPANY
CLIENT:
WEYERHAEUSER PAPER CO.
■ 220–223

DESIGNER:
JIM MIHO
CLIENT:
CHAMPION INTERNATIONAL CORP.
■ 224-227

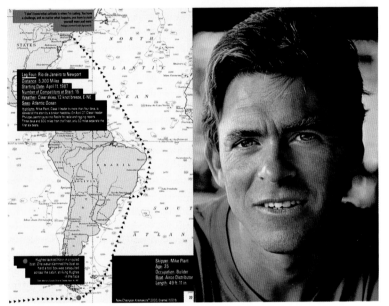

■ 220-223 Cover and double spreads from the Weyerhaeuser Paper Company's promotional brochure. (USA)

■ 224-227 With photographs and sketches from the log book of a sailing regatta, a manufacturer of paper publicizes its new quality *Kromekote 2000*. (USA)

■ 220-223 Umschlag und Doppelseiten einer Werbebroschüre der Weyerhaeuser Paper Company. (USA)

■ 224-227 Mit Photos und Tagebuchaufzeichnungen einer Segelregatta wirbt ein Papierhersteller in dieser Broschüre für seine neue Papiersorte *Kromekote 2000*. (USA)

■ 220-223 Couverture et doubles pages d'une brochure publicitaire du papetier Weyerhaeuser Paper Company. (USA)

■ 224-227 Dans cette brochure, un papetier met en vedette son nouveau papier *Kromekote 2000* en l'utilisant comme support d'un reportage illustré sur une régate. (USA)

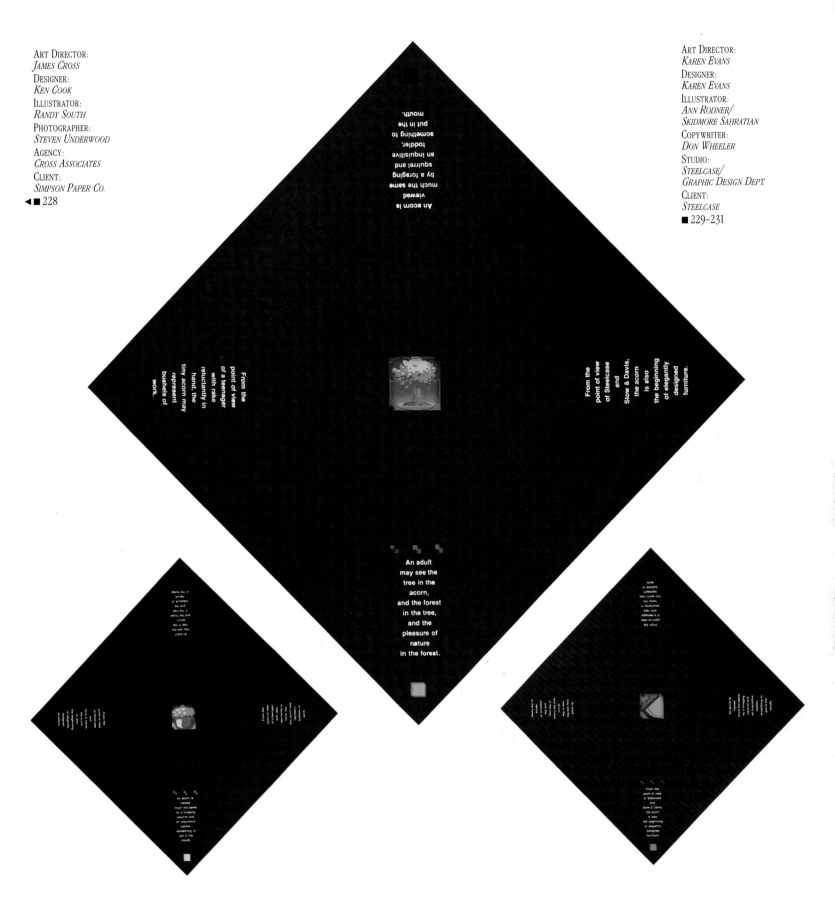

ART DIRECTOR:
JAMES CROSS
DESIGNER:
KEN COOK
ILLUSTRATOR:
RANDY SOUTH
PHOTOGRAPHER:
STEVEN UNDERWOOD
AGENCY:
CROSS ASSOCIATES
CLIENT:
SIMPSON PAPER CO.
◀ ■ 228

ART DIRECTOR:
KAREN EVANS
DESIGNER:
KAREN EVANS
ILLUSTRATOR:
ANN RODNER/
SKIDMORE SAHRATIAN
COPYWRITER:
DON WHEELER
STUDIO:
STEELCASE/
GRAPHIC DESIGN DEPT.
CLIENT:
STEELCASE
■ 229-231

■228 Promotional material for the Simpson Paper Co. as conceived for graphic designers. The folder, with two textile closures, has been made from transparent, grooved plastic and printed in color. The contents consist of a brochure, a spiral notebook, and small folders with cut-outs on the front sides. (USA)

■229-231 Invitation to visit the Steelcase, Stow & Davis showroom during CONEXION 87 - a furniture trade fair. The black card-board has cut-outs. According to its position, it reveals various pictures of an oak or an acorn. The texts in the corner describe how the oak tree is seen by the firm, an adult, a teenager, and by a squirrel. (USA)

■228 An Graphik-Designer gerichtetes Werbematerial des Papierherstellers Simpson Paper Co. Die Mappe ist aus transparentem, gerilltem Plastik, farbig bedruckt, und hat zwei Textilverschlüsse. Der Inhalt besteht aus einer Broschüre und einem Block mit Spiralbindung sowie aus kleinen Faltmappen mit Ausstanzungen auf der Vorderseite. (USA)

■229-231 Einladung zu einer Möbel-Fachschau. Der schwarze Karton ist mit Ausstanzungen versehen und lässt je nach Position im Zentrum verschiedene Bilder der Eiche bzw. der Eichel sichtbar werden. Das Thema der Texte in den Ecken: die Eiche aus der Sicht der Firma, eines Erwachsenen, eines Jugendlichen und eines Eichhörnchens. (USA)

■228 Matériel publicitaire du papetier Simpson Paper Co. destiné aux graphistes. Le dossier en plastique cannelé transparent imprimé en couleurs est doté de deux fermetures textiles. Il renferme une brochure, un bloc à reliure spirale et des mini-dossiers dont la couverture est agrémentée de motifs en découpe. (USA)

■229-231 Invitation à une exposition d'ameublements réservée aux professionnels. Le carton noir est muni de découpes révélant selon la position au centre diverses représentations du chêne et du gland. Le sujet des commentaires apparaît dans les coins: le chêne du point de vue de l'entreprise, d'un adulte, d'un adolescent et d'un écureuil. (USA)

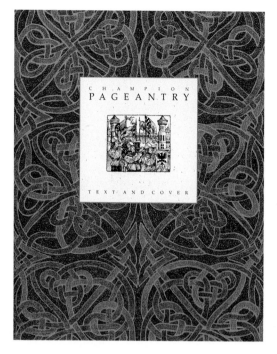

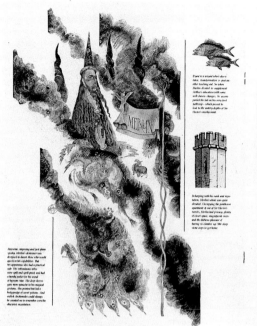

MERLIN

ART DIRECTOR:
WOODY PIRTLE/JOE RATTAN

DESIGNER:
JOE RATTAN/WOODY PIRTLE

ILLUSTRATOR:
JOE RATTAN/GREG KING 232
JACK UNRUH 233

COPYWRITER:
MARY LANGRIDGE

STUDIO:
PIRTLE DESIGN

CLIENT:
CHAMPION INTERNATIONAL CORP.
▲ ■ 232, 233

ART DIRECTOR:
STEVEN TOLLESON

DESIGNER:
STEVEN TOLLESON/
NANCY PAYNTER/SUSAN GROSS

AGENCY:
TOLLESON DESIGN

CLIENT:
SIMPSON PAPER CO.
▼ ■ 234–236

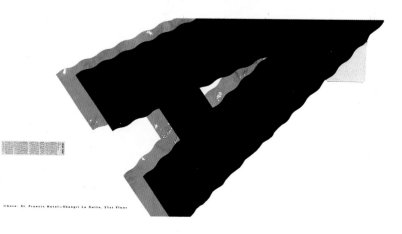

ART DIRECTOR:
CHRISTOPHER GARLAND
DESIGNER:
CHRISTOPHER GARLAND
PHOTOGRAPHER:
AARON CHANG/
J. GRANT BRITTAIN/
STEVE WILKINGS/
PAUL GALLAHER/CHRIS NOBLE
AGENCY:
XENO
CLIENT:
CONSOLIDATED PAPERS, INC.
■ 237–242

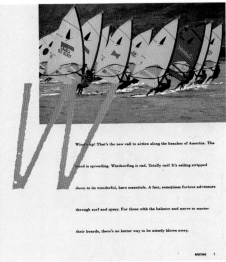

■ 232, 233 Cover and double spread from a promotional brochure. It has been designed for a manufacturer of paper for the introduction of *Pageantry* as a new product. (USA)

■ 234–236 The invitation card to an AIGA convention as used by Simpson, a paper manufacturer. The illustration shows the front and back sides, closed and opened. (USA)

■ 237–242 Cover and double spreads from a promotional brochure of Consolidated Papers. Inc. (USA)

■ 232, 233 Umschlag und Doppelseite einer Werbebroschüre eines Papierherstellers, mit der die neue Papiersorte *Pageantry* vorgestellt wird. (USA)

■ 234–236 Geschlossene und geöffnete Einladung (Vorder- und Rückseite) des Papierherstellers Simpson zu einer AIGA-Konferenz. (USA)

■ 237–242 Umschlag und Doppelseiten einer Werbebroschüre der Consolidated Papers, Inc. (USA)

■ 232, 233 Couverture et double page d'une brochure publicitaire conçue pour un papetier. On y présente une nouvelle qualité de papier baptisée *Pageantry.* (USA)

■ 234–236 Invitation montrée fermée et ouverte (recto et verso). Il s'agit d'une conférence de l'AIGA à laquelle le papetier Simpson convie les intéressés. (USA)

■ 237–242 Couverture et doubles pages d'une brochure publicitaire de Consolidated Papers, Inc. (USA)

ART DIRECTOR:
Thomas Kluepfel/
Stephen Doyle
DESIGNER:
Drenttel Doyle Partners
PHOTOGRAPHER:
Chris Callis 246
George Hein 247
Victor Schrager 248
AGENCY:
Drenttel Doyle Partners
CLIENT:
Drenttel Doyle Partners
■ 243-248

13
COCKTAILS
PUNCH

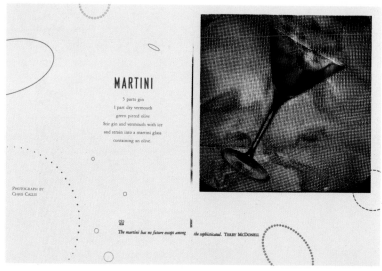

Those after-hour meetings are, for us, a way of exploring the symbolic commitment of breaking bread. Of course one offers not offers a bit of one's self over that cocktail—leaving business chance of that moment leading to others. It is in this spirit Friends, both photographers and writers, were invited to "join interpretation of that drink with us. We offered each a as responsible hosts. Meetings take place in these pages: a recipes as icebreakers. Sometimes the conversation is natural, just don't have a lot in common, but we're glad they had the

possibilities of friendship without the larger and more only to buy, but, more importantly, one behind and risking a personal moment, with the that this book was conceived. us for a drink", and to share their personal particular cocktail and proceeded to act dialogue of words, pictures, and design .... with sometimes we have to prompt, and sometimes our friends chance to meet. It's that chance we salute.

WE SHOULD GET TOGETHER SOME NIGHT FOR A DRINK.

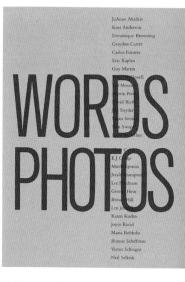

WORDS PHOTOS

COCKTAILS 13

JoAnne Akalitis
Kurt Anderson
Dominique Browning
Graydon Carter
Carlos Fuentes
Eric Kaplan
Guy Martin
J. Moon
Martin Perez
David Rieff
Snyder
Susan Sontag
Sweo
E.J. Camp
Mitch Epstein
Jerald Frampton
Lee Friedman
George Hein
Britta Hill
Len J
Karen Kuehn
Joyce Ravid
Maria Robledo
Bonnie Schiffman
Victor Schrager
Neil Selkirk

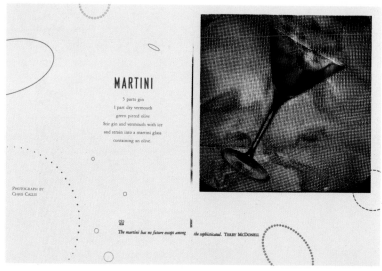

MARTINI

5 parts gin
1 part dry vermouth
green pitted olive
Stir gin and vermouth with ice
and strain into a martini glass
containing an olive.

PHOTOGRAPH BY
CHRIS CALLIS

The martini has no future except among *the sophisticated.* TERRY McDONELL

C·U·B·A

(Homage to G.C.I.)

The secret to making a good Cuba Libre is the Coca-Cola. Without the genuine stuff, even a Cuba Libre made

2 ounces rum

with the noblest rum on the island is little more than glucose with an extra gear. Unfortunately, It was just one of

Coca-Cola

those wretched concoctions which served as my introduction to the Cuba Libre. And in Cuba to boot. Alas, the

½ fresh lime

Coca-Cola company had itself gotten the boot some years before and Cubans were mixing their fine Havana

Pour rum into a tall glass.

Club rum with some Godless, caramel-colored ooze made, I firmly believe, out of the nectar of Bulgarian date

Squeeze the lime and drop in

palms. This bastard concoction could give you a hangover before you'd taken your first sip. - So much for the

Add ice and fill

Cuba Libre. There is still the question of Cuba libre—and what a difference that missing article and lower-

with Coca-Cola

cased / makes—which itself has certain ineluctable connections with the Coca-Cola company. From a product

label, one can infer the world. Thus the question: Can you get a good Cuba Libre in Cuba libre?

David Rieff

people have been wondering about that, with no very happy result, since January 1st, 1959, when Fidel

George Hein

Castro, a man who drinks Greek brandy (Metaxa, to be precise), swallowed Havana like a cocktail olive.

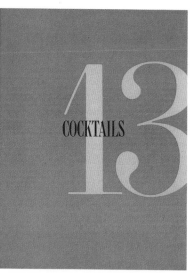

When I was a rancher in the West I would drive my herd along by blowing a huge bubble and keeping it moving in front of them. Each cow saw her own reflection in the bubble and was so enchanted she followed it wherever I blew. It happened though in Nevada one summer that an ill wind blew my bubble across the dunes and my herd stampeded after it into the desert.

So I took the only re-course open to me and that night lit a fire, took off my clothes and sought communion with the coyotes. They were coy at first, lingering in the sage at the edge of the fire's light. I knew they were secretly fond of ambergris though, and put my ambergris idol of a squatting Teonanacti on the ground in front of me. Soon their king loped out of the shadows and told me what had happened with my cattle. He said the earth is asleep and its mouth is off in the desert, seventy-five miles north of Elko, breathing out fairies. One of these fairies had stolen my cows and taken them to the mouth to take part in an ageless chthonic ceremony. He told me I could recover them if I remembered the charm Torpedo Cocktail but if I ever offered one of these drinks to anyone I would be lost.

I left the next morning and in seven days came to the gorge that was the mouth of circled weaving cows.

TORPEDO COCKTAIL

The first guardian of the ceremony who was a bull of fire within a shell of ice within a mist of fragrance asked me the riddle "What is it that is cold and then hot?" and I gave the answer "A torpedo cocktail, because it is cold on the lips and then hot in the heart." And I drank one and advanced the first step to the ultimate center.

The second guardian of the ceremony who was a titanic toad with the head of a clock then asked me the riddle "What is it that is fast and then slow?" and I rowe the answer "A torpedo cocktail because it shoots to your body's center and then creeps out to the periphery." And I drank another and advanced the second step to the ultimate center.

Then the third guardian of the ceremony, who was a huge cocktail shaker with fur and big teeth asked me another riddle which slipp my memory, only the answer was torpedo cocktail. Then I advanced the last step to the edge of the earth's mouth. I was so happy I whooped and danced and made a big wassail and finally threw a cocktail over the edge. The last I remembered the coyote king's warning not to offer a drink to anyone. The earth got drunk and belched and then it yawned and I plummeted to fairyland below.

1½ OUNCES SCOTCH
make scotch with fine ice and strain into an old-fashioned glass. Add a twist of lemon.

BY TORPEDO

ERIC KAP

■ 243-248 Fourteen authors and photographers were asked by Drenttel Doyle Partners to suggest their interpretations of a specific cocktail drink. The recipes for the cocktails are mentioned in part. "13 Cocktails and a Punch" is a brochure for the agency's own promotion. (USA)

■ 249 Folder with hardcover in linen for the promotion of a new Design District in Dallas, Texas. It is shown open and closed. (USA)

■ 250-253 Cover and double spreads from a self-promotional brochure of the Bradley Printing Co. (USA)

■ 243-248 Vierzehn Autoren und Photographen wurden von der Agentur Drenttel Doyle Partners gebeten, einen bestimmten Cocktail, dessen Rezept jeweils angegeben ist, zu interpretieren. Die Broschüre «13 Cocktails und ein Punch» wird für Eigenwerbungszwecke verwendet. (USA)

■ 249 Faltmappe mit festem Leinenumschlag - geschlossen und geöffnet gezeigt - als Werbung für einen neuen Design-Distrikt in Dallas. (USA)

■ 250-253 Umschlag und Doppelseiten aus einer Werbebroschüre der Bradley Printing Co. (USA)

■ 243-248 Quatorze auteurs et photographes ont été invités par l'agence Drenttel Doyle Partners à interpréter un cocktail déterminé dont la recette est indiquée à chaque fois. La brochure qui en est résultée, «13 Cocktails et un punch», sert aux besoins promotionnels de l'agence. (USA)

■ 249 Dossier pourvu d'une couverture pleine toile, montré ouvert et fermé. Publicité pour un nouveau quartier de Dallas où s'agglomèrent les studios de design. (USA)

■ 250-253 Couverture et doubles pages d'une brochure publicitaire de l'imprimerie Bradley Printing Co. (USA)

ART DIRECTOR:
WALTER HORTON
DESIGNER:
WALTER HORTON/
COLLETTE MICHAUD
AGENCY:
SIBLEY/PETEET DESIGN
CLIENT:
DALLAS MARKET CENTER
■ 249

ART DIRECTOR:
STEVEN LISKA
DESIGNER:
STEVEN LISKA
PHOTOGRAPHER:
CHARLES SHOTWELL
COPYWRITER:
JEANNETTE LOCURTO
AGENCY:
LISKA & ASSOCIATES
CLIENT:
BRADLEY PRINTING CO.
■ 250-253

REFLECTIONS OF INSPIRATION

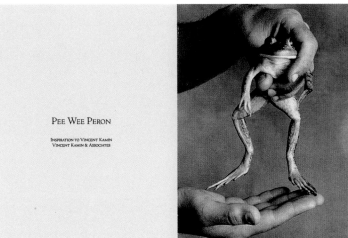

PEE WEE PERON

INSPIRATION TO VINCENT KAMIN
VINCENT KAMIN & ASSOCIATES

ANNIE

INSPIRATION TO WENDY PRESSLEY-JACOBS
PRESSLEY JACOBS DESIGN, INC.

The Mason jar was first patented in 1858

A TOOL IS PERHAPS THE ULTIMATE EXAMPLE OF AN OBJECT WHOSE DESIGN IS DICTATED PRIMARILY BY FUNCTION.

Shaped for maximum strength and for rolling, the barrel is like a container on wheels.

ART DIRECTOR:
KIT HINRICHS/NEIL SHAKERY
DESIGNER:
KIT HINRICHS/NEIL SHAKERY
PHOTOGRAPHER:
JIM BLAKELEY/STEVEN HELLER
COPYWRITER:
DELPHINE HIRASUNA/
MAXINE GAIBER/JOHN DREYFUSS
AGENCY:
PENTAGRAM DESIGN
CLIENT:
ART CENTER COLLEGE
OF DESIGN, PASADENA
■ 254-260

■ 254-260 The educational program offered by the Pasadena (California) Art Center of Design is publicized in two brochures and a folder entitled "Why the Art Center?" and "Why Design?" (USA)

■ 254-260 Mit zwei Broschüren («Warum das Art Center?» und «Design, warum?») und einem Faltprospekt wirbt das Art Center College of Design, Pasadena, Kalifornien, für sein Ausbildungsangebot. (USA)

■ 254-260 Deux brochures intitulées respectivement «Pourquoi l'Art Center?» et «Le design, pourquoi?» et un dépliant sont mis au service de la campagne de recrutement d'étudiants de l'Art Center College of Design de Pasadena. (USA)

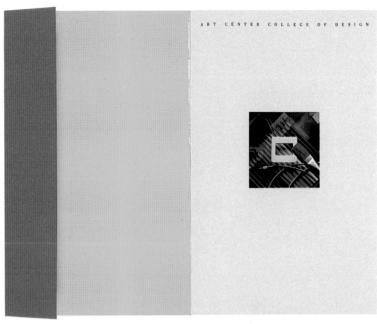

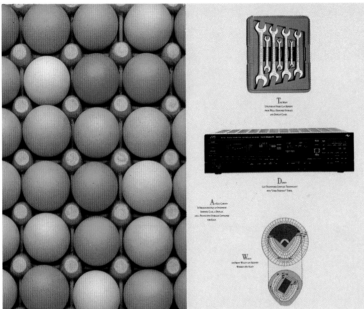

George Bernard Shaw overstated the case when he said, "Love of economy is the root of all virtue." But, as usual, he made his point. It is a point not lost on designers, who know they can offer manufacturers and consumers excellence without breaking the bank.

The role of design in helping clients and consumers hang onto their money seldom is recognized by the general public.

Designers find the least expensive materials to do a job well, and work with engineers to discover the most economical methods of assembling those materials, thereby minimizing production costs.

Designers advise manufacturers about personnel matters related to factory working environments that affect worker productivity, thereby minimizing labor costs.

Designers offer expert advice on packaging, distribution and merchandising, thereby minimizing marketing costs.

Design's relationship to saving money is obvious in products like disposable razors and good looking, inexpensive wristwatches. It is less obvious, but no less important, in big ticket items like factory machinery and automobiles.

The designer's role in cutting production, labor, and marketing costs results in more prosperous clients and a buying public that can get more value for less money.

In short, economics effected by designers make people richer, more successful, and happier. The designer's role reflects Samuel Johnson's comment that "without frugality, none of us can be rich."

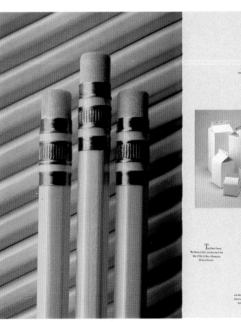

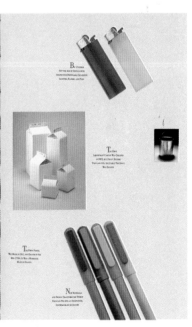

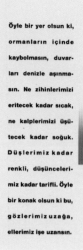

Öyle bir yer olsun ki, ormanların içinde kaybolmasın, duvarları denizle aşınmasın. Ne zihinlerimizi eritecek kadar sıcak, ne kalplerimizi üşütecek kadar soğuk. Düşlerimiz kadar renkli, düşüncelerimiz kadar tarifli. Öyle bir konak olsun ki bu, gözlerimiz uzağa, ellerimiz işe uzansın.

1 9 8 8

ART DIRECTOR:
BÜLENT ERKMEN
DESIGNER:
BÜLENT ERKMEN
ILLUSTRATOR:
HAYDAR KARABEY
COPYWRITER:
MELTEM AHISKA/
HAYDAR KARABEY
AGENCY:
REKLAMEVI
CLIENT:
REKLAMEVI
■ 261-263

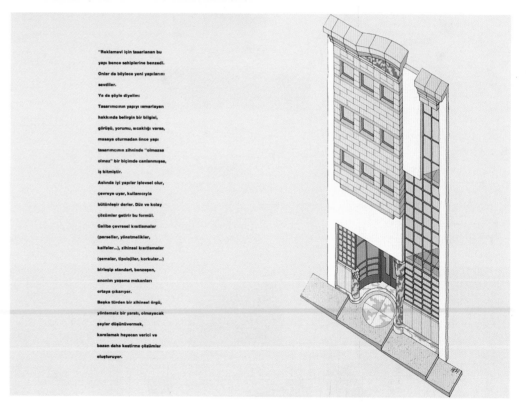

"Reklamevi için tasarlanan bu yapı bence sahiplerine benzedi. Onlar da böylece yeni yapılarını sevdiler.
Ya da şöyle diyelim:
Tasarımcının yapıyı ısmarlayan hakkında belirgin bir bilgisi, görüşü, yorumu, sıcaklığı varsa, masaya oturmadan önce yapı tasarımcının zihninde "olmazsa olmaz" bir biçimde canlanmışsa, iş bitmiştir.
Aslında iyi yapılar işlevsel olur, çevreye uyar, kullanıcıyla bütünleşir derler. Düz ve kolay çözümler getirir bu formül.
Galiba çevresel kısıtlamalar (parseller, yönetmelikler, kalfalar...), zihinsel kısıtlamalar (şemalar, tipolojiler, korkular...) birleşip standart, benzeşen, anonim yaşama mekanları ortaya çıkarıyor.
Başka türden bir zihinsel örgü, yöntemsiz bir yaratı, olmayacak şeyler düşünüvermek, karalamak heyecan verici ve bazen daha kestirme çözümler oluşturuyor.

■ 261-263 Cover and double spreads from a Turkish advertising agency's brochure for its own promotion. (TUR)

■ 264-267 Promotional prospectus, folded in an unusual way, for Archetype, the Boston architectural firm. (USA)

■ 261-263 Umschlag und Doppelseiten einer Broschüre für Eigenwerbungszwecke einer türkischen Werbeagentur. (TUR)

■ 264-267 Aussergewöhnlich gefalteter Werbeprospekt des Bostoner Architekturbüros Archetype. (USA)

■ 261-263 Couverture et pages doubles de la brochure autopromotionnelle d'une agence de publicité turque. (TUR)

■ 264-267 Prospectus publicitaire du bureau d'architecture Archetype de Boston. On notera le pliage inhabituel. (USA)

ART DIRECTOR:
Nancy Skolos
DESIGNER:
Nancy Skolos
COPYWRITER:
Nina Tovish
AGENCY:
Skolos, Wedell + Raynor
CLIENT:
Archetype Architecture
■ 264–267

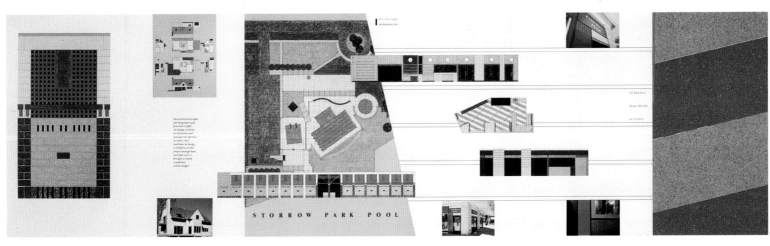

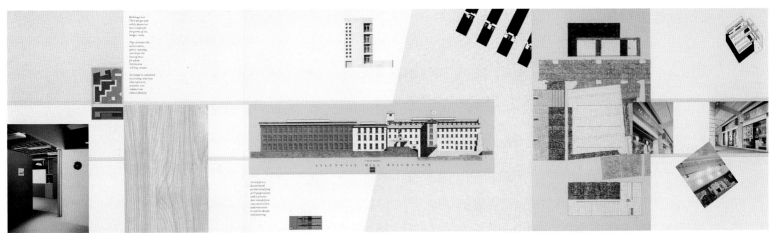

ART DIRECTOR:
KEN WHITE
DESIGNER:
LISA LENN
COPYWRITER:
AILEEN FARNAN ANTOINER
AGENCY:
WHITE + ASSOCIATES
CLIENT:
COLE MARTINEZ CURTIS
■ 268-270

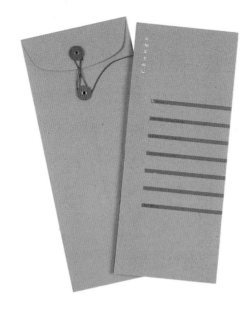

ART DIRECTOR:
LESLIE SMOLAN
DESIGNER:
ALYSSA A. ADKINS
ARTIST:
MARK KOSTABI 271
JACK GOLDSTEIN 273
ROGER BROWN 274
AGENCY:
CARBONE SMOLAN ASSOCIATES
CLIENT:
SMITH BARNEY
► ■ 271-274

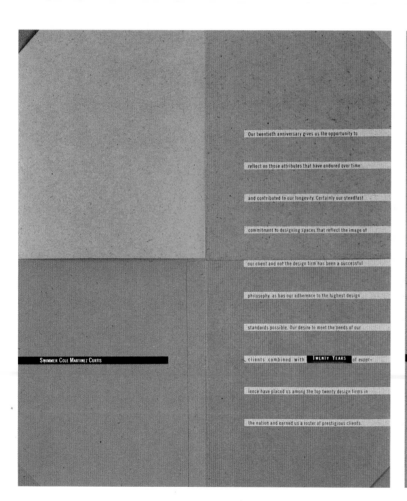
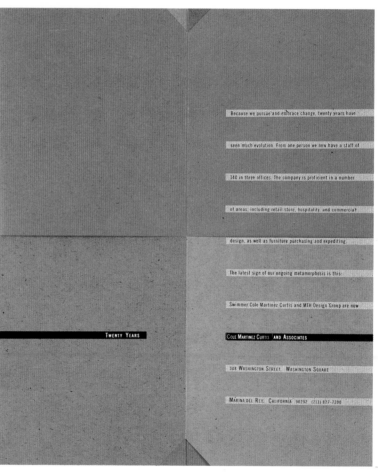

■ 268-270 Notification of the merger of two firms and the announcement of the new name. Cover and folding card are made from a paper with a clearly visible wood structure and which has been cut in a special way. The firm's new name is displayed in the cut-out. (USA)

■ 271-274 Mergers and acquisitions are the themes of this brochure. The cover and three of the double spreads are shown. The pages on the right hand side *(273, 274)* cover only half of the succeeding pages. (USA)

■ 268-270 Ankündigung des Zusammenschlusses zweier Firmen und Bekanntgabe des neuen Namens. Umschlag und Faltkarte sind aus stark holzhaltigem Papier, das einen besonderen Zuschnitt sowie eine Ausstanzung für den neuen Namen hat. (USA)

■ 271-274 Fusionen und Akquisitionen sind das Thema dieser Broschüre für Smith Barney. Hier der Umschlag und drei Doppelseiten. Die rechten Seiten *(273, 274)* verdecken jeweils nur die Hälfte der folgenden Seiten. (USA)

■ 268-270 Annonce de la fusion de deux entreprises et du nouveau nom du groupe ainsi constitué. La couverture et la carte dépliante ont une forte teneur en pâte mécanique et comportent une découpe pour la nouvelle raison sociale Cole Martinez Curtis and Associates. (USA)

■ 271-274 Cette brochure pour Smith Barney traite des fusions et acquisitions d'entreprises. Couverture et trois doubles pages. Les pages de droite *(fig. 273, 274)* ne recouvrent que la moitié des pages qui suivent. (USA)

At Smith Barney, we earn it. We earn it *for our clients*. Our philosophy is predicated on a commitment to meeting the growth and development objectives of our clients, as opposed to maximizing fee income in a transaction-oriented environment. This commitment to our clients' best interests is demonstrated by creative ideas, thorough analysis, professionalism and hard work. Our Firm's unique quality is that it is large enough to provide the full array of investment banking services, but small enough to focus our resources effectively and quickly on behalf of the client. The Mergers and Acquisitions Group constantly draws on:

— The Firm's Corporate Finance Department, maintaining senior level relationships with most U.S. corporations, broad industry expertise, superior knowledge of current financing techniques, and assistance in acquisition financing.

— The Firm's extensive securities trading departments, providing current assessments of securities markets' reactions to proposed transactions and financing alternatives.

— Smith Barney's top-ranked Research Department, providing invaluable industry expertise as well as close relationships with companies followed by our research analysts.

— Smith Barney International, with offices throughout Western Europe and a leading presence in Japan, providing a wealth of contacts with foreign corporations and assistance in cross-border transactions.

2

Smith Barney's Mergers and Acquisitions Group has successfully handled all types of major business combinations. Our expertise in each of these areas is described in more detail on the following pages.

Corporate Restructuring and Takeover Defense Preparation

Buyer Representation—Negotiated Acquisitions

Buyer Representation—Leveraged Buyouts

Buyer Representation—Unilateral Tender Offers

Takeover Defense

Seller Representation

Cross-Border Transactions

Joint Ventures

Representation of Block Shareholders

Fairness Opinions and Valuation

Takeover Defense

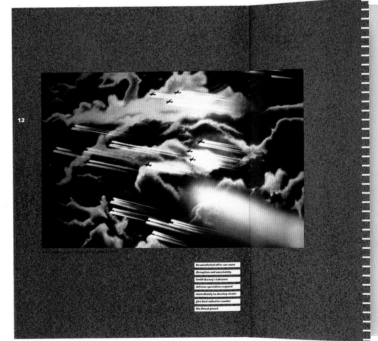

An unsolicited takeover contest is the most demanding situation that any company, its management and its Board of Directors ever experience. The pressures are intense, as management and the Board must make hard decisions in a very limited time period. A target company needs the best advice it can get from experienced advisors who are familiar with the company and committed to devoting unlimited energy and resources to its defense.

The central issue is whether a target company should remain independent, if possible, or seek to maximize value in the short term through a sale of the company to a white knight. Smith Barney's primary objective, when possible, is to assist its clients in remaining independent, so that the management and the Board of Directors can maximize value for shareholders through the implementation of a long-term strategic plan. Over 55% of Smith Barney's clients who have been the target of an unsolicited tender offer, a stock accumulation program or a proxy fight for control have remained independent. In 35% of our defense assignments, where management and the Board decided to sell the company, Smith Barney has maximized value by finding a white knight or conducting an auction. In two instances, the original bidder did acquire control of a client, but at a higher price than the original bid in a negotiated transaction approved by the Board.

An unsolicited offer can cause disruption and uncertainty. Smith Barney's takeover defense specialists respond immediately to develop strategies best suited to counter the threat posed.

12   13

Cross-Border Transactions

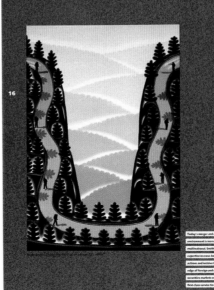

Merger and acquisition activity across international borders has become more prevalent for many reasons. Business growth on an international scale has continued to be a major priority for both American and foreign companies, as they seek to penetrate new markets. In many industries, a strong international presence is critical to maintaining competitiveness in a global marketplace. Additionally, foreign companies have always been attracted to the growth potential and political stability of investments in corporate America.

Smith Barney has strong expertise in consummating international merger and acquisition transactions. This effort requires a broad understanding of the differences between business practices in America and abroad, as well as foreign currency and exchange rate issues and the complexities of securities trading in foreign markets. The Mergers and Acquisitions Group works closely with Smith Barney International, which has offices throughout Western Europe and a leading presence in Japan, providing an invaluable source of contacts and expertise to effect cross-border transactions.

Today's merger and acquisition environment is increasingly multinational. Smith Barney's expertise in cross-border transactions and incisive knowledge of foreign and domestic securities markets ensure first class service to our clients.

16   17

The friends of Bonnie Legco invite you to a shower in her home at 320 Morris Ave. in Lutherville, Maryland on Sunday, February 22 at 3 P.M. RSVP soon to Cathy Cage at 301-592-8260. And please don't tell. Because with you at the shower it'll be a big splash.

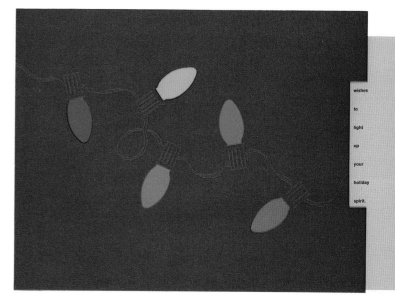

wishes
to
light
up
your
holiday
spirit.

JULIA TAM DESIGN

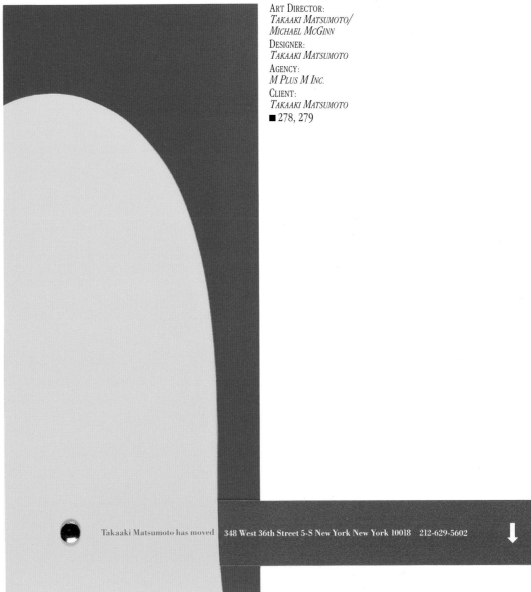

ART DIRECTOR:
TAKAAKI MATSUMOTO/
MICHAEL McGINN
DESIGNER:
TAKAAKI MATSUMOTO
AGENCY:
M PLUS M INC.
CLIENT:
TAKAAKI MATSUMOTO
■ 278, 279

Takaaki Matsumoto has moved

Takaaki Matsumoto has moved · 348 West 36th Street 5-S New York New York 10018 212-629-5602

ART DIRECTOR:
RON SULLIVAN
ILLUSTRATOR:
DARREL KOLOSTA
COPYWRITER:
MAX WRIGHT
AGENCY:
SULLIVAN PERKINS
CLIENT:
BONNIE LEGRO
▲■275

ART DIRECTOR:
JULIA TAM
ILLUSTRATOR:
JULIA TAM
COPYWRITER:
JULIA TAM
AGENCY:
JULIA TAM DESIGN
◀■ 276, 277

■ 275 A baby shower in celebration of a new birth occasioned this invitation which has been conceived in the form of a shower curtain. (USA)

■ 276, 277 Envelope with cut-outs and a movable card which "lets the lights burn". Created by a design studio as a Christmas card and for its own promotion. (USA)

■ 278, 279 Card announcing a change of address. The movable part indicates the new address. (USA)

■ 275 Eine «Baby Shower» (wörtlich Baby-Dusche) ist Anlass dieser als Duschvorhang konzipierten Einladung zur Feier einer Geburt. (USA)

■ 276, 277 Umschlag mit Ausstanzungen und beweglicher Karte, die die Lichter «brennen» lässt, als Weihnachtsgruss und Eigenwerbung eines Design-Studios. (USA)

■ 278, 279 Umzugsanzeige mit einem beweglichen Teil, auf dem die neue Adresse angegeben ist. (USA)

■ 275 Cette invitation à fêter une naissance prend la forme d'un rideau de douche et annonce que les réjouissances commenceront par une «Baby Shower». (USA)

■ 276, 277 Couverture à découpes; la carte mobile «allume» les bougies de Noël. Autopromotion d'un studio de design qui transmet ainsi ses vœux de fin d'année. (USA)

■ 278, 279 Avis de déménagement; la partie mobile comporte l'indication de la nouvelle adresse. (USA)

■ 280 Various brochures for "The 21 Club" in New York. They include a menu card which is shown both from the front and from the inside, a brochure containing information for private banquets, and a brochure which relates the club's history. (USA)

■ 281-283 The wine list from a brasserie. The cover and the unfolded card are illustrated as well as the complete back side of the menu card from the same restaurant. Both cards are fully laminated. (AUS)

■ 280 Verschiedene Broschüren für «The 21 Club» in New York. Es handelt sich um die Speisekarte, die hier von vorne und aufgeschlagen gezeigt ist, eine Informationsbroschüre für private Banquetts und eine Broschüre über die Geschichte des Clubs. (USA)

■ 281-283 Vorderseite und auseinandergefaltete Weinkarte einer Brasserie sowie die vollständige Rückseite der Menükarte des gleichen Lokals. Beide Karten sind vollständig laminiert. (AUS)

■ 280 Diverses brochures pour le «21 Club» de New York: on voit ici tout d'abord le recto d'un menu, qui est aussi présenté ouvert; une brochure d'information pour l'organisation de banquets privés; et une brochure relatant l'histoire du Club. (USA)

■ 281-283 Recto de la carte des vins d'une brasserie, que l'on montre également dépliée; verso complet du menu du même restaurant. Ces deux cartes sont entièrement laminées. (AUS)

ART DIRECTOR:
BARRIE TUCKER

DESIGNER:
BARRIE TUCKER/CAZ TILLY

ILLUSTRATOR:
ROBERT MARSHALL

STUDIO:
BARRIE TUCKER DESIGN

CLIENT:
DISCOVERY BAY DEVELOPMENTS

▶■ 281-283

ART DIRECTOR:
PETER HARRISON/
SUSAN HOCHBAUM

DESIGNER:
SUSAN HOCHBAUM

ILLUSTRATOR:
PAUL DAVIS

COPYWRITER:
JOHN BERENDT

AGENCY:
PENTAGRAM DESIGN

CLIENT:
THE '21' CLUB

◀■ 280

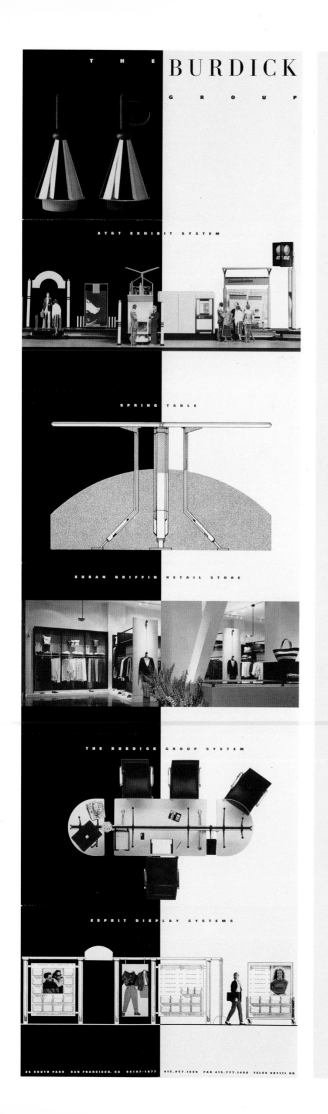

ART DIRECTOR:
Susan K. Burdick/
Bruce Burdick
DESIGNER:
Cindy Steinberg
PHOTOGRAPHER:
Various
COPYWRITER:
Susan K. & Bruce Burdick
STUDIO:
The Burdick Group
CLIENT:
The Burdick Group
■ 284, 285

THE BURDICK GROUP

● ● ●

The Burdick Group looks for ways to accomplish meaningful changes for our clients by using the tools of design. These changes are accomplished for clients who wish to separate themselves from their competition in a stronger way than can be achieved by simply changing external form.

The work of The Burdick Group has altered the perception of what a desk, a retail space or an exhibition system can be. It may seem that the conceptual development and design processes for such diverse projects are not related – but they are.

In each case The Burdick Group looks for functional changes that will produce useful changes of form – the inherent solution that lies within the problem. In each we search for a "fit" – an appropriateness of things and their parts – approaching these problems with the perceptions and resources of the arts and technology.

An example of visual change growing from function is the tableware designed by The Burdick Group. Large stem-like glasses of stainless steel and soft plastic bowls on the reverse side have turning heads that grind pepper and salt while they fit the hand and grace the table.

AT&T EXHIBIT SYSTEM

AT&T needed an exhibit system to be used for each of its divisions, to display and interconnect their diverse product range. The system will be used at exhibitions ranging in size from 200 to 10,000 square feet.

To express both visually and functionally the products' interconnectivity, The Burdick Group developed a modular track system. Each track module connects to the next one (somewhat like a set of train tracks). After the track units are joined, display and communication elements, products and lighting can be located at any point along them. Interconnectivity of products to each other takes place in the space between the tracks, which carries electrical and data cabling.

The Burdick Group developed the graphic standards for the system which provides for a planned order of resources, with color-coded headlines differentiating display areas, and graphic panels containing product identification, diagrams and illustration.

SPRING TABLE

The Burdick Group developed the Spring Table, with its "knee-bend" leg, which combines the benefits of both a pedestal and leg support system. Manufactured by Herman Miller, Inc., it can be used for conferencing, working and dining. Utilizing advances in technology, materials and manufacturing techniques, the table is designed so that its various parts (tops, edge, edge inserts, legs, feet) can be specified in different colors and materials, providing different finish combinations based upon the table's use.

SUSAN GRIFFIN RETAIL STORE

The Burdick Group designed the interior, display elements and graphics for Susan Griffin's and John Lazaro's new store in San Francisco, based upon their merchandising concept – to display clothing by collections.

Vertical display elements, which create individual collection areas, rest on a continuous display curb that runs throughout the store as a unifying element. The end result is a composition of refined display elements, constructed from a limited palette of materials which are separated and juxtaposed within the space. The interior differentiates "Susan Griffin" from the competition by using the visual clarity and order of the display elements to create an environment where the clothes can be "seen" and understood.

The Burdick Group developed the store identity program for "Susan Griffin," in which two typefaces are combined, reflecting the sophisticated combination of materials and merchandise to be found within the store.

THE BURDICK GROUP SYSTEM

The Burdick Group observed that we spend more time behind our desks than we do in our automobiles. However, no desk offered the matching of detail with function found in a Porsche or BMW. Existing desks – flat surfaces to write on, with assorted storage opportunities – use contemporary materials, but do not solve contemporary needs.

Working from this observation, The Burdick Group set out to design a new type of desk – a personal work tool for management – with the capacity to integrate the computer with working and conferencing. The furniture is based on a beam support system, which allows beams to be connected in a variety of configurations. Electrical and communication cables are carried underneath the beams so that computers and telephones can be located where required – at a work or meeting area.

The location of work surfaces, computer tables and storage, which are supported by the beams, can be changed as the user's needs change. Paper handling elements, such as letter trays, snap into place along the beams, requiring no tools for movement. Top surfaces come in glass, wood, laminate or marble, allowing the user's environment to be personalized.

ESPRIT DISPLAY SYSTEMS

Esprit wanted merchandising and display elements, for use in their Super Stores and in department stores, to separate them visually and functionally from other merchandise. The displays are changed weekly, monthly or even daily to accommodate their ever-changing line of clothing.

The Burdick Group designed two groups of elements – Movable Platforms and the Perimeter System – which define Esprit's environments while displaying clothing and graphics. The Movable Platforms, with soft edges on the platforms (bumpers and large, colorful castors), come in three different heights to create different types of spaces. Their perforated display panels support baskets, hang rods and accessories, which snap into place.

The Perimeter System bolts on the reverse side, accommodates the same merchandising items as the Platforms. Its construction of columns, lintels and portals has an architectural rhythm, creating a strong visual presence. Platforms, for shoppers, contribute to the expression of the energetic and lively environment.

ART DIRECTOR:
Rick Biedel/Bill Bonnell
DESIGNER:
Rick Biedel/Lisa Bernich
PHOTOGRAPHER:
Various
AGENCY:
Bonnell Design Assoc.
CLIENT:
Koch + Lowy
■ 286–289

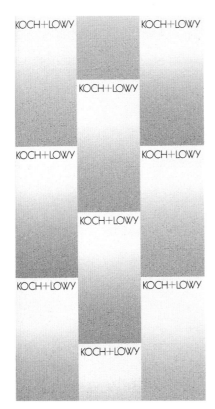

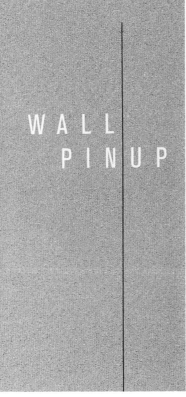

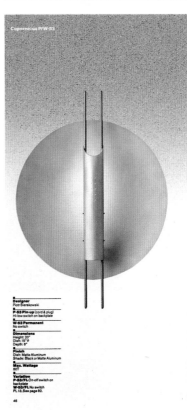

■ 284, 285 Front and back sides of a folder for the Burdick Group, designers of systems for exhibitions, display and store furnishings. (USA)

■ 286–289 Cover and double spreads from a catalog for lamps and lighting fixtures from Koch + Lowy. (USA)

■ 284, 285 Vorder- und Rückseite eines Faltprospekts für The Burdick Group, eine Gruppe, die sich mit Ausstellungssystemen, Ladeneinrichtungen etc. befasst. (USA)

■ 286–289 Umschlag und Doppelseiten aus einem Katalog für Lampen von Koch + Lowy. (USA)

■ 284, 285 Un dépliant du Burdick Group spécialisé dans les matériels de présentation pour exposants et dans l'aménagement de locaux de vente, magasins, etc. (USA)

■ 286–289 Couverture et doubles pages d'un catalogue des éclairagistes Koch + Lowy. (USA)

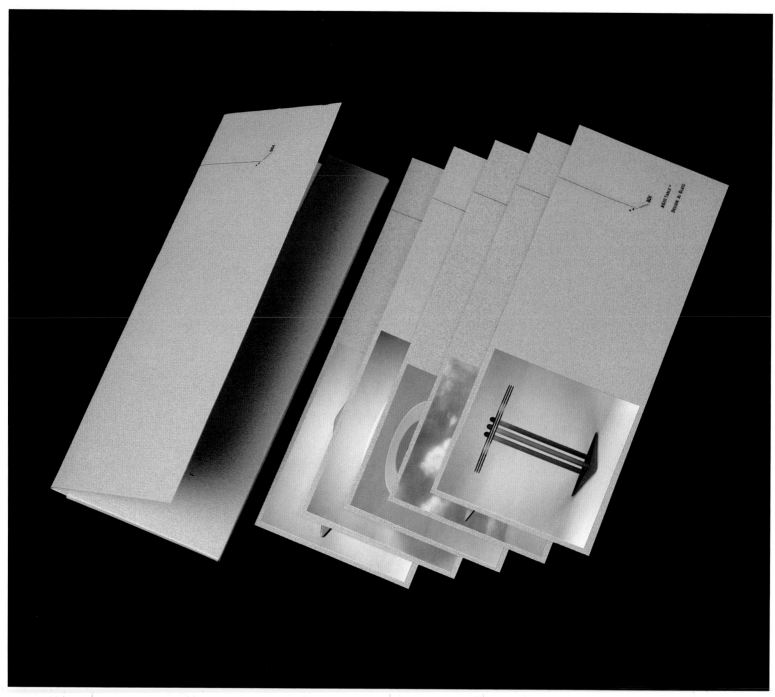

Art Director:
Al Glass
Designer:
Al Glass/Jim Keaton
Photographer:
Ed Castle/Peter Garfield
Studio:
Glass & Glass, Inc.
Client:
Becker Designed, Inc.
■ 290

■ 290 Cover of a small folder and its contents. Photographs mounted on loose gray cardboard sheets illustrate a collection of tables by Becker Designed Inc. (USA)

■ 291-294 Catalog presenting the table collection *Möbelle.* The cover is protected by a wrapping of transparent paper. Some of the double spreads are also shown. (GER)

■ 290 Umschlag einer Faltmappe und der Inhalt, lose Blätter aus grauem Karton mit aufgeklebten Photos, für eine Kollektion von Tischen der Firma Becker Designed. (USA)

■ 291-294 Mit Transparentpapier geschützter Umschlag und Beispiele der Doppelseiten für einen Katalog mit der Tischkollektion *Möbelle.* (GER)

■ 290 Couverture d'un dossier et son contenu, des feuilles mobiles de carton gris illustrées de photos collées pour une gamme de tables Becker Designed, Inc. (USA)

■ 291-294 Couverture à jaquette de protection transparente et doubles pages types d'un catalogue publié par le fabricant de tables *Möbelle.* (GER)

Möbelle

ART DIRECTOR:
PIT FRANKE/KARL KÖNIG
PHOTOGRAPHER:
CLAUDIA TERSTAPPEN/THEO
BENTGENS/STEPHAN HOFER
AGENCY:
DAS IDEEN-SYNDICAT
CLIENT:
MÖBELLE
■ 291–294

ELIX

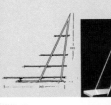

Der eine sieht in dem Objekt ein Kunstwerk, der andere will nur von einem Gebrauchsgegenstand, eben von einem Regal wissen. Beide haben Recht. Dennoch tun beide, durch ihre festgelegte Betrachtungsweise, dem Objekt Abbruch.

Selbst wenn der Gedanke von einem Regal ausging, so muß man hier auch von einem Objekt sprechen, das Attribute der Kunst geltend macht. Das optisch Reduzierte akzentuiert nicht nur die Eigenständigkeit des kreativen Vorgangs, sondern auch vor allem eine Fülle von Formen. Formen, die durch unterschiedliche Anordnungen im Raum entstehen und die das Regal und den Raum zugleich ergänzen.

So wird dieses Regal von dem Benutzer immer neue geistige Anforderungen verlangen. Dadurch, daß es jederzeit zu unterschiedlichen Plazierungen herausfordert und somit neue Raumeindrücke erzeugt, ist es Kunstwerk und Gebrauchsgegenstand zugleich: zwei Eigenschaften, die die Kreativität erheben.

Die Auseinandersetzung zwischen den Designern und ihrem Werk endet nicht nach der Fertigstellung, sondern setzt sich fort. Egal, wo immer man es aufstellen mag, dieses Regal wird seiner Umgebung neue Definitionsmöglichkeiten verleihen.
El Loko, Bildhauer.

Elix gibt es in 3 Oberflächen-Variationen: Grün/seidenmatt (Abbildung), Dunkelblau/hochglanz und Birke natur mit Lackversiegelung.
Elix kostet: 2.800,– DM

HUNDERTFADEN

Es gibt verschiedene Möglichkeiten, am Schreibtisch zu arbeiten. Die einen schwören darauf, sich hinter Bergen von Akten und einem Anschein von Geschäftigkeit zu verbergen und beklagen, daß der Schreibtisch eigentlich nie übergenug Fläche verfügt. Andere sind energische Vertreter der These, daß nur eine leergefegte Schreibtischfläche klare Gedankengänge und Konzentration ohne Ablenkung ermöglicht. Die meisten Schreibtische bieten eine Kompromißlösung an: Schubladen, kleine und große, möglichst bis zum Boden. Schubladen nicht nur für das Notwendigste, sondern auch für das, was auch noch morgen oder übermorgen erledigt werden kann, für das, was später einmal von Wichtigkeit sein könnte oder genauerer Überlegung bedarf. Wenn sich eines Tages auch die letzte, ohnehin schwer zu erreichende Schublade weigert, sich weiterhin schließen zu lassen, wandert ein großer Teil des Schubladeninhalts in den Papierkorb. Und man stellt sich vor: es müßte einen Schreibtisch mit großer Fläche geben, dessen Schubladen in Griffhöhe nur Platz für das Notwendige bieten.
Christiane Paul, Dr. Phil.

Hundertfaden gibt es in 3 Oberflächen-Variationen: Dunkelblau/hochglanz (Abbildung), Grün/seidenmatt und Birke natur mit Lackversiegelung.
Hundertfaden kostet: 3.900,– DM

KÜMPE

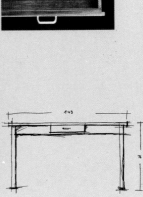

Ja, Mensch, der Kümpe, der täte auch bei mir reinpassen, und da würd' ich dann mal dem Zuccini-Nudel-Auflauf essen weil, man nimmt 400 g grüne Bandnudeln, kocht sie 10 Minuten, gießt, schreckt und tropft sie ab. Dann ein klitzekleines Bündchen Basilikum abpulen, trockentupfen, in Streifchen schneiden und 200 g Gorgonzola, 100 g gemahlene Nüsse, hmmm, 200 g Schlagsahne, 200 g Ricotta, Pfeffer und 2 Eßl. Weinbrand cremig rühren und mit Salz abschmecken. Halt, stop, bei soviel naschen! Jetzt 8 kg 750 g kleine Zuccini waschen, mit Haushaltspapier trockentupfen, die Enden abschneiden und kräftig losgeraspelt. Dann jeweils ein Drittel der Nudeln, der Zuccini und der Basilikumstreifen und der Käsecreme in die gefettete Auflaufform schichten. Den Vorgang zweimal wiederholen. Haben Sie? Jetzt noch die oberste Schicht Käsecreme mit Semmelmehl und mit Butterflöckchen belegen und rein das Ganze für 50 Minuten in den Backofen auf 225 Grad. Bon appetit!
Michael Weigert, Texter.

Ich, Kümpe, gehöre zum Grundbestand des menschlichen Mobiliars. Eine gelungene häusliche Stelle für mich wäre die Küche. Ist sie doch besonders als Ort geeignet, auch und gerade dort im engeren und weiteren Sinne zu kochen. Im engeren am Herd und im weiteren im gespannten Gespräch, im doppelten Sinn also, um mich herum. Frei von jeglichem Begriffsgestrüpp denke ich mir so die Küche als einen Ort der handfesten Utopie.
Manfred Trinkl, Monteur.

Kümpe gibt es in 3 Oberflächen-Variationen: Birke natur mit Lackversiegelung (Abbildung), Dunkelblau/hochglanz und Grün/seidenmatt.
Kümpe kostet: 2.600,– DM

MARTEX

© Mad Marti Ragowell, 1987

ART DIRECTOR:
JAMES SEBASTIAN
DESIGNER:
JAMES SEBASTIAN/
JUNKO MAYUMI
INTERIOR DESIGNER:
WILLIAM WALTER
PHOTOGRAPHER:
BRUCE WOLF
AGENCY:
DESIGNFRAME INC.
CLIENT:
MARTEX/
WEST POINT PEPPERELL
◄■ 295-297

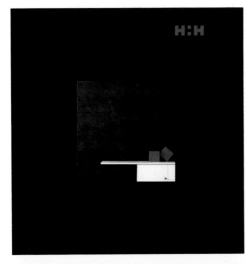

■ 295-297 Hardcover catalog for *Martex* home furnishing fabrics. A photograph has been mounted on the cover. Table of contents and a double spread are also shown. (USA)

■ 295-297 Umschlag mit aufgeklebten Photos, die Inhaltsseite und ein Beispiel der Doppelseiten aus einem hochformatigen Katalog mit festem Einband, für *Martex*-Heimtextilien. (USA)

■ 295-297 Couverture illustrée de photos collées, page de sommaire et double page type d'un catalogue en hauteur relié pleine toile, pour les textiles d'intérieur *Martex*. (USA)

ART DIRECTOR:
FRÉDÉRIC KLEIN
DESIGNER:
NICOLE MORISSETTE
PHOTOGRAPHER:
FRÉDÉRIC KLEIN
STUDIO:
STUDIO 70
CLIENT:
THREE H MANUFACTURING LTD.
■ 298-301

■ 298-301 Cover and some of the double spreads from a prospectus for a furniture program from Three H Manufacturers. (CAN)

■ 298-301 Umschlag und Beispiele der Doppelseiten aus einem Prospekt für Möbelprogramme der Three H Manufacturers. (CAN)

■ 298-301 Couverture et pages doubles d'un prospectus publicitaire des ameublements canadien Three H Manufacturers. (CAN)

ART DIRECTOR:
JOHN CASADO
DESIGNER:
JOHN CASADO
PHOTOGRAPHER:
RUDI LEGNAME
COPYWRITER:
JOHN CASADO
AGENCY:
CASADO INC.
CLIENT:
HAWORTH, INC.
■ 302–308

■ 302–308 A box of heavy, cut-out cardboard and the brochure for *Cata+lyst* furniture which it was designed to contain. The brochure has a spiral binding and its cardboard cover has been similarly decorated with cut-outs. One of its pages can be unfolded like a poster. *303–308* show some of the double spreads. (USA)

■ 302–308 Mit Ausstanzungen versehener Schuber aus starkem Karton und die darin enthaltene Broschüre für *Cata+lyst*-Möbel. Sie hat eine Spiralbindung und ihr Kartonumschlag hat ebenfalls Ausstanzungen. Eine der darin enthaltenen Seiten lässt sich wie ein Plakat auseinanderfalten. *303–308* zeigen Beispiele der Doppelseiten. (USA)

■ 302–308 Emboîtage à découpes, en carton fort, et son contenu, une brochure de présentation des meubles *Cata+lyst*, dotée d'une reliure spirale et comportant également des découpes dans sa couverture cartonnée. L'une de ses pages se déplie comme une affiche. Les fig. *303–308* montrent des pages doubles de cette publication. (USA)

ART DIRECTOR:
CLANE GRAVES
DESIGNER:
CLANE GRAVES
PHOTOGRAPHER:
RODNEY RASCONA
COPYWRITER:
LESLIE JOHNSON
AGENCY:
FORMAZ
CLIENT:
ROCKFORD CORP.
■ 309–311

■ 309–311 Recto d'un dépliant montré également mi-ouvert et complètement déplié, pour les haut-parleurs *Acoustat-Spectra*, véritable «technosculpture». (USA)

■ 312–317 Brochure affectant le format d'un journal, pour les haut-parleurs *Canton;* couverture et pages doubles choisies. (GER)

■ 309–311 Vorderseite, der halb- und der vollständig geöffnete Faltprospekt für *Acoustat-Spectra*-Lautsprecher: «Eine technologische Skulptur, deren Funktion Musik ist.» (USA)

■ 312–317 In Journal-Format gestaltete Broschüre für *Canton*-Lautsprecher; hier der Umschlag und Beispiele der Doppelseiten. (GER)

■ 309–311 Front page of the half and fully opened folder for *Accoustat-Spectra* loudspeakers illustrating the phrase "Technological sculpture whose function is music". (USA)

■ 312–317 This brochure has been designed in the format of a journal. The cover and some of the double spreads reproduce different models of *Canton* loudspeakers. (GER)

ART DIRECTOR:
Christof Gassner

DESIGNER:
Christof Gassner

ILLUSTRATOR:
Christof Gassner/
Bernd Ciepluch

PHOTOGRAPHER:
Ulfert Beckert

COPYWRITER:
Dieter Skerutsch

CLIENT:
Canton Elektronik

■ 312–317

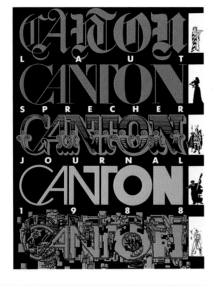

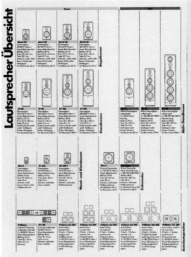

Noch nie hat jemand gehört, wie ein Verstärker klingt. Kein Mensch hat je die Töne vernommen, die ein Plattenspieler produziert. Einzig die Lautsprecher sind es, die das Ohr wahrnimmt; und nur durch sie hindurch – wie durch ein Fenster – die anderen Geräte der HiFi Anlage. Also hängt naturgetreue Wiedergabe am Ende davon ab, wie ungefärbt und durchlässig diese Fenster sind; also bilden die Lautsprecher die wichtigsten Bausteine der Anlage. Jedoch, so scheint es, auch die langweiligsten. Keine Tasten zu drücken, keine Knöpfe zu drehen, keine Skalen abzulesen: Über Lautsprecherboxen gibt es nicht viel zu sagen ... Oder etwa doch? Erfahren Sie in diesem Heft, daß Lautsprecher nicht nur die wichtigsten, sondern auch die interessantesten HiFi Geräte sind. Welche Typen es gibt. Wie man sie auswählt. Worauf man hören sollte. (Und worauf nicht.) Wie man sie bestens aufstellt. Was beim Betrieb von Lautsprechern zu beachten ist – und vieles mehr.

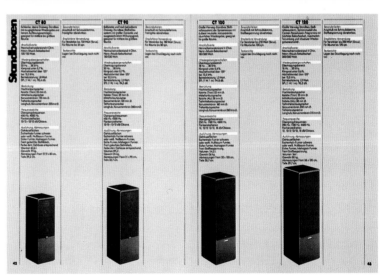

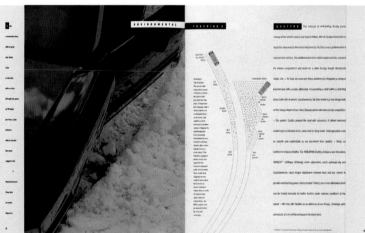

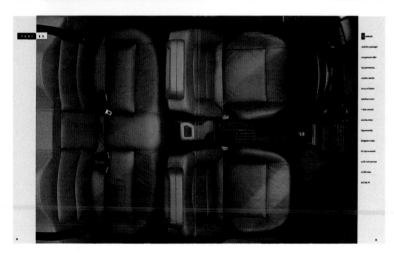

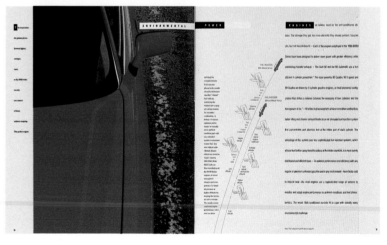

ART DIRECTOR:
BARRY SHEPARD

DESIGNER:
BARRY SHEPARD/STEVE DITKO/
KARIN BURKLEIN ARNOLD/
DOUGLAS REEDER

PHOTOGRAPHER:
RICK RUSING/RICK GAYLE

COPYWRITER:
STEVE HOGAN

STUDIO:
SHR COMMUNICATIONS
PLANNING & DESIGN

CLIENT:
AUDI OF AMERICA, INC.
■ 318-322

ART DIRECTOR:
RANDOLPHE NOLTE

DESIGNER:
RANDOLPHE NOLTE

PHOTOGRAPHER:
PETER KNAUPP

COPYWRITER:
PETER GOLDAMMER

AGENCY:
RANDOLPHE NOLTE CREATIVE
CONSULTANTS

CLIENT:
SCHÖNWALD
►■ 323

■ 318-322 Cover and double spreads from a catalog introducing the new series of *Audi 80/90*. (USA)

■ 323 Folder with loose sheets publicizing *Schönwald* porcelain. They illustrate scenes from the production, the line of porcelain known as "Form 98" and its creation. (GER)

■ 318-322 Umschlag und Doppelseiten aus einem Katalog, mit dem die neue *Audi-Serie 80/90* vorgestellt wird. (USA)

■ 323 Faltmappen mit losen Blättern als Werbung für *Schönwald*-Porzellan. Die Themen: Szenen aus der Herstellung, die Linie «Form 98» und deren Entstehung. (GER)

■ 318-322 Couverture et doubles pages d'un catalogue de présentation de la nouvelle série *Audi 80/90*. (USA)

■ 323 Dossiers comportant des feuilles mobiles, pour la publicité des porcelaines *Schönwald*. Les sujets: étapes de fabrication, la gamme «Form 98» et son développement. (GER)

Schönwald

Hemingway hat es benutzt.
Die Queen hat es benutzt.
Sie haben es benutzt.

Das Hotelporzellan.

Auf Schönwald trifft man fast überall. Kein anderes Porzellan steht häufiger auf dem Tisch, wenn man ins Hotel geht. Oder ins Restaurant, oder in die Gaststätte, oder ins Krankenhaus, oder in die Luft – mit der Lufthansa oder einer anderen Fluggesellschaft. Dieser Erfolg hat eine lange Geschichte; es ist die Geschichte des Hotelporzellans: Bis zu den dreißiger Jahren gab es für Hotels und Gaststätten kein eigenes Geschirr. Was benutzt wurde, besaß nur eine Besonderheit: Es war besonders klobig, um länger haltbar zu sein. Mehr nicht. Das wollte man bei Schönwald ändern. Systematisch wurden zum ersten Mal die Form und Funktion von Hotelporzellan untersucht und neue Formen gestaltet. 1936 wurden diese Entwicklungsarbeiten beendet. Das Ergebnis war eine gelungene Verbindung von schöner Form und intelligenter Funktion: Form 98. Das erste systematische Hotelgeschirr der Welt. Schon nach wenigen Jahren wird es international ausgezeichnet. Weitere ausgezeichnete Formen folgen. Von Jahr zu Jahr benutzten mehr Menschen Hotelporzellan von Schönwald. Hemingway hat es benutzt. Die Queen hat es benutzt. Sie haben es benutzt.

Schönwald

Form 98 für die Zukunft.

Schönwald

Wer ist der Herr
mit dem komischen Hut?

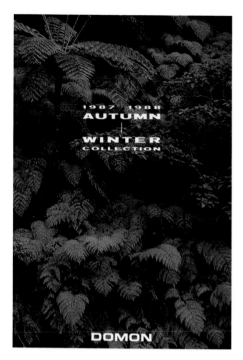

ART DIRECTOR:
MASAMI SHIMIZU
DESIGNER:
MASAMI SHIMIZU
PHOTOGRAPHER:
YOSHIHIKO UEDA
CLIENT:
JUN CO., LTD.
■ 324–327

■ 324–327 Some of the double-spread photographs from a hard-cover catalog for the fall and winter collection of men's clothing as designed by *Domon*. (JPN)

■ 324–327 Doppelseitige Aufnahmen aus einem Katalog mit festem Einband für die Herbst/Winter-Kollektion von Herrenoberbekleidung der Marke *Domon*. (JPN)

■ 324–327 Photos double page qui illustrent un catalogue relié pleine toile pour la collection d'automne/hiver des modes masculines *Domon*. (JPN)

ART DIRECTOR:
MASAMI SHIMIZU
DESIGNER:
MASAMI SHIMIZU
PHOTOGRAPHER:
YOSHIHIKO UEDA
CLIENT:
JUN CO., LTD.
■ 328–331

■ 328–331 Full-page black-
and-white photographs
from the *Domon* catalog of
men's spring and summer
fashions for 1987. (JPN)

■ 328–331 Schwarzweiss-
aufnahmen aus dem Katalog
für die Herrenkollektion
von *Domon* für Frühjahr
und Sommer 1987. (JPN)

■ 328–331 Photos pleine
page en noir et blanc pour le
catalogue printemps/été
1987 des modes masculines
Domon. (JPN)

LEFT
32912
SHORT CIRCLE SKIRT
ABOVE
33412C
CHILD'S DANCE DRESS

LEFT
33014
LONG CHIFFON SKIRT
ABOVE
32914
SHORT CHIFFON SKIRT

THE GRECIAN COLLECTION

LEFT
33312
SHORT TANK DRESS
ABOVE
33212
LONG SLEEVE DRESS

LEFT
3171
LOW BACK LEOTARD
ABOVE
3171
LOW BACK LEOTARD

ART DIRECTOR:
Frank Young
PHOTOGRAPHER:
Kyle Ericksen
COPYWRITER:
Regina Ovesey
AGENCY:
Ovesey and Company
CLIENT:
Ballet Makers, Inc.
■ 332-336

THE CAPEZIO®
ANNIVERSARY COLLECTION
BALLET MAKERS, INC.

ART DIRECTOR:
MICHAEL PATRICK CRONAN
DESIGNER:
MICHAEL PATRICK CRONAN/
CINDY STEINBERG
PHOTOGRAPHER:
THOMAS HEINSER
AGENCY:
CRONAN DESIGN
CLIENT:
LEVI STRAUSS & CO.
■ 337, 338

■ 332–336 Double spreads with black-and-white photographs and the cover of a brochure for ballet wear. (USA)

■ 337, 338 Front and back covers of two different, yet similarly designed brochures for *Levi's* jeans clothing. The chipped and faded colorings of the old wall are an allusion to the washed-out look of this style. (USA)

■ 332–336 Doppelseiten mit Schwarzweissaufnahmen und der Umschlag einer Broschüre für Ballettkleidung. (USA)

■ 337, 338 Vordere und hintere Umschlagseite von zwei verschiedenen Broschüren im gleichen Stil für *Levi's*-Jeanskleidung. Die abgeblätterte Farbe der alten Mauern ist eine Anspielung auf den verwaschenen Look dieser Mode. (USA)

■ 332–336 Doubles pages illustrées de photos noir et blanc, et couverture d'une brochure pour les tutus *Capezio*. (USA)

■ 337, 338 Première et quatrième pages de couverture de deux brochures réalisées dans le même style pour les jeans *Levi's*. La peinture des vieux murs qui s'en va par plaques entières évoque le look délavé de la nouvelle mode. (USA)

ART DIRECTOR:
*DAVID EDELSTEIN/NANCY
EDELSTEIN/LANNY FRENCH*
DESIGNER:
*DAVID EDELSTEIN/NANCY
EDELSTEIN/LANNY FRENCH/
CAROL DAVIDSON/
D. THOM BISSETT*
PHOTOGRAPHER:
PETER GRAVELLE
COPYWRITER:
KATHY CAIN/NANCY EDELSTEIN
AGENCY:
EDELSTEIN ASSOCIATES ADVERTISING INC.
CLIENT:
GENERRA SPORTSWEAR
◄ ■ 339

ART DIRECTOR:
JENNIFER MORLA
DESIGNER:
MORLA/KOSSMAN
PHOTOGRAPHER:
JEFFREY NEWBURY
AGENCY:
MORLA DESIGN
CLIENT:
LEVI STRAUSS & CO.
■ 340

ART DIRECTOR:
ROBERT VALENTINE
DESIGNER:
ROBERT VALENTINE
ILLUSTRATOR:
DAVE CALVER
COPYWRITER:
AMIE VALENTINE
STUDIO:
BLOOMINGDALE'S
CLIENT:
BLOOMINGDALE'S
■ 341

■ 339 "The *Generra* Fashion System" – a case containing various pamphlets and promotional material for its line of sports-wear. (USA)

■ 340 A sales catalog for jeans clothing from Levi Strauss. It has been designed as a loose-leaf binder. (USA)

■ 341 *Bloomingdale's* department store chose the bear as a mascot for its children's section. The story book and hang tag tell the story of the bear. (USA) .

■ 339 «Das *Generra*-Modesystem» ist der Titel dieser Schachtel mit verschiedenen Broschüren und Werbematerial für eine Sportbekleidungslinie. (USA)

■ 340 Als Ringordner gestalteter Verkaufskatalog für Jeanskleidung von Levi Strauss. (USA)

■ 341 *Bloomingdale's* wählte den Bär als Maskottchen für die Kinderabteilung; hier ein Etikett und ein Büchlein, in dem die Geschichte des Bären erzählt wird. (USA)

■ 339 Boîte intitulée «Le Système mode de *Generra*»: on y trouve diverses brochures et autres éléments publicitaires pour une gamme de vêtements sport. (USA)

■ 340 Catalogue de vente des jeans Levi Strauss réalisé sous forme d'un classeur à feuillets mobiles. (USA)

■ 341 Les grands magasins *Bloomingdale's* ont opté pour le nounours comme mascotte du rayon enfants: étiquette et mini-album relatant l'histoire du nounours. (USA)

ART DIRECTOR:
ROBERT CIPRIANI
ILLUSTRATOR:
CALDERWOOD & PREG
PHOTOGRAPHER:
LOU GOODMAN 342
JACK RICHMOND 343, 344
■ 342-344

ART DIRECTOR:
SETH JABEN
ILLUSTRATOR:
SETH JABEN
COPYWRITER:
SETH JABEN
▼■ 345

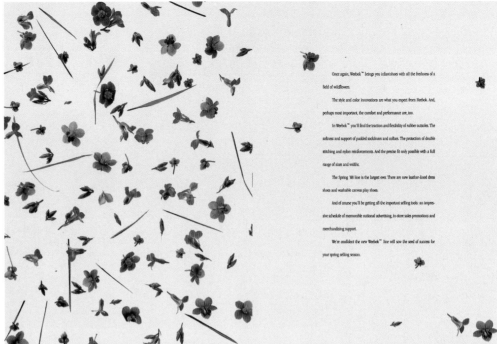

ART DIRECTOR:
JOANNE BIRON
DESIGNER:
JOANNE BIRON/JULIE EDWARDS
PHOTOGRAPHER:
ANNIE LEIBOVITZ/MYRON
AGENCY:
HELLER BREENE
CLIENT:
REEBOK
■ 346–348

■ 342–344 Covers from different brochures for *Cole Haan* shoes. *342* is for the men's fall collection, *343* for the women's collection, and *344* for the men's spring collection. (USA)

■ 345 Promotional material designed to be used as catalogs, and partly as counter displays for socks and hosiery from E.G. Smith. (USA)

■ 346–348 "Once again, Weebok brings you infant shoes with all the freshness of a field of wildflowers." From a catalog for *Weebok* children's shoes. (USA)

■ 342–344 Umschläge von Broschüren für Schuhe der Marke *Cole Haan*. *342* ist für die Herren-Herbstkollektion, *343* für die Damen- und *344* für die Herren-Frühjahrskollektionen. (USA)

■ 345 Werbematerial mit der Funktion von Katalogen und zum Teil von Laden-Displays für Socken und Strümpfe von E.G. Smith. (USA)

■ 346–348 Umschlag und zwei Doppelseiten aus einem Katalog für *Weebok*-Kinderschuhe, «mit der ganzen Frische eines Feldes wilder Blumen». (USA)

■ 342–344 Couvertures de brochures réalisées pour le chausseur *Cole Haan*. *342* désigne la collection messieurs d'automne, *342* la collection dames et *344* la collection messieurs de printemps. (USA)

■ 345 Matériel publicitaire utilisable comme catalogue et partiellement comme présentoir pour les chaussettes et bas commercialisés sur la marque E.G. Smith. (USA)

■ 346–348 Couverture et deux pages doubles d'un catalogue des chaussures d'enfants *Weebok* imprégnées de «toute la fraîcheur d'un champ de fleurs sauvages». (USA)

ART DIRECTOR:
STEVE MISKA
DESIGNER:
TIM GIRVIN/STEPHEN PANNONE
ILLUSTRATOR:
TIM GIRVIN
PHOTOGRAPHER:
JIM CUMMINS
AGENCY:
TIM GIRVIN DESIGN
CLIENT:
GENERRA CORP.
■ 349-351

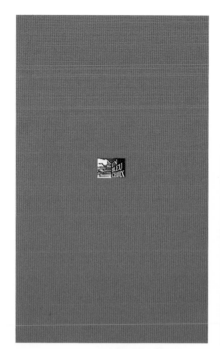

■ 349-351 Cover and pages from a brochure which is intended for buyers. It presents *Un Bleu Choix,* the new line of blue jeans from Generra Corp. (USA)

■ 352, 353 First and second cover pages as well as a black-and-white photograph from a sales brochure for *Wallman* clothing. A mat paper revealing its wood structure has been used. (USA)

■ 354, 355 Cover with cut-outs and embossed vignette as well as a double spread from a sales brochure for *Sevens,* a new and elegant line of apparel from Levi Strauss. (USA)

■ 349-351 Umschlag und Seiten aus einer für Einkäufer bestimmten Broschüre, mit der die neue Jeans-Linie, *Un Bleu Choix,* der Generra Corp. vorgestellt wird. (USA)

■ 352, 353 Erste und zweite Umschlagseite sowie eine der Schwarzweissaufnahmen aus einer Verkaufsbroschüre für *Wallman*-Kleidung. Es wurde mattes, holzhaltiges Papier verwendet. (USA)

■ 354, 355 Umschlag mit Ausstanzungen und blindgeprägter Vignette sowie eine Doppelseite aus einer Verkaufsbroschüre für *Sevens,* eine Bekleidungslinie von Levi Strauss. (USA)

■ 349-351 Couverture et pages d'une brochure de présentation de la nouvelle ligne de jeans *Un Bleu Choix* de la Generra Corp. à l'intention des acheteurs. (USA)

■ 352, 353 Première et deuxième pages de couverture et photo noir et blanc illustrant une brochure de vente des vêtements *Wallman.* Le papier mat a une proportion élevée de pâte mécanique. (USA)

■ 354, 355 Couverture à découpes et vignette gaufrée à sec, ainsi qu'une page double d'une brochure de vente pour *Sevens,* une ligne d'habillement de Levi Strauss. (USA)

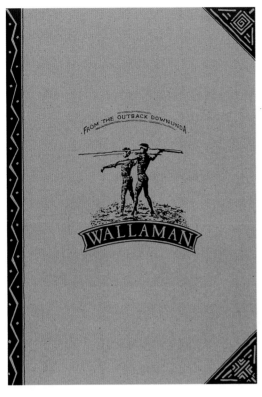

ART DIRECTOR:
JENNIFER MORLA
PHOTOGRAPHER:
DAVID ROBIN
COPYWRITER:
JENNIFER MORLA
AGENCY:
MORLA DESIGN
CLIENT:
BRADMILL USA, LTD.
■ 352, 353

ART DIRECTOR:
JENNIFER MORLA
PHOTOGRAPHER:
JEFFREY NEWBURY
COPYWRITER:
JENNIFER MORLA
AGENCY:
MORLA DESIGN
CLIENT:
LEVI STRAUSS & CO.
▼ ■ 354, 355

ART DIRECTOR:
Keizo Matsui
DESIGNER:
Keizo Matsui/Hitomi Nagao
PHOTOGRAPHER:
Hiroshi Murakami
COPYWRITER:
Keiko Arai
AGENCY:
Keizo Matsui & Associates
CLIENT:
Hiroko Koshino
International Corp.
■ 356–359

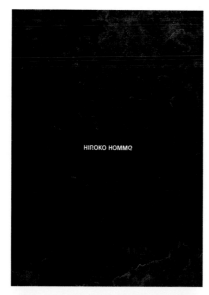

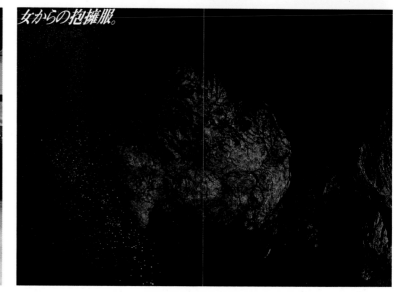

■ 356-359 Cover and double spreads from a large-scale brochure for men's fashion from the Japanese manufacturer Hiroko Koshino International. (JPN)

■ 360 The advertising material of *Reebok* weekend wear as presented in this zippered folder. One of the loose sheets contained in it is shown as well. (USA)

■ 356-359 Umschlag und Doppelseiten aus einer grossformatigen Broschüre für Männermode des japanischen Herstellers Hiroko Koshino International. (JPN)

■ 360 Mit einem Reissverschluss versehene Faltmappe und eines der losen Blätter als Werbung für Freizeitkleidung der Marke *Reebok*. (USA)

■ 356-359 Couverture et doubles pages d'une brochure au grand format pour les modes masculines du fabricant japonais Hiroko Koshino International. (JPN)

■ 360 Dossier à tirette-éclair et l'une des feuilles mobiles qu'il contient: documentation publicitaire pour les vêtements de loisirs *Reebok*. (USA)

ART DIRECTOR:
Cheryl Heller
DESIGNER:
*Cheryl Heller/
Rose DiSanto*
PHOTOGRAPHER:
Herb Ritts
COPYWRITER:
Jerry Cronin
AGENCY:
Heller Breene
CLIENT:
Reebok
■ 360

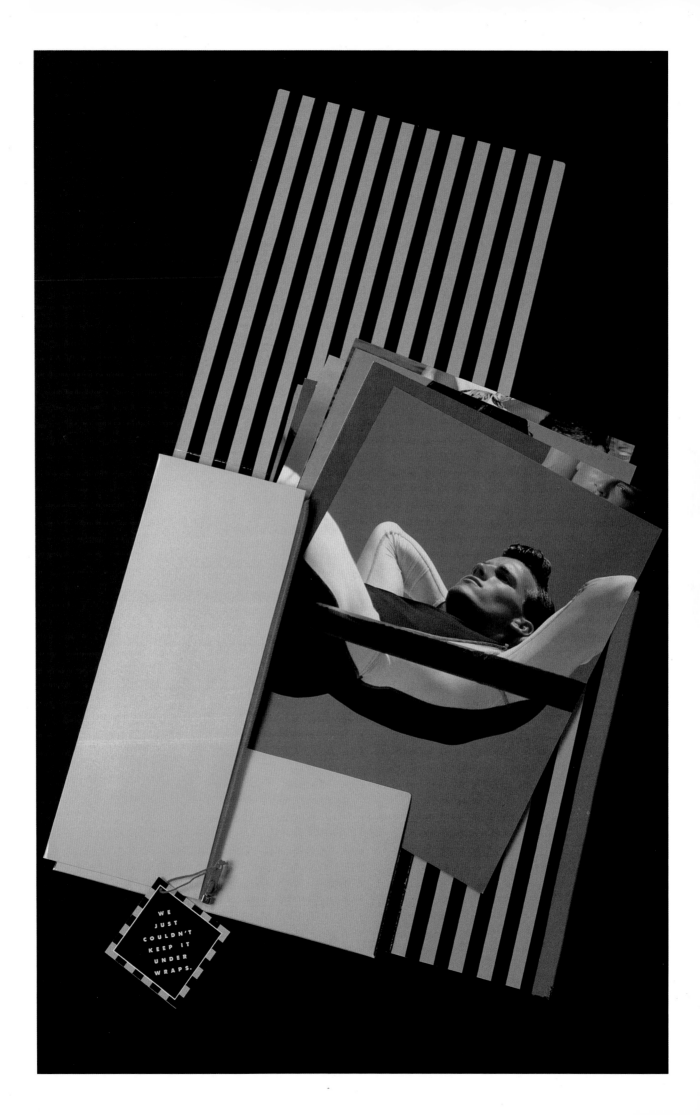

MÄNNER-MODE
mit der man was erleben kann!
(I/S'80)

JOCKEY

ART DIRECTOR:
Uli Weber
DESIGNER:
Ursula Koch
PHOTOGRAPHER:
Werner Pawlok/
Celia von Hornstein
COPYWRITER:
Brigitte Fussnegger
AGENCY:
Leonhardt + Kern
CLIENT:
Jockey, Volma
Wirkwaren GmbH
■ 361-364

DIE GESETZE
des freien FALLS

ABGESCHLOSSENER KURZROMAN
VON JOCKEY, 7450 NECHINGEN.

RAYMOND	...sucht was
RITA	...findet was
AMALFI	ist eine Badehose von Jockey, die einen aufregenden Fall vor sich hat

Rita hatte weder Busen noch Po, sie hatte die Schönheiten dieser Welt in ihrem Kopf. Ihre tellergroßen Augen waren grün, ihre zündholzkurzen Haare waren rot. Und wenn sie sich ärgerte, harmonierte´ihre Nasenspitze farblich mit ihrem Haar.

Rita hatte einen kleinen Buchladen. Eines Tages ging die Tür auf. Und da stand er. Sie wußte sofort: Mit diesem Mann werde ich die nächsten hundert Jahre verbringen.

Er: »Ich such´ Literatur über die Gesetze des freien Falls.« – Sie: »Bei mir finden Sie nix Füsikalisches, das könnte ich schon in der Schule nicht leiden.« – Er: »Ich muß aber ganz schnell wissen, mit welcher Geschwindigkeit und in welcher Zeit ein Apfel vom 18. Stockwerk fällt.« – Sie: »Sind Sie Obsthändler?« – Er: »Nein, Architekt.«

»Nun, vielleicht kann ich Ihnen weiterhelfen«, sagte Rita und musterte ihn so verwegen, daß er marzipanweiche Knie bekam.

»Gesetzt den Fall«, begann Rita, »Sie sind einssechsundachtzig groß und 78 Kilo schwer und springen 37 Meter tief ins Meer, dann nehmen wir s gleich einhalb g mal t Quadrat, jetzt formen wir das um in t Quadrat gleich zwei s durch g, dann t gleich Wurzel aus zwei s durch g, also Wurzel aus zwei mal 37 durch 9,81, dann wären Sie also in 2,75 Sekunden im Wasser. Und v ist g mal t, also 9,81 mal 2,75 gleich 26,94 Meter pro Sekunde, das wäre eine Stundengeschwindigkeit von 96,9 Kilometer.«

Raymond war sprachlos. Worauf Rita sagte: »Wir fliegen jetzt schnurstracks nach

Mexiko, da gibt´s bei Acapulco eine Schlucht mit einem Felsen überm Meer. Dort springen Sie schnell mal runter, und ich stopp´ die Zeit.«

Gesagt, getan. Raymond, wie der inzwischen Verliebte hieß, stand zwei Tage später mit seiner eleganten blaugrünrotgelbschwarzkarierten Badehose von Jockey auf jenem Felsen, 37 Meter unter ihm lag das Meer.

Während er sprang, saß Rita mit ihrer Stoppuhr unten im Boot. Sie wurde plötzlich kreidebleich. Hatte sie doch verdammt noch mal vergessen, den Luftwiderstand sowie den aufkommenden Südwestwind mit zu berücksichtigen. Was bedeutete, daß ihre Theorie von der Praxis eingeholt wurde.

Als Raymond mit seiner eleganten Jockey-Badehose auf sie zuschwamm, wartete sie mit einem Ring. Es war kein Rettungsring.

JOCKEY
MÄNNER MODE, MIT DER MAN WAS ERLEBEN KANN!

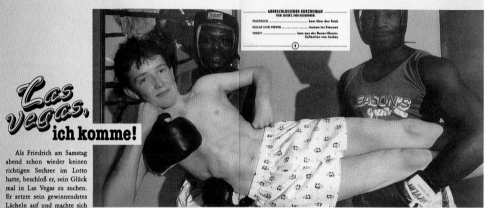

ABGESCHLOSSENER KURZROMAN
VON JOCKEY, 7450 NECHINGEN.

FRIEDRICH	kam über den Teich
SUGAR UND PEPPER	kommen ins Staunen
TEDDY	kam aus der Boxer-Shorts-Collection von Jockey

Las Vegas,
ich komme!

Als Friedrich am Samstag abend schon wieder keinen richtigen Sechser im Lotto hatte, beschloß er, sein Glück mal in Las Vegas zu suchen. Er setzte sein gewinnendstes Lächeln auf und machte sich schnurstracks auf den Weg zu den Spielhöllen des Wilden Westens.

Als erstes spielte er mit dem Gedanken, sich eine Hollywood-Villa, einen Rolls und einen Butler anzuschaffen. Dann spielte er Bakkarat, Roulette und Black Jack. Bald ging nichts mehr: Friedrich hatte nur noch ein paar Cents, die er einem Spielautomat, so einem einarmigen Banditen, erfolglos in den Rachen warf. Darauf versetzte Friedrich peu à peu alles, was er noch besaß: seinen

weich gefütterten Blouson, seine nagelneue Strickweste, sein kariertes Baumwollhemd, seine graue Flanellhose (übrigens alles hochnobel und von Jockey). Nun stand er nur noch mit seinen witzigen Boxer-Shorts (ebenfalls von Jockey) da.

Aber Friedrich wollte auch jetzt noch kein Spielverderber sein. Er überlegte, wie er seine Boxer-Shorts kapitalisieren könnte. So kam er auf die naheliegende Idee, in einer der berühmtberüchtigten Boxer-Shows mitzumischen.

Er bot sich dem Profigespann Sugar und Pepper als Sparringspartner und Show-Spieler an. »Na, den machen wir doch mit links nieder«, dachten sich die beiden und nahmen seinen Vorschlag mit Vergnügen an. Als Friedrich im Ring stand, das Scheinwerferlicht und 6219 Augen auf ihn gerichtet, wuchs er sozusagen über sich selbst hinaus und mähte erst Sugar, dann Pepper mit seiner scheint´s aus dem Nichts kommenden Rechten nieder.

Auch das Publikum war völlig geplättet und schrie »da capo, da capo«. Sugar und Pepper waren einerseits schwer irritiert und andererseits hellauf begeistert über so viel Nachwuchstalent. Sie trugen Friedrich durch die jubelnde Menge und sagten ihm, seiner Rechten und seinen witzigen Boxer-Shorts noch eine glanzvolle Karriere in den einschlägigen Kreisen voraus.

JOCKEY
MÄNNER-MODE, MIT DER MAN WAS ERLEBEN KANN!

ABGESCHLOSSENER KURZROMAN
VON JOCKEY, 7450 NECHINGEN.

AMBROSIUS BLÜMEL	will keine Neurose, sondern eine neue Rose
ROSALIA, SEINE FRAU	ist damit einverstanden
BASTIAN	ein Schlafanzug von Jockey, der einen blühenden Blödsinn erlebt

ENTSCHEIDUNG UM
MITTERNACHT.

Es war einmal ein Finanzchef in einem weltumspannenden Konzern, der hieß Ambrosius Blümel. Je tiefer er in seinen Bilanzen steckte, um so mehr bekam er Sehnsucht, seinem Namen alle Ehre zu machen. Und so beschloß er an einem schönen Mai, beruflich umzusteigen.

»Rosalia«, sagte er zu seiner Frau, »laß uns in ein hübsches Dorf ziehen und Gärtner werden.« Sein Ziel war dornenreich. »Ich will die Rosen aller Rosen züchten, und die soll Rosa Rosalia heißen.«

Ambrosius Blümel besorgte sich Rosenreiser aus Antibes, Sissinghurst, Schiras. Er korrespondierte mit Botanikern aus aller Welt. Er okulierte, propfte, kreuzte, veredelte und schnipselte.

Nach Jahr und Tag, es war wieder Mai, hatte er endlich das Gefühl, seine Rose geschaffen zu haben. Abends zog Blümel seinen neuen Schlafanzug von Jockey an, der aus feinster mercerisierter Baumwolle war, und stellte sein Rosenpflänzchen neben sein Bett, so, wie

man das immer mit seinem Jüngsten macht. Er küßte seiner Rosalia die rosa Nasenspitze und schlief zufrieden ein.

Mitternachts wachte er an einem ohrenbetäubenden Rosenduft auf. »Rosalia, bist Du´s?« Als er das Licht anknipste, lag er in einem Rosenbett bzw. in einem Rosenbeet, das ganz sachte rauschte und summte und wuchs und wuchs.

Ambrosius und Rosalia konnten sich in letzter Minute aus der dornigen Umarmung retten. Sie liefen zur Treppe. Doch die Rosen waren fast so schnell wie sie, ja, sie verfolgten sie durchs ganze Haus, in den Garten, auf die Straße.

Die Nachbarn eilten herbei. Die Feuerwehr kam tatütata. Die Presse machte erste Sensationsfotos in der Geschichte des Dorfes.

Und weil es in dieser Gegend bis dato keinerlei Tourismus gab, entschied der Bürgermeister schnell und einstimmig: »Eine Rose ist eine Rose! Das heißt, wir lassen diesem blühenden Blödsinn seinen Lauf! Zudem können wir doch für dieses Wunder ab morgen ein bißchen Eintritt verlangen!!!«

Mann, war Ambrosius froh, daß er bei so viel nächtlichem Aufsehen seinen schönen neuen Schlafanzug aus feinster mercerisierter Baumwolle von Jockey anhatte. Und nicht so dastand wie seine Frau, nämlich ganz schön nackt.

JOCKEY
MÄNNER-MODE, MIT DER MAN WAS ERLEBEN KANN!

■ 361-364 Promotional documentation for *Jockey* men's wear. It was designed for retail in the form of an over-sized newspaper. Front page and double spreads with photographs, which are always accompanied by humorous "short stories". (GER)

■ 365-367 A prospectus conceived for dealers to enhance the image of *Carat,* the young fashion line of Tiffany's. A continuing story appears throughout. The cover and two double spreads with colored black-and-white photographs are shown. The pages, which are bound with a clip, can be used individually for decoration. (GER)

■ 361-364 An den Handel gerichtete, im Format einer übergrossen Zeitung gestaltete Werbedokumentation für *Jockey*-Männermode. Hier die Vorderseite und Beispiele der Doppelseiten; zu den Photos werden jeweils amüsante «Kurzgeschichten» erzählt. (GER)

■ 365-367 Imageprospekt für die junge Modelinie *Carat* von Tiffany's, für den Fachhandel bestimmt. Der Prospekt enthält eine durchgehende Geschichte. Gezeigt sind der Umschlag und zwei Doppelseiten mit kolorierten Schwarzweissphotos. Die mit einer Klemmleiste gebundenen Seiten lassen sich auch als Dekoration verwenden. (GER)

■ 361-364 Documentation publicitaire au format d'un maxi-journal; relative aux modes masculines *Jockey,* elle est destinée aux commerçants. Première page de couverture et doubles pages choisies. Les photos sont accompagnées de textes amusants. (GER)

■ 365-367 Prospectus de prestige pour la jeune ligne mode *Carat* de Tiffany's, destiné aux professionnels. On y trouve un récit complet. On voit ici la couverture et deux doubles pages illustrées de photos noir-blanc coloriées. Les pages réunies par un fermoir à pince font également office d'éléments de décoration. (GER)

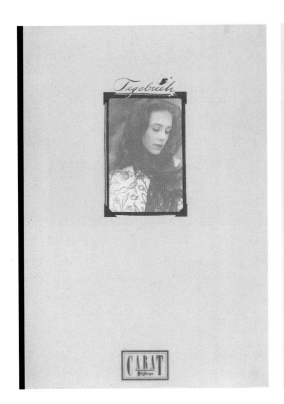

ART DIRECTOR:
BIRGIT UNTERWEGER
DESIGNER:
BIRGIT UNTERWEGER
PHOTOGRAPHER:
CLAUS RUDOLPH
COPYWRITER:
MANFRED UNTERWEGER
AGENCY:
ART·WORK
CLIENT:
PASSPORT/TIFFANY'S
■ 365-367

"Sometimes working with Jimmy drives me crazy. Like yesterday, I sent him for these No. 2 bags and he was gone for over 10 minutes. I wanted to kill him...until I found out he stopped to help some old lady carry groceries to her car. Yeah, I guess he's an okay guy."

UPGRADE

"In jr. high, all you had to do was be cool to be a star. Now, it definitely helps to be cool, but I know it takes more than that to get where and what I want."

FAST

ART DIRECTOR:
Wendy Edwards Lowitz
DESIGNER:
Wendy Edwards Lowitz
PHOTOGRAPHER:
Marc Hauser/Jack Perno
AGENCY:
Moira & Company
CLIENT:
Uniforms To You
■ 368, 369

■ 368, 369 Front pages from laminated prospectuses of a manufacturer of working uniforms. (USA)

■ 370-374 The 1987 spring and summer collection of the fashion designer Ex Jun is the subject of this catalog. The newest fashions are presented here with the help of black-and-white photographs of well-known personalities. Miles Davis appears on the cover. Gregory Hines, Ian McKellen, Annie Leibovitz and Allen Ginsberg are pictured on the double spreads. (USA)

■ 368, 369 Vorderseiten von laminierten Prospekten für einen Hersteller von Arbeitsuniformen. (USA)

■ 370-374 Die Frühjahrs- und Sommerkollektion 1987 des Modeschöpfers Ex Jun ist Gegenstand dieses Katalogs, in dem Mode mit Hilfe von schwarzweissen Porträtaufnahmen bekannter Persönlichkeiten präsentiert wird. Auf dem Umschlag ein Porträt von Miles Davis, auf den gezeigten Doppelseiten Gregory Hines, Ian McKellen, Annie Leibovitz und Allen Ginsberg. (USA)

■ 368, 369 Rectos de prospectus laminés pour un fabricant d'uniformes de travail. (USA)

■ 370-374 La collection de printemps et d'été 1987 du grand couturier Ex Jun est le sujet de ce catalogue où la mode est présentée à travers les portraits noir et blanc de personalités connues: en couverture, le musicien Miles Davis; les doubles pages qui suivent sont illustrées par Gregory Hines, Ian McKellen, Annie Leibovitz et Allen Ginsberg. (USA)

PORTRAITS
SPRING AND SUMMER COLLECTION 1987

EX JUN BY YUKIKO TAMURA

ART DIRECTOR:
Masami Shimizu
DESIGNER:
Masami Shimizu
PHOTOGRAPHER:
Yoshihiko Ueda
CLIENT:
Jun Co. Ltd.
■ 370–374

ALLEN GINSBERG

ANNIE LEIBOVITZ

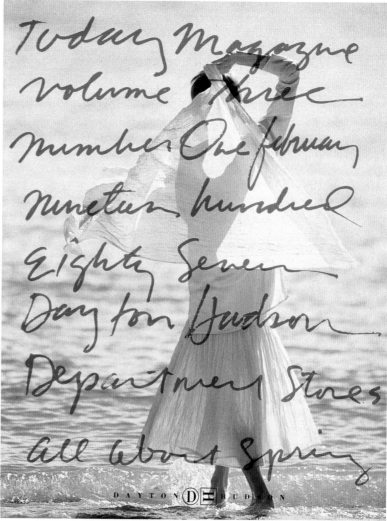

ART DIRECTOR:
Robert Valentine
DESIGNER:
Robert Valentine
PHOTOGRAPHER:
William Garett/James Wojcik
COPYWRITER:
Vicki Ross/Cathy Berg
AGENCY:
Robert Valentine, Inc.
CLIENT:
Dayton/Hudson
■ 375, 377

ART DIRECTOR:
Robert Valentine
DESIGNER:
Robert Valentine
PHOTOGRAPHER:
Jim Reiher/Rick Strauss
COPYWRITER:
Cathy Berg/Vicki Ross
AGENCY:
Robert Valentine, Inc.
CLIENT:
Dayton/Hudson
■ 376, 378

■ 375–378 A cover page and a double spread from each of two catalogs for fashion and accessories from Dayton/Hudson. They were sent as promotional material in a direct mailing for its fall and spring collection. (USA)

■ 379, 380 Promotional material used by Hallmark in its effort to recruit creative co-workers. "Discover Hallmark, discover yourself". The cover is shown as it is closed by a textile closure, and opened. (USA)

■ 375–378 Umschlagseiten und jeweils eine Doppelseite aus zwei Katalogen für Kleidung und Accessoires von Dayton/Hudson. Sie wurden als Direktwerbung für die Herbst- und die Frühjahrskollektion verschickt. (USA)

■ 379, 380 Geschlossener (Textilverschluss) und geöffneter Umschlag für Promotionsmaterial der Firma Hallmark, das für die Rekrutierung kreativer Mitarbeiter eingesetzt wird: «Entdecke Hallmark, entdecke dich selbst.» (USA)

■ 375–378 Pages de couverture et une double page type de deux catalogues présentant les vêtements et accessoires commercialisés par Dayton/Hudson. Publicité directe pour les collections d'automne et de printemps. (USA)

■ 379, 380 Enveloppe fermée et ouverte pour le matériel de promotion de l'entreprise Hallmark utilisé pour le recrutement de collaborateurs créatifs: «Partez à la découverte de Hallmark, partez à la découverte de vous-même.» (USA)

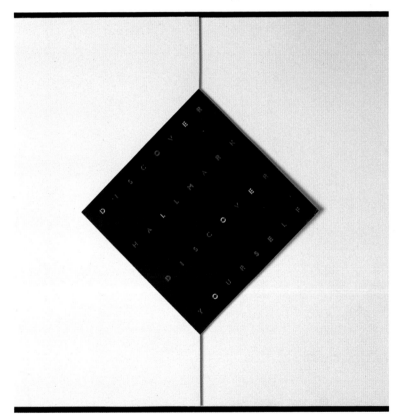 

ART DIRECTOR:
JOHN MULLER/MARK SACKETT
DESIGNER:
MARK SACKETT
PHOTOGRAPHER:
DAVID BIEGELESON
AGENCY:
MULLER + CO.
CLIENT:
HALLMARK CARDS
■ 379, 380

VALAN

Art Director:
Hiromi Inayoshi
Designer:
Hiromi Inayoshi
Illustrator:
Hiroki Taniguchi
Photographer:
Yutaka Sakano
Copywriter:
Haruo Yoshida
Agency:
Dentsu Inc.
Client:
*Wig's Fashion Gallery
Valan Ginza*
■ 381-384

■ 381-384 Cover and double
spreads from a large-sized
brochure showing wigs by
Valan. (JPN)

■ 381-384 Umschlag und
Doppelseiten aus einer
Broschüre für Perücken von
Valan. (JPN)

■ 381-384 Couverture et
pages doubles d'une brochure
réalisée pour la promotion
des perruques *Valan.* (JPN)

MY FAVORITE STYLE
She's always fresh. Performing makes her more beautiful.
And wigs brighten her more and more.

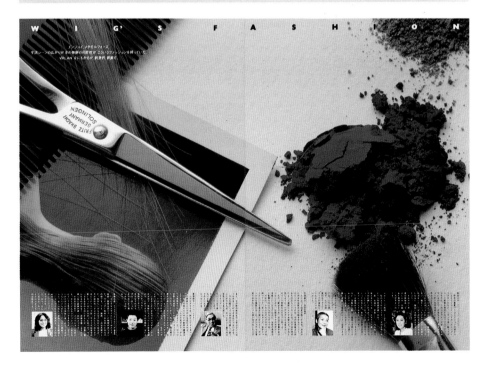

Styled with the look of the cockpit instrument panel where readings match heartbeats. Men's watch with brushed silver case and screws and polished gold bezel, lugs and crown. Swiss quartz movement. Baton hands. Arabic numerals. Perpetual calendar. Glass crystal. Water resistant. Khaki twill band with interchangeable pigskin band.

The spirit of laughing fear in the face before catapulting into the landscape of clouds where danger lurked. Men's watch with brushed silver case and polished bezel. Swiss quartz movement. Contemporary black dial with polished baton hands. Glass crystal. Water resistant. Textured pigskin band.

Styled for on-the-go jump-in-the-cockpit wind-whipped-flag excitement. Men's watch with silver and navy enameled case. Swiss quartz movement. Two-tone baton hands with baton center seconds. Perpetual calendar. Glass crystal. Water resistant. Khaki twill band and interchangeable pigskin band.

Poised for flight into the vast expanse of derring-do sky. Men's and women's insignia watch with polished silver case. Swiss quartz movement. Antique ornate lugs. RAF wing symbol dial. Polished baton hands. Antique crown with genuine sapphire. Glass crystal. Water resistant. Khaki twill band with interchangeable pigskin band.

■ 385–388 Pages from a brochure for *RAF* watches. The company takes its name from that of the Royal Air Force. Scenes from the pioneer days of aviation evoke the association of the product with its namesake. (USA)

■ 389 Jewelry by Sartori & Ruchswurm. Double spread from a promotional folder which was sent as an invitation in connection with a trade fair. (AUT)

■ 385–388 Seiten aus einer Broschüre für Uhren der Marke *RAF* Die Royal Air Force stand Pate für diesen Namen. Als Hintergrund für die Produktaufnahmen wurden Szenen aus den Pioniertagen der Fliegerei gewählt. (USA)

■ 389 Doppelseite aus einer Werbemappe für Schmuck von Sartori & Ruchswurm, die anlässlich einer Messe mit einer Einladung versandt wurde. (AUT)

■ 385–388 Pages d'une brochure de présentation des montres *RAF* sigle emprunté à la Royal Air Force. En arrière-plan des photos de produits, des scènes de l'histoire héroïque des premiers temps de l'aviation. (USA)

■ 389 Double page d'un dossier publicitaire pour les créations des joailliers Sartori & Ruchswurm accompagnant l'invitation à une foire-exposition. (AUT)

DESIGNER:
MIKE PETERSON
PHOTOGRAPHER:
AL PITZNER
COPYWRITER:
ROBERT TRUE
AGENCY:
SANDVIN TRUE PRUITT
CLIENT:
PETERSON IMPORTS INC.
◀ ■ 385–388

ART DIRECTOR:
WALTER BOHATSCH
DESIGNER:
WALTER BOHATSCH/
CLEMENS SCHEDLER
COPYWRITER:
CLEMENS SCHEDLER
CLIENT:
SARTORI & RUCHSWURM
■ 389

k.one

ART DIRECTOR:
Ciriano Zanoni
DESIGNER:
Ciriano Zanoni
PHOTOGRAPHER:
*Alberto Facchi/
Franco Cardin*
COPYWRITER:
Anna Pellizzari
AGENCY:
*Zan On Design
Communication*
CLIENT:
K. one
■ 390-393

■ 390-397 Sunglasses of
k.one as shown in two catalogs with spiral bindings.
Both have cut-out covers
and *390* has an additional
embossment. (ITA)

■ 390-397 Zwei Kataloge
mit Spiralbindung und aus-
gestanztem Umschlag *(390*
mit zusätzlicher Prägung)
für Sonnenbrillen der Marke
k. one. (ITA)

■ 390-397 Deux catalogues
à reliure spirale et couverture à découpes *(390* en
gaufrage) pour les lunettes
de soleil de la marque
k. one. (ITA)

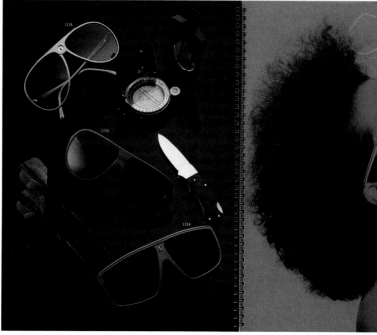

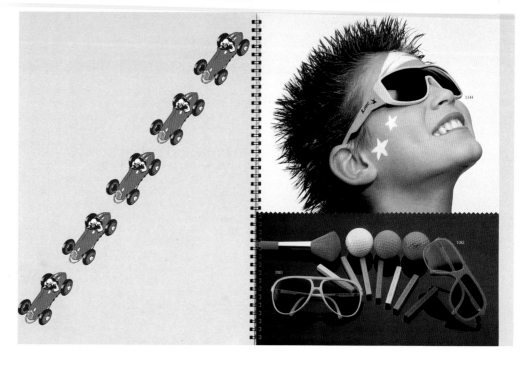

k.one

ART DIRECTOR:
Ciriano Zanoni

DESIGNER:
Anna Paola Pellizzari

PHOTOGRAPHER:
Gianni Baccega

COPYWRITER:
Anna Pellizzari

AGENCY:
*Zan On Design
Communication*

CLIENT:
K. ONE
■ 394-397

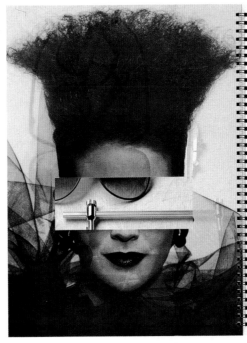

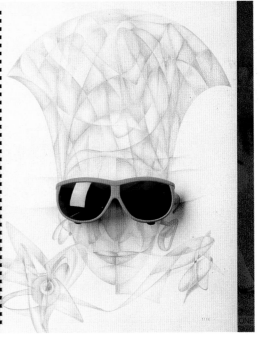

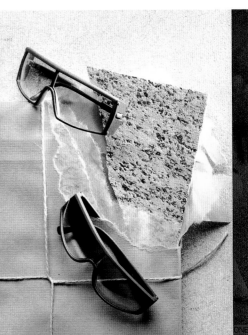

ART DIRECTOR:
GREGOIRE PHILIPIDHIS
DESIGNER:
GREGOIRE PHILIPIDHIS/
DEBORAH FAY
PHOTOGRAPHER:
MARIO TESTINO
AGENCY:
SONCINI & GINEPRO
CLIENT:
MARINA SPADAFORA
■ 398-402

■ 398-402 Front side of the wrapping paper cover, the title page, and double spreads from a narrow brochure for fashions by Marina Spadafora. (ITA)

■ 398-402 Vorderseite des Packpapierumschlags, die Titelseite und Beispiele der Doppelseiten aus einer schmalen Broschüre für Mode von Marina Spadafora. (ITA)

■ 398-402 Première page de la couverture en papier kraft, page de titre et pages doubles choisies d'une mince brochure de présentation des modes Marina Spadafora. (ITA)

EDITORIAL DESIGN

REDAKTIONELLES DESIGN

DESIGN DE PERIODIQUES

NOTES FROM UNDERGROUND

IN THE SOVIET ECONOMY, IT'S WHAT YOU DON'T SEE THAT COUNTS

G R E E D

ON the morning that the vodka went on sale, the man with the scarf woke up tired and hurting all over. Eyes full of foam said that he'd tanked up on cheap Russian vodka the night before, the syrupy kind that makes you feel mean and ugly for the next 48 hours. He darted through a convoy of large trucks, his legs sagging like punctured inner tubes, until he found himself a place at the end of a line of 200 men outside an open liquor store in the Moscow of Mikhail Sergevich Gorbachev. The men at the front of the line were working every deal imaginable to get a bottle.

The Soviet premier's yearlong crackdown on the sale and consumption of vodka (it's part of a broad attempt to curtail all income that isn't controlled by the state) has forced the bureaucrats at the Ministry of Food/Vice Ministry of Beer, Mineral Water, Alcoholic Beverages, and Soft Drinks to cut back on the manufacture and sale of distilled potato juice for domestic use, making a flask of vodka more prized than a gallon of wartime gasoline. Vodka is the prime agent of Russian life, a liquid buffer against the harsh realities of life in a police state. Gorbachev made the Soviet Union an almost dry country practically overnight, and the Russian people have been scrambling for the stuff with the zeal of oil brokers in a short market.

Stores that sell wine, beer, and cognac are open from 2:00 P.M. until 8:00 P.M. on weekdays and from 11:00 A.M. on weekends, but stores that sell vodka are now forbidden to open until 4:00 P.M. Shorter hours, cutbacks in production, and price increases have combined to create a flourishing vodka black market; vodka is sometimes even sold under-the-counter in stores that sell only lighter alcoholic beverages.

There's no reliable or rational price structure in the Russian vodka market. Off-the-shelf vodka sells for 10 rubles ($15) a half liter, but the street price can reach $60, depending upon the demand. Anyone who wants to monopolize the free market needs plenty of rubles, although a dealer who doesn't have the money to buy in large quantities can arrange to borrow the capital, usually in return for selling the vodka at a discount back to the lender.

On this morning in late October, the heavily bundled Russian women shambling past the liquor store to buy vegetables at the nearby produce mall watched the juggling and judging of the vodka market gain momentum. Over the course of a few minutes the 200 people had ballooned to 300, blocking the narrow sidewalk next to Sadovo Samotechnaya. Many of them clenched fistfuls of rubles. The shouting, shoving, and fighting to gain entrance through the store's slender door smacked of the gold action on the COMEX floor. The line was a battle, and the people at the end of it knew they had lost.

By the time the man with the scarf made it to the front of the line, someone

"YO, COMRADE, WANNA BUY LEVIS? MEAT?" IN AN ECONOMY THAT'S STARVED FOR VIRTUALLY EVERYTHING, SOVIET BLACK MARKETEERS SOLD ABOUT $7 BILLION WORTH OF GOODS AND SERVICES LAST YEAR.

BY A. CRAIG COPETAS

ILLUSTRATIONS BY DAVID SHANNON

ART DIRECTOR:
FRED WOODWARD
DESIGNER:
JOLENE CUYLER
ILLUSTRATOR:
DAVID SHANNON
PUBLISHER:
REGARDIE'S
■ 403

COMING HOME

By Annette Insdorf

AFTER TEN YEARS IN HOLLYWOOD,
Louis Malle
RETURNED TO THE LAND OF HIS BIRTH AND THE MEMORIES OF HIS YOUTH TO CREATE A MASTERPIECE

S LOUIS MALLE MORE FRENCH OR MORE AMERICAN? LAST September, on the occasion of the premiere of *Goodbye, Children (Au Revoir les enfants)*, his first French film in ten years, Malle addressed that question at the Telluride Film Festival. "I come from the heart of the French bourgeoisie. But nobody asked me," he said wryly, "and I wish I hadn't been born in France. I've tried to resist the horror of French culture—especially this philosopher Descartes. I hate to hear my work defined as quintessentially French. I've worked in India, Mexico, and Italy. . . . I tried to run away and came to America."

A few months after the Colorado event, Malle was back in the New York apartment he shares with his wife, Candice Bergen, and their two-year-old daughter, Chloe. Now that *Goodbye, Children* had opened in Paris to glowing reviews and growing audiences, the French were claiming him as a prodigal son. But the 55-year-old director of such films as *Pretty Baby*, *Atlantic City*, *My Dinner With André*, *And the Pursuit of Happiness*, and *Alamo Bay*—all made in the U.S.—wasn't claiming anything about the reasons for his departure from or return to his native country.

"You *could* say I left France because *Black Moon* [1975] was a gigantic flop, but that's not the reason," Malle says of his experimental film. "Actually, I decided to move to the States because I

PHOTOGRAPHED BY
Jeanne Louise Bulliard

ART DIRECTOR:
DAVID WALTERS
DESIGNER:
ROBERT BEST/
DAVID WALTERS
PHOTOGRAPHER:
JEANNE LOUISE BULLIARD/
SYGMA
PUBLISHER:
PREMIERE PUBLISHING
■ 404

■ 403 Introductory double spread for an article on the black market in the Soviet Union. (USA)

■ 404 Photograph from *Au Revoir les enfants,* a film directed by Louis Malle. The article describes the return of Louis Mallé to his native France after a ten-year stay in Hollywood. (USA)

■ 405 Title page of the American magazine *Scene.* (USA)

■ 406 Cover of the Dutch monthly magazine *Avenue.* (NDL)

■ 403 Einleitende Doppelseite eines Artikels über den Schwarzmarkt in der Sowjetunion. (USA)

■ 404 Aufnahme aus dem Film *Au Revoir les enfants* des französischen Filmemachers Louis Malle. Das Thema des Artikels ist die Rückkehr dieses Regisseurs nach Frankreich nach 10-jährigem Aufenthalt in Hollywood. (USA)

■ 405 Titelseite der amerikanischen Zeitschrift *Scene.* (USA)

■ 406 Umschlag des holländischen Magazins *Avenue.* (NLD)

■ 403 Double page initiale d'un article où il est question du marché noir en Union Soviétique. (USA)

■ 404 Photo tirée du film *Au revoir les enfants* du cinéaste français Louis Malle. L'article paru dans le magazine américain *Premiere* traite du retour du réalisateur en France, au terme de dix années d'activité à Hollywood. (USA)

■ 405 Page de titre du magazine américain *Scene.* (USA)

■ 406 Couverture du mensuel hollandais *Avenue.* (NLD)

ART DIRECTOR:
Owen Hartley
DESIGNER:
Frances Melendez
PHOTOGRAPHER:
Rudolf Vandome
PUBLISHER:
Fairchild Publications
■ 405

ART DIRECTOR:
Hans van Blommestein
PHOTOGRAPHER:
Carrie Branovan
PUBLISHER:
De Geïllustreerde Pers B.V.
■ 406

ART DIRECTOR:
Phyllis Schefer
PHOTOGRAPHER:
Gilles Bensimon
PUBLISHER:
Elle Magazine
■ 407–409

■ 407–411 Covers and double spreads from various issues of the American edition of the fashion magazine *Elle*. On the double spread in the upper right, new fabrics for the fall collections are shown. An article on bathing suits in black and white is below it. (USA)

■ 407–411 Umschläge und Doppelseiten verschiedener Nummern der amerikanischen Ausgabe der Modezeitschrift *Elle*. Auf der Doppelseite rechts oben werden die neuen Gewebe für die Herbstmode vorgestellt. Unten ein Beitrag über die Bademode in Schwarz und Weiss. (USA)

■ 407–411 Couvertures et doubles pages de différents numéros de l'édition américaine du magazine de mode *Elle*. La double page de droite, en haut, renseigne sur les nouveaux tissus d'automne. En bas, les modes de bains en noir et blanc. (USA)

SILVER

HOT FLASH
Everything that glitters is silver this season: lean legs sheathed in liquid lamé, sweaters shot with spaced-out shimmer. Charged up and ready for blast-off? Out of sight! Day or night! Page 276

KNITS

ROYAL PLUSH
Luxe Fifties sweater sets double up for the Eighties. Think Grace Kelly in *High Society*, Gidget at the sock hop. Vests, cardigans, and crews—ELLE winks at retro for Eighties sweater girls! Page 252

LEATHER

CON BRIO
Classico con twist. Car coat goes wind-breaker, blazer goes vest, and jackets aren't just jackets anymore. Take to the streets in romantic Roma colors—burnt oranges and browns. Bravissimo! Page 272

JEANS

BLACK ATTACK
The darker side of denim, made in the heavenly shade—of bleached black. Beyond stone-washing, to a new sophistication. Softened with the poetry of posies and Chaplinesque bowlers, sharpened with stripes. Page 258

VELVET

VELOUR TOUJOURS
From blue velvet to new velvet, from formal to fun. Rich velvet takes a royal detour and gets down, sporting a new attitude. Slip into velvet like you would your favorite old jeans. Page 266

PLAIDS

MIXED MEDIA
It's a clash act: mismatched mis-mates in glad, mad plaids. Anything goes, as long as it doesn't go together. From minikilts with menswear to tartan-topping flower-pot hats. Blanket plaid-itudes! Page 234

A spell is in the air this fall—and the magic is woven in the shape of classics gone a bit mad (perhaps it's the harvest moon?). Sweet pleated plaids clash in kaleidoscopic pile-ons;

ELLESTYLE

classic denim bleaches black. Let's go retro: Sweater sets—remember them?—now suit up for the Eighties. Coats take on a new twist, and shout! Our luxe night-novas—plush velvet and smashing silver—are metamorphosed for day. *Bonjour, richesse.* What else is there to stir about? Nip-and-tuck suits, glittering accessory prizes. And beauty's bathed in rosy pinks, the shade just ripe for picking. This autumn's harvest: going against the grain!

AUTUMN WEAVES

GEOMETRICS

BLACK AND WHITE

The hottest color combo to hit the beach: bold black and white, guaranteed not to fade into the background. Look for it in swimsuits, bathing caps, sunglasses—everything under the sun!

Cotton/Lycra geometric bathing caps by special order from Whittall & Shon, NYC, $40 each. Black and white sunglasses by Alain Mikli Ltd., $90 to $125 per pair. For details and more stores, see Shopping Guide. Best beauty bet: Sun-soaked skin needs protection—especially if you're heading south from chillier climes. For color, just a hint on lips does it. All "assets" by Estée Lauder. On faces: Oil-Free Tanning Formula. On lips: Protective Lip Shield, topped with Automatic Lipshine in, near right, Mulled Claret; second from right, Misty Mauve; far right, Beige Shimmer.

ART DIRECTOR:
PHYLLIS SCHEFER
PHOTOGRAPHER:
OLIVIERO TOSCANI/
GILLES BENSIMON/
MARC HISPARD
PUBLISHER:
▲ *ELLE MAGAZINE*
▲■ 410

ART DIRECTOR:
PHYLLIS SCHEFER
PHOTOGRAPHER:
GILLES BENSIMON
PUBLISHER:
ELLE MAGAZINE
■ 411

ART DIRECTOR:
Angelica Blechschmidt
PHOTOGRAPHER:
Albert Watson
CLIENT:
Deutsche VOGUE
PUBLISHER:
Condé Nast Verlag GmbH
■ 412

ART DIRECTOR:
Alberto Nodolini
PHOTOGRAPHER:
Piero Gemelli
CLIENT:
VOGUE Italia
PUBLISHER:
Condé Nast S.P.A.
▼ ■ 413, 414

■ 412 Cover page of the 1986 Christmas issue of the German edition of *Vogue*. (GER)

■ 413, 414 From an article on new make-up colors in the Italian edition of *Vogue*. (ITA)

■ 415, 416 Double spreads from two articles on beauty published in the Italian *Vogue*. (ITA)

■ 412 Titelseite der Weihnachtsnummer 1986 der deutschen Ausgabe der Modezeitschrift *Vogue*. (GER)

■ 413, 414 Aus einem Beitrag in der italienischen Ausgabe der Zeitschrift *Vogue* über neue Make-up Farben. (ITA)

■ 415, 416 Doppelseiten aus zwei Artikeln zum Thema Schönheit in der italienischen *Vogue*. (ITA)

■ 412 Page de titre du numéro de Noël de l'édition allemande de *Vogue*. (GER)

■ 413, 414 Pour un article de l'édition italienne de *Vogue*: présentation des nouveaux coloris de maquillage. (ITA)

■ 415, 416 Pages doubles tirées de deux articles de l'édition italienne de *Vogue* consacrés à la beauté. (ITA)

ART DIRECTOR:
Alberto Nodolini
PHOTOGRAPHER:
Javier Vollhonrat
CLIENT:
Vogue Italia
PUBLISHER:
Condé Nast S.P.A.
■ 415

DOWN TOWN
BEAUTY

Un photographe est toujours voyeur; la bellezza mi seduce quando meno ne sento l'intenzione, quando più ho il sentimento di sorprenderla. Magari in un contesto sgradevole come può esserlo un ingorgo a Place de la Concorde. Mi può colpire un profilo scorto nel deflettore, una capigliatura dietro un finestrino appannato dalla pioggia. Enigmi, perché

il movimento del traffico non mi permetterà un secondo sguardo, mai saprò cosa nasconde la tesa del suo cappello, come finisce la curva della sua nuca. La mia immaginazione galoppa tra semafori e sensi unici e penso al poema di Baudelaire «A une passante» che finisce con «... oh toi que j'eusse aimée oh toi qui le savais...».

DETTAGLI DI BELLEZZA RUBATI ALLA BRUTALITÀ DEL QUOTIDIANO, RACCONTATI CON PAROLE E IMMAGINI DI FRANK HORVAT.

Frank Horvat

208

Smagliante di luce opalescente questa «apparizione» firmata Chanel. Il makeup è quello nuovissimo per la prossima primavera-estate: Poudre Douce, nella sfumatura Beige Rosé per esaltare la carnagione, ombretti Les Mats — opachi e delicatissimi — per ombreggiare lo sguardo, rossetto Rouge à Lèvres Brun Insolent in armonia con lo smalto omonimo. Tubino e giacca in paillettes di Chanel.

ART DIRECTOR:
Alberto Nodolini
PHOTOGRAPHER:
Frank Horvat
CLIENT:
Vogue Italia
PUBLISHER:
Condé Nast S.P.A.
■ 416

BELLEZZA

Lo sa bene chi conduce vita da single. Dopo aver provveduto agli optional tecnologici — dall'ultimo impianto stereo al video registratore, all'idromassaggio computerizzato — si scopre improvviso e ineluttabile il bisogno di un supporto affettivo e quasi sempre si finisce per scegliere un «compagno» simile. La tenerezza e lo stupore di un gatto si specchiano anche negli occhi del suo ospite. Qui, l'associazione è resa ancora più evidente dal makeup, l'ultimo creato dal Yves Saint Laurent, che ha nome Fauve, «Belva», con ombretto n. 65 alleggerito dalla poudre Pressé n.7. Per le guance un velo di fard à Joues Poudres n. 20. Plaid in cachemire di Faliero Sarti. Gattino gentilmente prestato dallo Zoo Benaggi, Milano.

190

·R·E·M·

IN THE REAL WORLD
ROCK'S MOST INFLUENTIAL COLLEGE BAND GRADUATES

It's a warm, clear fall afternoon in New York City; R.E.M.'s guitarist, Peter Buck, is shopping in midtown Manhattan, trying to answer the young clerk who is ringing up his Jim Carroll and John Waters paperbacks and keeps asking, "Are you from Boston? Do you know any musicians in Boston?" Unfailingly polite, Buck hems and haws, says that he knows a few Boston musicians and adds that he is him-

ART DIRECTOR:
FRED WOODWARD
DESIGNER:
KAREN SIMPSON
PHOTOGRAPHER:
BRIAN SMALE
PUBLISHER:
ROLLING STONE
■ 417

INHUMAN
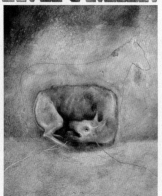

The Animal Liberation Front believes that meat is murder, that science is torture, that animals have the same rights as humans. In the last six years this underground band of ordinary people has freed

BONDAGE

BY MIKE SAGER
ILLUSTRATIONS BY MATT MAHURIN

ART DIRECTOR:
FRED WOODWARD
DESIGNER:
DENNIS ORTIZ-LOPEZ
(LETTERING)
ILLUSTRATOR:
MATT MAHURIN
PUBLISHER:
ROLLING STONE
■ 418

GEORGE HARRISON
— *Gets Back* —

"I DIDN'T THINK IT WAS THAT STUPID," MUTTERS A puzzled George Harrison during a halt in a video shoot, as a battery of eight Warner Bros. Records employees hastens to reassure him. The mood in the skylighted, wood-paneled room at Warner Bros. headquarters in beautiful Burbank, California, is a heady mix of exhilaration and tension. Harrison has just delivered *Cloud Nine*, his first album in five years, to the label. The record is Harrison's finest since his first solo outing after the Beatles' breakup – the three-album set *All Things Must Pass*, in 1970. With good reason, Warner Bros. holds big commercial hopes for it.

Aside from those considerations of art and potential sales, the mere presence of the mysterious ex-Beatle at his record company's offices has propelled the place into a dazzling spin. For the two days that Harrison has been on the scene meeting the press and talking business with the label's bigwigs, the staff has been buzzing. Admirers peek around doorways to catch glimpses of him, and a steady stream of devotees has presented him with albums and other memorabilia to autograph. "In the past week there's been more Beatles records around here

The mystical ex-Beatle rides 'Cloud Nine' back into the material world

than Warner Bros. records," one staffer says jokingly.

But if Harrison's legendary stature has sparked the mood of exhilaration, it's also charged the undercurrent of tension. The video interview being filmed is not for MTV – it's a promotional clip for the annual Warner Elektra/Atlantic (WEA) sales convention in Miami. Featuring segments with a host of premier Warner Bros. acts, the video is intended to "get the troops up, raise the level of morale, motivate the salespeople for the fourth quarter," according to Adam Somers, the vice-president of creative services at Warner Bros., who is coordinating the filming.

To achieve those all-important ends – the holiday season is crucial to the bottom line throughout the record industry – Warner Bros. has recruited fast-talking NBC West Coast sportscaster Fred Roggin and conceived a quasi-comical baseball theme to link the artists' skits. In the year of the lively ball and corked bats, that theme is, What is Warner Bros. Records putting into its vinyl to give the company so many big "hits"? Get it? Perhaps you do, but Harrison – being British and all – doesn't. Still, because of the priority the label is placing on *Cloud*

BY ANTHONY DECURTIS
PHOTOGRAPHS BY WILLIAM COUPON

ROLLING STONE, OCTOBER 22ND, 1987 · 57

ART DIRECTOR:
FRED WOODWARD
DESIGNER:
FRED WOODWARD
PHOTOGRAPHER:
WILLIAM COUPON
PUBLISHER:
ROLLING STONE
■ 419

■ 417–422 Double spreads and covers from various issues of the American magazine *Rolling Stone*. (USA)

■ 417–422 Doppelseiten und Umschläge verschiedener Ausgaben der amerikanischen Zeitschrift *Rolling Stone*. (USA)

■ 417–422 Doubles pages et couvertures de divers numéros du magazine américain *Rolling Stone*. (USA)

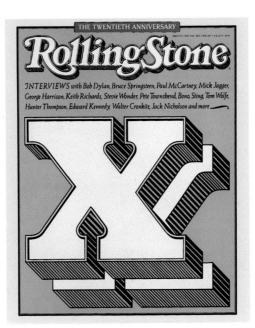

ART DIRECTOR:
FRED WOODWARD
ILLUSTRATOR:
ANITA KUNZ
PUBLISHER:
ROLLING STONE
■ 420

ART DIRECTOR:
FRED WOODWARD
ILLUSTRATOR:
JIM PARKINSON
PUBLISHER:
ROLLING STONE
■ 421

ART DIRECTOR:
FRED WOODWARD
PHOTOGRAPHER:
HERB RITTS
PUBLISHER:
ROLLING STONE
■ 422

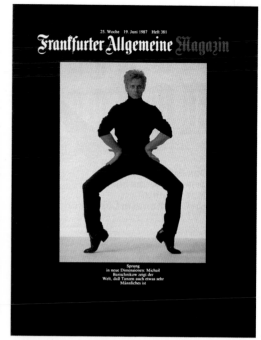

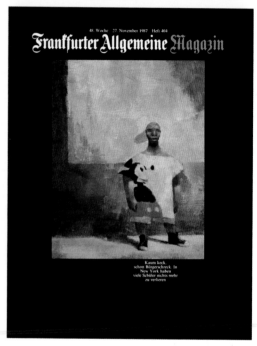

■ 423-431 Covers and double spreads of various issues of the weekly magazine of the *Frankfurter Allgemeine.* Right page top: From a feature on the English poet and painter Edward Lear (1812-1888) who, with his fanciful limericks, was the originator of nonsense-poetry. Middle: Introductory double spread to an article on Liza Minelli who is described by the author as being "seductive, sharp as a knife, ready to fight and full of hope". Bottom: Illustration from a feature on the tradition and mystic importance of ball games in Mexico. (GER)

■ 423-431 Umschläge und Doppelseiten verschiedener Ausgaben des *Frankfurter Allgemeine Magazins.* Rechte Seite oben: Aus einem Artikel über den englischen Dichter und Maler Edward Lear (1812-1888), der mit seinen pointierten Limericks zum Begründer der Nonsense-Verse wurde. Mitte: Einleitende Doppelseite zu einem Artikel über Liza Minelli, von der der Autor sagt, sie sei «verführerisch, messerscharf, kampfbereit und voller Hoffnung». Unten: Illustration zu einem Artikel über die Tradition und mystische Bedeutung des Ballspiels in Mexiko. (GER)

■ 423-431 Couvertures et doubles pages de divers numéros du *Frankfurter Allgemeine Magazin.* Page de droit, en haut: pour un article sur le poète et peintre anglais Edward Lear (1812-1888), qui fonda la poésie de l'absurde en créant nombre de limericks pince-sans-rire. Au centre: double page initiale d'un article consacré à Liza Minelli que l'auteur trouve «séduisante, péremptoire, combative et pleine d'espoir». En bas: illustration d'un article étudiant la tradition du football et des jeux de balle en général au Mexique et la signification mystique qu'ils y revêtent. (GER)

ART DIRECTOR:
Hans-Georg Pospischil

ILLUSTRATOR:
Kurt Ard 424
Brad Holland 428

PHOTOGRAPHER:
Jürgen Röhrscheid 423
Annie Leibovitz 425
Frank Horvat 427

PUBLISHER:
*Frankfurter Allgemeine
Zeitung GmbH*

◀■ 423–428

ART DIRECTOR:
Hans-Georg Pospischil

ILLUSTRATOR:
Edward Lear 429
José Cruz 431

PHOTOGRAPHER:
Annie Leibovitz 430

PUBLISHER:
*Frankfurter Allgemeine
Zeitung GmbH*

■ 429–431

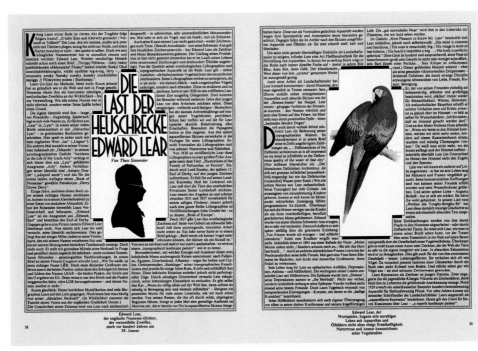

SHIRYŪ MORITA

Zeichen für
Glück: Der japanische
Schreibmeister denkt es –
und lebt es

Shiryū Morita
war gerade fünfzig Jahre alt, als
wir einander auf dem Frankfurter
Flughafen zum ersten Mal begegneten, vor Jahrzehnten. Heute gehört er zu den großen Avantgarde-Altmeistern der Schreibkunst, die
in ganz Ostasien, besonders aber in
Japan, noch immer einen hohen
Stellenwert besitzt und nicht mit
Kalligraphie zu verwechseln ist.

Von
Irmtraud Schaarschmidt-
Richter
Fotos Wilfried Bauer

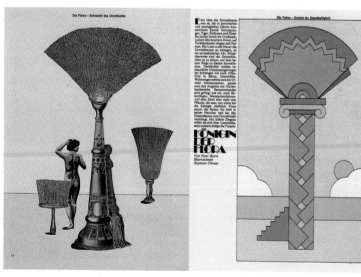

■ 432-440 Additional double spreads from the *Frankfurter Allgemeine Magazin*. On the left side, the introductory double spreads are for articles on the Japanese master scribe Morita, the palm as a symbol of steadfastness, and on the young Spanish designer Sybilla Sorondo who is known as the muse of Spanish fashion. The photographs and illustrations on the right side are from articles on unintentional humor in religion *(435)*, the Russian dancer Mikhail Barishnikov who emigrated to the United States in 1974 *(436)*, greyhounds *(437)*, ski teachers *(438)*, twins *(439)*, and the fishing harbor of Zanzibar *(440)*. (GER)

■ 432-440 Weitere Doppelseiten aus dem *Frankfurter Allgemeine Magazin*. Linke Seite: Doppelseiten zu Artikeln über den japanischen Schreibmeister Morita, über die Palme – Symbol der Standhaftigkeit – und über die junge spanische Mode-Designerin Sybilla Sorondo, die als Muse der spanischen Mode bezeichnet wird. Die Photos und Illustrationen auf der rechten Seite stammen aus Artikeln über die unfreiwillige Komik der Religion *(435)*, den 1974 nach USA emigrierten russischen Tänzer Michail Barishnikow *(436)*, Windhunde *(437)*, Skilehrer *(438)*, Zwillinge *(439)* und über den Fischereihafen von Sansibar *(440)*. (GER)

■ 432-440 Autres pages doubles du *Frankfurter Allgemeine Magazin*. Page de gauche: Doubles pages initiales d'articles sur le maître calligraphe japonais Morita; le palmier symbole de la persévérance; la jeune dessinatrice de mode espagnole Sybilla Sorondo, qualifiée de muse de la mode de son pays. Les photos et illustrations de la page de droite sont tirées d'articles où il est question des aspects comiques involontaires de l'exercice de la religion *(435)*, du danseur russe Mikhaïl Barishnikov émigré aux Etat-Unis en 1974 *(436)*, de lévriers *(437)*, de moniteurs de ski *(438)*, de jumeaux *(439)* et du port de pêche de Zanzibar *(440)*. (GER)

ART DIRECTOR:
Hans-Georg Pospischil

ILLUSTRATOR:
Shiryu Morita 432
Seymour Chwast 433

PHOTOGRAPHER:
Susan Lamèr 434

PUBLISHER:
Frankfurter Allgemeine
Zeitung GmbH

◄■ 432–434

ART DIRECTOR:
Hans-Georg Pospischil

ILLUSTRATOR:
Heinz Edelmann 435, 438
Brad Holland 437
Alfons Holtgreve 440

PHOTOGRAPHER:
Annie Leibovitz 436
Abe Frajndlich 439

PUBLISHER:
Frankfurter Allgemeine
Zeitung GmbH

▼■ 435–440

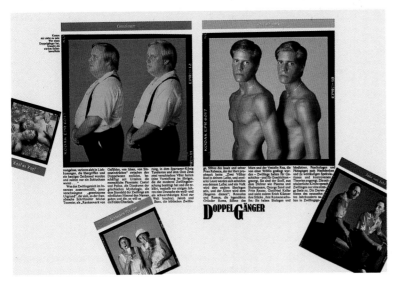

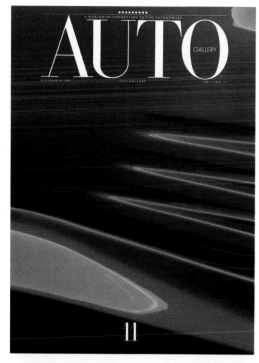

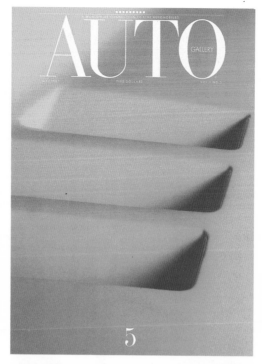

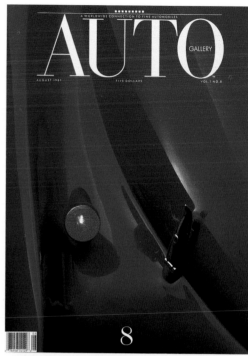

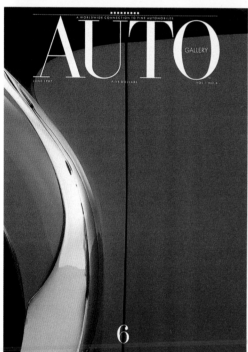

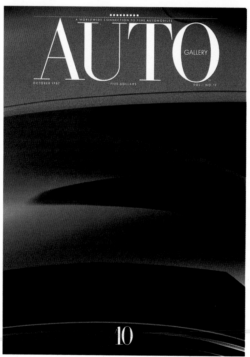

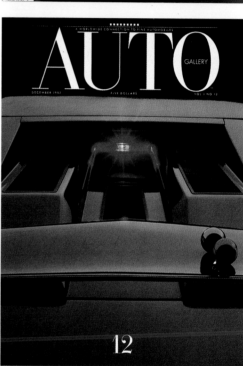

ART DIRECTOR:
MICHAEL BROCK
DESIGNER:
MICHAEL BROCK
PHOTOGRAPHER:
BRUCE MILLER 441
GLEN MCCALLISTER 442
CINDY LEWIS 443-445
JOHN PAUL ENDRESS 446
TIM HARGROVE 447
AGENCY:
MICHAEL BROCK DESIGN
PUBLISHER:
AUTO GALLERY PUBLISHING CO.
■ 441-447

■ 441-447 Cover pages for various issues of the American magazine *Auto Gallery.* (USA)

■ 441-447 Umschlagseiten verschiedener Ausgaben der amerikanischen Zeitschrift *Auto Gallery.* (USA)

■ 441-447 Couvertures de divers numéros de la revue américaine *Auto Gallery.* (USA)

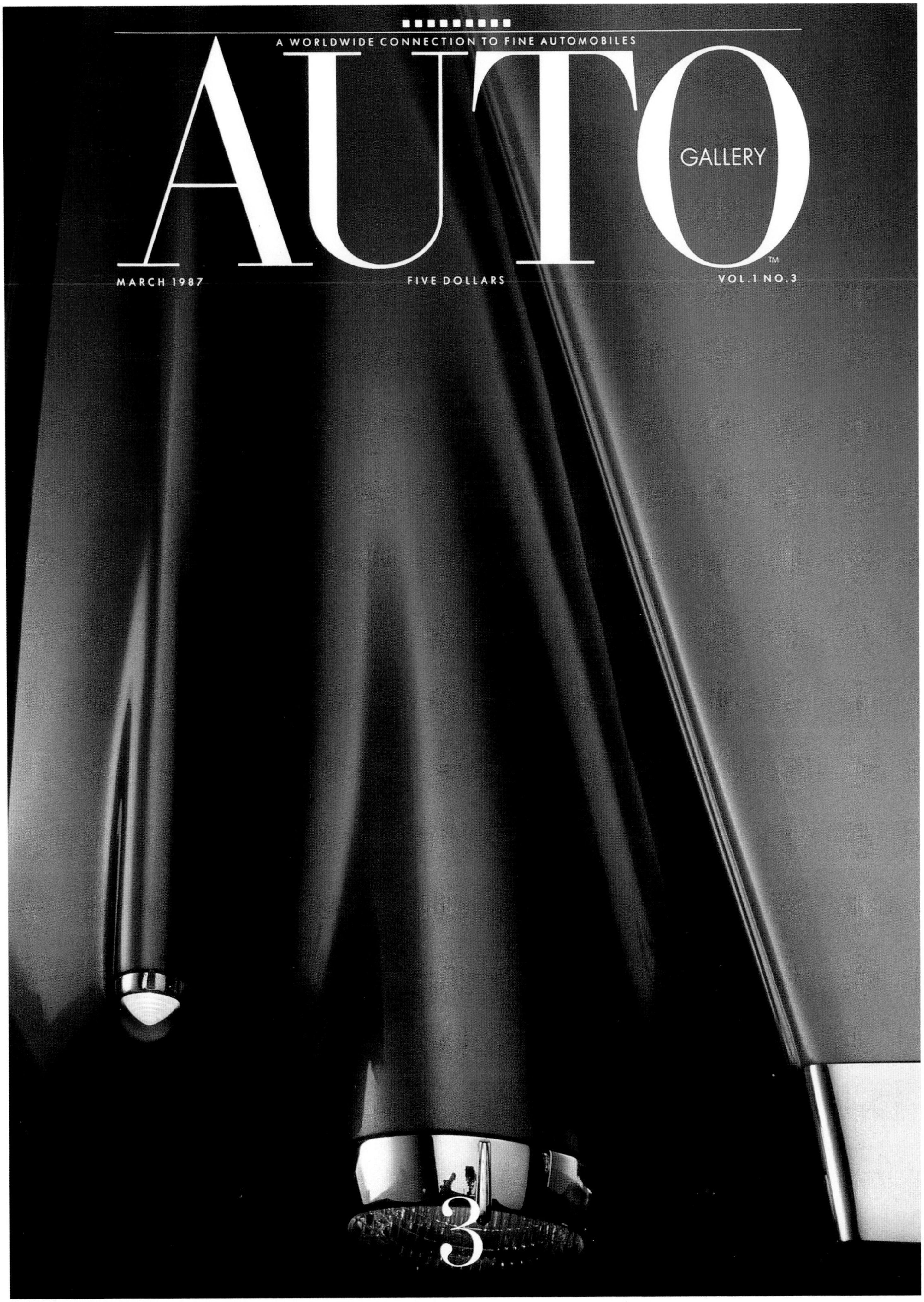

A WORLDWIDE CONNECTION TO FINE AUTOMOBILES

AUTO

GALLERY

™

MARCH 1987   FIVE DOLLARS   VOL. 1 NO. 3

3

ART DIRECTOR:
KIT HINRICHS

DESIGNER:
KIT HINRICHS/LEONORE BARTZ

PHOTOGRAPHER:
STEVEN A. HELLER

AGENCY:
PENTAGRAM DESIGN

PUBLISHER:
*ART CENTER COLLEGE
OF DESIGN, PASADENA*

■ 448

ART DIRECTOR:
KIT HINRICHS

DESIGNER:
KIT HINRICHS/LEONORE BARTZ

ILLUSTRATOR:
WALID SABA/JOHN MATTOS

PHOTOGRAPHER:
HENRIK KAM (COVER)

COPYWRITER:
*SUSAN HOFFMAN/
JEAN KEEFE PARRY*

AGENCY:
PENTAGRAM DESIGN

PUBLISHER:
*ART CENTER COLLEGE
OF DESIGN, PASADENA*

■ 449, 450

ArtCenter

NEWS

Reader response to our first issue of *Review* was overwhelmingly positive. Clearly the publication is helping to meet the growing need to widen and deepen communication lines between Art Center and its graduates. But *Review* is just one step in that direction. Others, in varying stages of development include a new alumni directory, an alumni survey, with results to be published in *Review*, an exhibition of alumni work, and a comprehensive history of Art Center slated for release in 1990. The biggest step – or leap – was the first-ever Alumni Reunion held at the college on September 26. Reminiscing, reconnecting, rekindling old friendships, and kindling new ones were the order of the day. There were almost tangible feelings of pride and excitement about the new spirit at Art Center and its promise for the future. A full report of the day's (and night's) activities will follow in *Review* 3.

Upcoming Events

Fall Exhibitions
Changing Light: The Sixth Arango International Design Exhibition, Main Campus, 1700 Lida, September 28 – October 31
Preview Opening: September 27, 4 – 7 P.M.
Duane Michals, Art Center/Downtown Gallery, 54 W. Colorado, November 4 – November 18

Lecture
William A. Reedy Memorial Lecturer and Photographer, Duane Michals, will speak on *Photography and Reality*, on November 18, 2 P.M. in the Robert H. Ahmanson Auditorium. Reception follows in the Atrium. Main Campus, 1700 Lida.

Banking on Our Students

To guarantee that no student of exceptional talent shall be denied an Art Center education on the basis of financial need, the college has launched a five-year, $25 million fund-raising campaign. The announcement was made on May 21.

The campaign will expand efforts already begun by David Brown, who since becoming president in 1985, has added new programs and facilities and committed the college to a $1 million budget for scholarships by 1990. Campaign revenues will increase this amount, with $20 million designated for endowment, its earnings going to scholarships and education programs. Four million dollars will augment tuition as operational income, and $1 million is earmarked for facilities and equipment upgrade.

Gifts to the campaign prior to the announcement total over $10 million, according to Khyl Smeby, chairman of Art Center's board of trustees.

"We live in a world which often takes design for granted," says Brown, "yet we are surrounded by objects, products, images, and space created by designers. This campaign is an invitation to help shape – very literally – how the world of the future will look, how it will work, and what it will be like to live in."

THE CAMPAIGN

Making a Business of Good Design

Bringing alive the past with computers and green florist foam may seem an unorthodox way to solve a design problem. But for Bob Gurr (Product Design '52) and his colleagues at Sequoia Creative, Inc., the challenge of creating a dinosaur that can bat an eyelid and a pterodactyl capable of flying requires unusual design skills.

Sequoia was founded 2½ years ago by ex-Disney creative managers Gurr, Tom Reidenbach, and Dave Schweninger. Described as a "full-service creator and producer of leisure time spectaculars," Sequoia has brought the extraterrestrial and prehistoric into the lives of millions of amazed spectators. The flying saucer for the closing ceremonies of the 1984 Olympics was their creation, and so are the King Kong at Universal Studios and 23 life-size dinosaurs installed in May at Knott's Berry Farm in Anaheim, California.

Since March, Sequoia has been bringing a little magic to Art Center. The latest business to join Design Associates, Sequoia now participates with 27 select businesses in a unique partnership with the college.

The firms are given the opportunity to work closely with professional designers of the future and to learn about the most recent developments in design. In turn, Art Center students are given "real-world" experience with practicing professionals.

Comments associate director of corporate relations Tim Butte, "Design Associates is a program for businesses that appreciate and understand the impact of good design on the marketability and acceptance of their products and services."

No 2

Reflections of a Place

After securing the permits and signing the contracts to build a 12-story office structure, developers in Woodland Hills, California realized they'd overlooked one thing: all the people overlooking their construction site from nearby offices.

Voit Developers decided to transform their construction fence into a mural dedicated to the neighbors. Local art students submitted proposals based on the theme of professional and recreational life in the San Fernando Valley.

Jill Field, 6th term Fine Arts major, won the competition with a composition that represents, in the first section, a scenic view of the region, in the second, the feet of people walking by the fence, and in the third, an abstract treatment of office windows.

Field's proposal so impressed Voit that they tripled Field's award to $3,000. Voit also contributed $2500 to Art Center and paid Field another $500 to hire two assistants: Art Center students Melissa Kretschmer (MFA candidate in Fine Arts) and Kendal Cronkhite (8th-term Illustration major).

Asked how the mural relates to her studio work, Field replied, "I'm interested in the viewer. With a mural, the viewer is most important, because the painting is for the community. I'm also interested in reflections and options of viewing the same space in different ways. With this mural, the space was the San Fernando Valley, which I interpreted as deep, then shallow, and then reflective space."

The mural, on view through the fall at 21550 Oxnard Street in Woodland Hills, has won other commissions for Field. Her second mural has changed a construction fence in Marina del Rey into a curbside exhibition of 13 photo-like paintings representing what Field calls "the heart of the Marina."

"I enjoy doing the murals," she said. "And the prize money is really appreciated because it's keeping me in school, paying the tuition and helping me support my studio work."

Joe Henninger Honored by S.I.L.A.

Close to 150 people gathered under the auspices of the Society of Illustrators of Los Angeles at the venerable Sportsman's Lodge on July 15 to honor Joseph Morgan Henninger, an amazingly influential illustrator and Art Center teacher and former department chairman. Many in the audience – themselves now successful illustrators and teachers – had been Henninger's students at Art Center.

Henninger, born in Wales, raised in Indiana, and trained at the Ecole des Beaux-Arts in Paris, began teaching at the Art Center School in 1937 as a substitute. In a fondly remembered and often cited anecdote, student interest in his knowledge and techniques jumped his class size from 8 to 30 in a few weeks' time, and he was invited to continue teaching on a permanent basis. Those 30 were the first of some 3,000 students Henninger was to teach over the next 40 years at Art Center.

Current S.I.L.A. president Craig Nelson (Illustration '70 and protégé and friend of Henninger's) chaired the evening and in his tribute reeled off the names of some of today's illustrators who studied under Henninger at Art Center. Among them: Robert M. Peak ('51), Phil Hays ('55), Isadore Seltzer ('56), Mark English ('60), Barron R. Storey ('61), and Bart Forbes ('63).

With Henninger at the ceremony, in which it was announced that S.I.L.A.'s annual "Best in Show" award will hence forward be known as the Joseph Morgan Henninger Award, was Danica Henninger, his wife of more than 50 years. Henninger continues to paint, working out of his studio in Pacific Palisades, producing sell-out shows of watercolors inspired by his far-ranging travels – and adding to his ever-growing collection of honors, awards, and thanks.

2

ArtCenter

Human Factors at Home

Dr. Kamran Abedini, Art Center faculty member specializing in human factors engineering, has developed a prototype for an improved remote control unit. Abedini presented his findings in May at Interface '87, a conference at which experts from industry and colleges discussed new ways to apply human factors engineering and industrial design to the development and design of consumer goods.

An abstract of Dr. Abedini's paper is reprinted here with permission of the author.

"Hand-held and -operated remote control units (RCUs) have become extremely popular in the present consumer market, with an estimated 98 percent of American homes using them.

"Despite their popularity, remote controls often intimidate the user by offering too many operating functions. One way to solve this confusion problem is to separate the TV and VCR functions on the display panel, add color and contrast coding, and, most importantly, establish a strong contrast between the symbols/labels or the buttons with the surface of the RCU.

"A change in the shape of the RCU is also recommended, as the existing rectangular model requires the user to point the top end of the unit at the TV/VCR to operate any function. This angle is uncomfortable for the wrist and makes the display panel hard to see. If the RCU were angled, as shown in the prototype, the wrist discomfort would be eliminated and the display panel could still be easily read."

The prototype was built by Art Center student Peter O'Rourke.

Subtle Communication in Japanese Advertising Photographs

Advertising Photography in Japan '86, a selection of 150 photographs created for print advertisements in Japan, was displayed at the college February 2 – 28. Chosen from the winning entries in the 1986 annual competition of the Japanese Advertising Photographers' Association, the works "merged an identifiably Japanese sensibility with a strong Western influence," according to Art Center's director of exhibitions Stephen Nowlin, who curated the exhibition with photography department chairman, Fred Hutton.

"In Japanese culture," Nowlin says, "blunt, aggressive communication is considered to be distasteful, and many photographs created for advertisements have little obvious connection with the products being sold. If portrayed, the products often become illuminated by the glow and strength of the image, rather than simply being illustrated by it." The photograph by Gan Fukuda reproduced here, for example, was an advertisement for Toshiba television sets.

Advertising Photography in Japan '86 was cosponsored by Canon, Inc., Canon U.S.A., Inc., and Kodak Nagase Co. Ltd. A second showing of the photographs was held in March at the Art Directors Club of New York.

Great Teachers Recognized at May Graduation

The graduates of the Spring '87 class honored eight faculty members with "Great Teacher" awards. Graduating students in each major voted for the instructor who had made, over the course of eight semesters at Art Center, an "extraordinary contribution" to their education.

Recognized at the May graduation were:
Martin Macdonald, Advertising
Barton Choy, Environmental Design
Gabor Kalman, Film
Hal Frazier, Graphic and Packaging Design
Sherri Nielsen, Illustration
Tim Bradley, Photography
Ted Youngkin, Product Design
Strother MacMinn, Transportation Design

Ted Youngkin, a faculty member at Art Center for 31 years, was also named a "Great Teacher" by members of the Fall '86 graduating class.

Educating Transportation Designers in the 21st Century

For visionary designers, the 21st century is on the drawing board today. And in Europe last spring, five leading industry executives and seven designers talked specifically about how best to educate the transportation designers of tomorrow.

A workshop entitled "Transportation in the 21st Century – The Challenge to Design Education," organized by Art Center (Europe), was held in Geneva on March 5 as part of the 57th International Motor Show. With a capacity crowd of 400 on hand, Uwe Bahnsen, Art Center (Europe) education director, moderated the panel discussion.

The conclusions? Design must be present at the "concept moment" of the product, according to Sergio Pininfarina, president, Pininfarina SpA. Transportation designers of the future must be part designer, part engineer, suggested Roger Forray, of S.N.C.F. And all agreed that the needs of the consumer – in particular, those of safety – must be combined in good design with a minimal harm to the environment.

Dr. Ferdinand Panik, director of Daimler-Benz AG, called attention to an ambitious safety program launched by the European automobile industry. Named Prometheus (Program for European Traffic with Highest Efficiency and Unprecedented Safety), the research is expected to lead to radically improved road transportation conditions in the 21st century.

21 CENTURY

The workshop is the first in a series planned by Art Center (Europe). The Italian magazine *Auto & Design* cosponsored the workshop. Additional funding was received from Du Pont de Nemours.

European Awards for Car Design

Art Center (Europe) advisors Giorgio Giugiaro and Claus Luthe were honored at the Geneva Motor Show as the recipients of the prestigious car design award Torino-Piemonte.

The award was established in 1984 by the City of Turin, Italy and the Region of Piedmont. It is given each year to the designer or design team who, during the previous year made the greatest contribution to the development of car/body design in the automotive industry.

Giugiaro and his company Ital Design won their award for the "Incas" prototype. Luthe was recognized for his work as chief designer for the BMW series "7."

President's Letter

S

Working in the Public Eye

GLENDALE POLICE

Residents of Glendale, California are feeling better about their police today, thanks in part to the public relations work of three Art Center students.

In an assignment for Vince Robbins' Graphic Design Workshop – designing for non-profits – 8th-term students Linda Joe-Cheung and Mimie F. Lee joined forces with Photo major Robert Cochran to design posters for the Glendale P.D.

The posters, which now stand in local shop windows, were partly funded by William Lambuth (Swain's Art Supplies) and Ralph Caravetta (Merget Printing).

On April 7, Glendale mayor Larry Zarian presented the students, Lambuth and Caravetta, with Certificates of Recognition for their work and donations.

Partners in Education

Sponsoring the publication of *Review* are ColorGraphics, Inc. and Kirk Paper, who have donated in full the costs of printing and paper. These gifts continue a long tradition of partnership between Art Center and the business and design communities, a hallmark of the college since its founding in 1930.

ColorGraphics/Los Angeles
150 North Myers Street
Los Angeles, California 90033
(213) 261-7171

ColorGraphics/San Francisco
2 Connecticut
San Francisco, California 94107
(415) 863-6066

National Press/Palo Alto
850 Hansen Way
Palo Alto, California 94304
(415) 493-0880

National Press/Santa Rosa
357 Sutton Place
Santa Rosa, California 95407
(707) 584-9444

Honolulu Graphic Arts
863 Halekauwila
Honolulu, Hawaii 96813
(808) 531-6467

Kirk Paper Company, Inc.
6550 East Washington Boulevard
Los Angeles, California 90040
(213) 685-7460

ColorGraphics, Inc.

3

■ 448–450 Covers and a double spread from *Review*, a magazine published by the Art Center College of Design, Pasadena, California. (USA)

■ 448–450 Umschläge und eine Doppelseite der vom Art Center College of Design, Pasadena, Kalifornien, herausgegebenen Zeitschrift *Review*. (USA)

■ 448–450 Couvertures et une double page du magazine *Review* publié par l'Art Center College of Design de Pasadena, en Californie. (USA)

ART DIRECTOR:
KIT HINRICHS
DESIGNER:
KIT HINRICHS/LEONORE BARTZ
ILLUSTRATOR:
GERALD HUERTE (PENCIL)
COPYWRITER:
SUSAN HOFFMAN/
JEAN KEEFE PARRY
AGENCY:
PENTAGRAM DESIGN
PUBLISHER:
ART CENTER COLLEGE
OF DESIGN, PASADENA
■ 451, 452

NEWS

BLACKSMITH

No 1

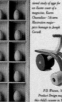
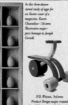

PROBLEM SOLUTION

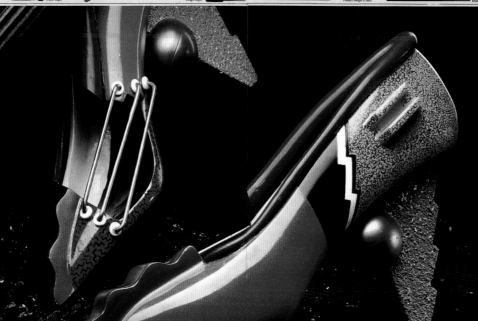

ART DIRECTOR:
KIT HINRICHS
DESIGNER:
KIT HINRICHS/LEONORE BARTZ
PHOTOGRAPHER:
STEVEN A. HELLER
COPYWRITER:
*SUSAN HOFFMAN/
JEAN KEEFE PARRY*
AGENCY:
PENTAGRAM DESIGN
PUBLISHER:
*ART CENTER COLLEGE
OF DESIGN, PASADENA*
■ 453, 454

■ 451–454 Additional double
spreads (see also p. 160/161)
from the magazine
Review. (USA)

■ 451–454 Weitere Doppel-
seiten (siehe auch S. 160/
161) aus der Zeitschrift
Review. (USA)

■ 451–454 Doubles pages
supplémentaires du maga-
zine *Review* (voir également
les pages 160/161). (USA)

PACIFIC

1987, No. 4

*Changing
Perspectives*

PACIFIC ✷ TELESIS
Group

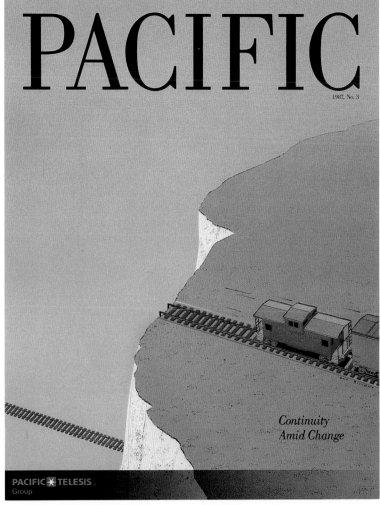

PACIFIC

1987, No. 3

*Continuity
Amid Change*

PACIFIC ✷ TELESIS
Group

PACIFIC

1987, No. 2

*The Network's
Changing Spectrum*

PACIFIC ✷ TELESIS
Group

PACIFIC

1987, No. 1

New Vantage Points

PACIFIC ✷ TELESIS
Group

ART DIRECTOR:
MICHAEL MABRY
DESIGNER:
*MICHAEL MABRY/RENÉE
WEN/PIPER MURAKAMI*
TOR:
UT

DESIGN

QUEENS

INDUSTRY
UPDATE

TRENDS · ISSUES · NEWS · DEVELOPMENTS

1987

As new CD's flood the market, the trend toward selection-oriented board packaging is unmistakable. "On an LP, you have 288-square inches for information," notes Ned Berndt, vice president of the Miami, FL-based Q Records and Tapes. "With a CD or cassette, a little package doesn't have that impact. The larger surface area of the board box is important for display."

Basing his judgment on the recent shipments of CD and cassette recordings, Berndt sees a clear shift away from the plastic clamshell—which had been favored by some manufacturers due to perceived anti-theft advantages—toward all board packaging with its superior graphics and selection orientation.

INDUSTRY TREND TOWARD BOARD VS. PLASTIC

MUSIC PACKAGING *is in the midst*

of a revolution—and its impact on record merchandisers is profound. As the music industry explodes with new and technically advanced formats of recorded music, such as compact disc and digital audio tape, record companies and retailers alike are seeking to maximize sales while meeting the demands dictated by these new configurations.

The LP, once the primary format, has taken a back seat to CDs and cassettes—which, according to RIAA, currently account for nearly 70 percent of industry sales, exclusive of singles—as record merchants make space for the influx.

The change in technology has also dictated a new approach to packaging. The trend towards greater sophistication in point-of-purchase packaging is reflected in the successful introduction of the CD 6-by-12-inch box. Not only does this format provide a greater area for graphic display, it addresses retailers' concerns of merchandising, cost and anti-theft.

For the same reasons, 4-by-12-inch boxes for cassettes are being made available on demand by savvy record industry marketers as more emphasis is being placed on merchandising cassettes—which have made a dramatic increase in volume over the last few years, and now represent more than 50 percent of the market.

As a result of the growth and strength of these formats, retailers are redesigning their stores to reflect this change. Many merchants have dramatically redistributed their selling space, as they move away from the focus on LPs and the past practice of keeping cassettes under lock and key. A large proportion of floor space is now allocated to displaying CD's and cassettes, making them directly accessible to consumers for full marketability. As the market continues to expand, packagers are working with the record companies to develop the kind of packaging that contributes to effective merchandising...

"Market research indicates that you stand a far higher chance of getting a consumer to purchase a product if you can get them to pick it up off the shelf," says Richard Roth, executive vice president of Queens Group, Inc., one of the nation's largest suppliers of printing and packaging to the music industry for 40 years. "Remember that 'Don't squeeze the Charmin' ad? Everybody did squeeze it, and then they bought it. Contemporary, high impact graphics have the same effect at the point of purchase—so it's crucial to use selection-oriented packaging that allows for as much 'eye-contact' as possible."

Roth points out that rack jobbers have also endorsed the 4-by-12-inch cassette box. The more rigid seal-end packaging now in use has reduced susceptibility to theft, and there's been wide discussion about incorporating anti-theft electronic article surveillance (EAS) targets directly into the packaging.

According to Roth, there is some indication that a two-tier system may de-

"...rack jobbers have also endorsed the 4-by-12-inch cassette box."

GRAPHICS

Critical Factor in CD and Cassette Packaging

velop with board packaging for new and important releases and selection-oriented generic boxes for less important titles. "We feel that future CD and cassette packaging will by and large be the board format," says Roth. "We anticipate a tremendous increase in our board packaging volume, and have committed ourselves to new equipment to meet the demand."

The 6" x 12" long box has gained wide acceptance in the industry. Savvy marketers look for the 4" x 12" box to house cassettes.

1

ART DIRECTOR:
TERRY KOPPEL
DESIGNER:
*TERRY KOPPEL/
ANNIKA LARSSON*
COPYWRITER:
MELISSA MOSO
AGENCY:
KOPPEL & SCHER
PUBLISHER:
QUEENS GROUP, INC.
■ 459

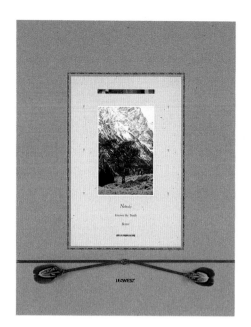

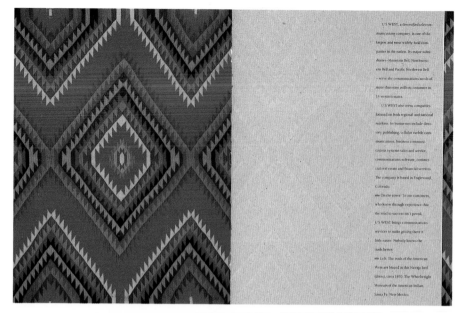

ART DIRECTOR:
J. DUFFY/C. ANDERSON
DESIGNER:
SHARON WERNER
PHOTOGRAPHER:
LYNN SCHULTE/C. AURNESS
AGENCY:
THE DUFFY DESIGN GROUP
CLIENT:
US WEST
■ 460–463

■ 460–463 Cardboard folder
with leather binding and
quail feathers for two
reports of the telecommunications company US West.
The narrower format of the
pages allows the pattern of
the Navajo blanket to
remain partly visible on the
insides of the covers. (USA)

■ 460–463 Kartonmappe
mit Lederband und Wachtel-
federn für zwei Berichte von
US West, Telekommunika-
tionen. Das Navajodecken-
muster auf den Innenseiten
der Umschläge bleibt dank
des schmaleren Formats der
übrigen Seiten teilweise
sichtbar. (USA)

■ 460–463 Chemise carton
avec ruban cuir et plumes
de cailles pour deux rapports
d'US West (télécommunica-
tions). Le dessin des pages 2
et 3 de couverture évoque
celui d'une couverture
navajo; il est visible grâce
au format réduit des pages
intérieures. (USA)

ART DIRECTOR:
MIKE WEYMOUTH
DESIGNER:
ELAINE PRATT
ILLUSTRATOR:
ELAINE PRATT
COPYWRITER:
ELLEN LYNCH
STUDIO:
WEYMOUTH DESIGN, INC.
CLIENT:
AUSIMONT
■464–467

■464–467 Cover and
double spreads from an
annual report of Ausimont,
a firm which is relatively
new to the specialized chemicals industry in the
United States. Photo collages
lend the report a note of
the unconventional. (USA)

■464–467 Umschlag und
Doppelseiten aus einem Jah-
resbericht für Ausimont, ein
Unternehmen, das im Spe-
zialchemikalien-Geschäft der
USA relativ neu ist. Die
Photocollagen geben dem
Bericht etwas Unkonventio-
nelles. (USA)

■464–467 D'un rapport
annuel d'Ausimont, qui a
rejoint récemment les rangs
des spécialistes en produits
chimiques spéciaux des E.-U.
Grâce aux collages photo, ce
rapport se détache nette-
ment de ses concurrents
plus conventionnels. (USA)

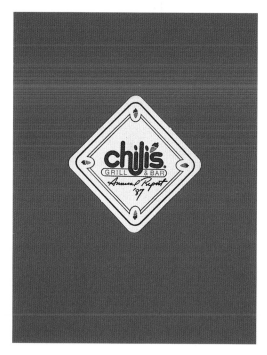

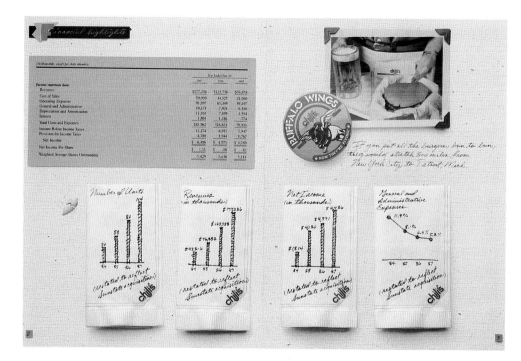

ART DIRECTOR:
BRIAN BOYD
DESIGNER:
BRIAN BOYD
PHOTOGRAPHER:
ROBERT LATORRE
COPYWRITER:
RICH FLORA
AGENCY:
*RICHARDS BROCK MILLER
MITCHELL & ASSOC./
THE RICHARDS GROUP*
CLIENT:
CHILI'S INC.
■ 468–471

■ 468–471 Cover and double spreads from the 1987 annual report of Chilis Grill & Bar. A style reminiscent of diary and photo album is achieved through the use of collages, and corresponds to the young image of this nationwide restaurant chain. (USA)

■ 468–471 Umschlag und Doppelseiten des Jahresberichtes 1987 von Chilis Grill & Bar. Dank der Collagen wirkt er wie eine Mischung aus Tagebuch und Photoalbum, ein Stil der dem jungen Image dieser landesweit präsenten Imbisskette entspricht. (USA)

■ 468–471 Couverture et doubles pages du rapport annuel 1987 de Chilis Grill & Bar. Les collages lui donnent un caractère mixte de journal et d'album photo – style qui colle très bien à l'image jeune de cette chaîne de snacks répandue à travers tout le pays. (USA)

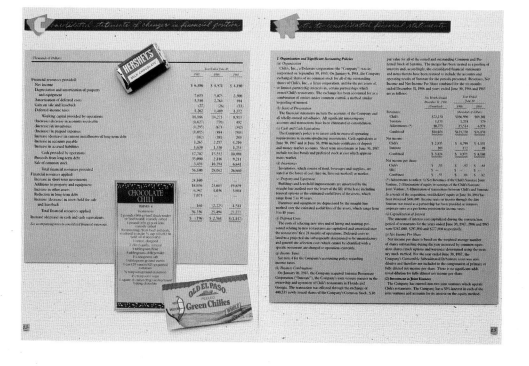

ILLUSTRATION

ILLUSTRATION

ILLUSTRATION

ART DIRECTOR:
JOHN DOLBY
ILLUSTRATOR:
GUY BILLOUT
AGENCY:
BBDM ADVERTISING
CLIENT:
SIGNODE CORP.
■ 472

ART DIRECTOR:
DENIS KITCHEN
DESIGNER:
ROBERT BURGER
ILLUSTRATOR:
ROBERT BURGER
PUBLISHER:
KITCHEN SINK PRESS
■ 473

■ 472 "Failure to assess and test our strengths inevitably leads to weakness". Signode, a manufacturer of industrial packaging, uses this slogan, and the illustration which accompanies it, for an advertisement. (USA)

■ 473 Cover for the *Death Rattle* comic book. (USA)

■ 474 Illustration used for the introduction of a new line of furniture by Keiser Newman. (USA)

■ 472 Die Firma Signode, Hersteller von Industrieverpackungen, verwendet diese Illustration für eine Anzeige, in der es um Selbsteinschätzung geht. Das Fazit: Signode kennt ihre starken Seiten. (USA)

■ 473 Für den Umschlag eines Comic-Heftes. (USA)

■ 474 Für die Ankündigung einer neuen Möbel-Linie von Keiser-Newman verwendete Illustration. (USA)

■ 472 La société Signode, qui produit des emballages industriels, utilise cette illustration pour une annonce, où elle se livre à l'examen et au contrôle de ses atouts, garants d'un développement dépourvu de faiblesses. (USA)

■ 473 Pour la couverture d'un magazine de B.D. (USA)

■ 474 Illustration utilisée pour le lancement d'une nouvelle gamme d'ameublements de Keiser-Newman. (USA)

ILLUSTRATION 171

ART DIRECTOR:
Sandra Hendler
DESIGNER:
Sandra Hendler
ILLUSTRATOR:
Sandra Hendler
AGENCY:
Sandra Hendler Inc.
CLIENT:
Keiser/Newman
■ 474

ART DIRECTOR:
HOLGER LOOF
ILLUSTRATOR:
PETER KRÄMER
AGENCY:
O.O.P.+P. WERBEAGENTUR
CLIENT:
TECHNIKER KRANKENKASSE
■ 475

DESIGNER:
CATHLEEN TOELKE
ILLUSTRATOR:
CATHLEEN TOELKE
CLIENT:
CATHLEEN TOELKE
■ 476

■ 475 From an advertisement for a health insurance plan for technicians encouraging the participation of those newly entering the profession. The slogan reads "a clear text". (GER)

■ 476 Illustration used by Cathleen Toelke for her own promotion. (USA)

■ 475 Aus einer Anzeige der Techniker Krankenkasse, die Berufsanfänger zum Eintritt bewegen soll. Der Slogan lautet: «Klartext». (GER)

■ 476 Als Eigenwerbung von Cathleen Toelke verwendete Illustration. (USA)

■ 475 Annonce de la Caisse-maladie des techniciens invitant les nouveaux venus à la profession à adhérer à une caisse dont les textes sont «en clair». (GER)

■ 476 Illustration que Cathleen Toelke, l'auteur, utilise pour sa promotion personnelle. (USA)

ILLUSTRATION 173

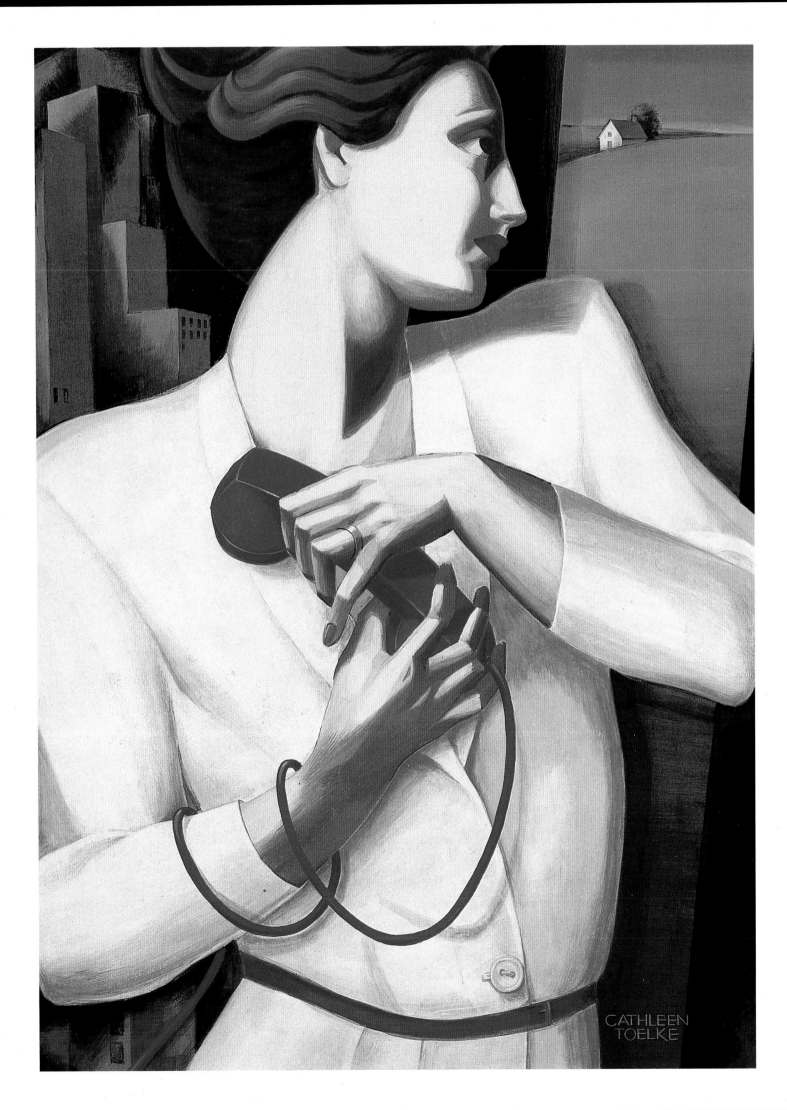

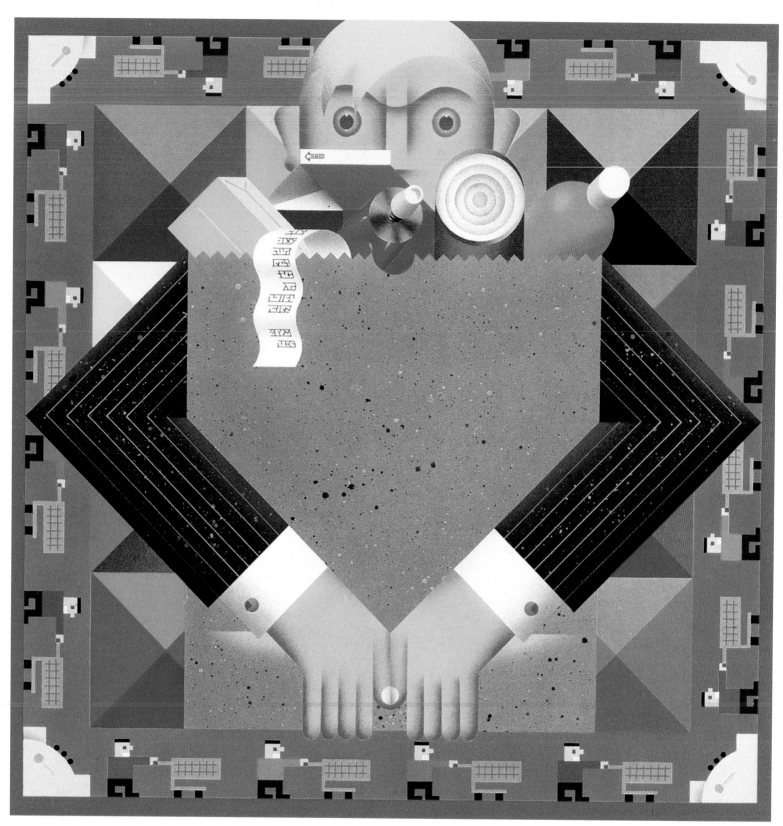

ART DIRECTOR:
SHARON GUSH
ILLUSTRATOR:
JOSE CRUZ
AGENCY:
PETERSON & BLYTH
ASSOCIATES INC.
CLIENT:
PETERSON & BLYTH
ASSOCIATES INC.
■ 477

ART DIRECTOR:
Hans-Georg Pospischil
ILLUSTRATOR:
Jose Cruz
PUBLISHER:
*Frankfurter Allgemeine
Zeitung GmbH*
■ 478

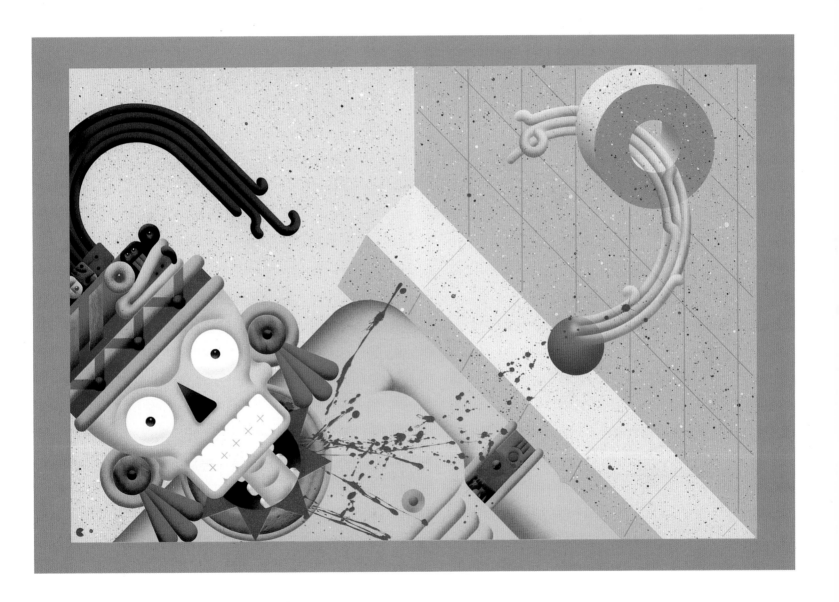

■ 477 Today's consumers have needs and purchasing patterns which are continuously changing. In the United
States, for example, man are presently responsible for 42%
of the grocery shopping. The illustration for this theme is
from a brochure by Peterson & Blyth, Design and Marketing
Communications. (USA)

■ 478 The corresponding article from the magazine of the
Frankfurter Allgemeine describes the Mexican "Lucha
libre", a variation of catch. The combat between good and
evil lends this spectator sport an appearance of extreme
brutality. (GER)

■ 477 Bedarf und Kaufverhalten der verschiedenen Konsu-
mentengruppen ändern sich praktisch von heut' auf morgen, z.B. tätigen gegenwärtig Männer 42% der Lebens-
mitteleinkäufe in den USA. Das ist das Thema dieser Illustration aus einer Broschüre von Peterson & Blyth, Design
und Marketing Communications. (USA)

■ 478 In dem zu dieser Illustration gehörenden Artikel
im *Frankfurter Allgemeine Magazin* geht es um die mexi-
kanische Lucha libre, eine Variante von Catch. Bei diesem
äusserst brutal wirkenden Schaukampf kämpft Gut gegen
Böse. (GER)

■ 477 Les besoins et les habitudes d'achat des divers
groupes de consommateurs sont extrêmement capricieux;
ainsi 42% des achats alimentaires aux Etats-Unis sont effec-
tués par des hommes. Illustration correspondante, pour
une brochure de Peterson & Blyth, Design and Marketing
Communications. (USA)

■ 478 Illustration pour un article du *Frankfurter Allgemeine Magazin* consacré à la lutte libre mexicaine, une
variété de catch. Spectacle haut en couleur, la lucha libre
incarne le combat du Bien et du Mal dans des scènes d'une
extrême violence. (GER)

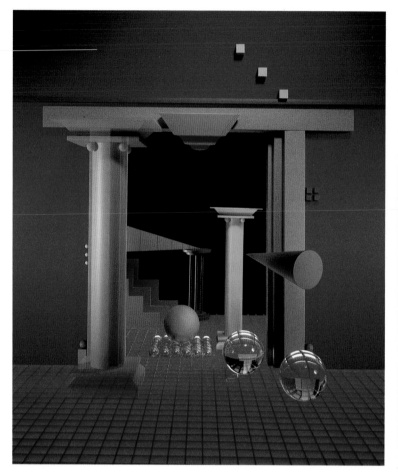

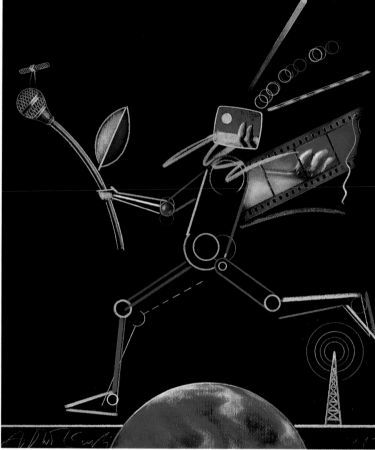

ART DIRECTOR:
Karen Kreiger
ILLUSTRATOR:
Thomas B. Wedell
AGENCY:
Skolos Wedell Raynor Inc.
PUBLISHER:
ID Magazine
■ 479

ART DIRECTOR:
Peter Hessler
DESIGNER:
Peter Hessler
ILLUSTRATOR:
Andrzej Dudzinski
AGENCY:
Beithan, Hessler, Lutz
CLIENT:
Messe Frankfurt GmbH
■ 480

■ 479 Illustration used for the cover of a magazine on international design. (USA)

■ 480 Cover illustration of a promotional brochure for the International Trade Fair for Film, Radio, Television in Frankfurt, which took place in October 1987. (GER)

■ 481 This illustration was used by Neutrogena, manufacturer of skin care products, for a promotional brochure and a poster. (USA)

■ 479 Für einen Umschlag einer Zeitschrift über internationales Design verwendete Illustration. (USA)

■ 480 Umschlagillustration einer Werbemappe für die Internationale Fachmesse für Film, Funk, Fernsehen, die im Oktober 1987 in Frankfurt stattfand. (GER)

■ 481 Diese Illustration wurde von Neutrogena, Hersteller von Hautpflegeprodukten, für eine Broschüre und ein Plakat verwendet. (USA)

■ 479 Illustration utilisée en couverture d'un magazine international de design. (USA)

■ 480 Illustration de couverture d'une brochure promotionnelle de la Foire internationale du cinéma, de la radio et de la télévision organisée à Francfort en octobre 1987. (GER)

■ 481 Illustration utilisée par Neutrogena, un fabricant de produits pour les soins de la peau, dans une brochure et comme sujet d'une affiche. (USA)

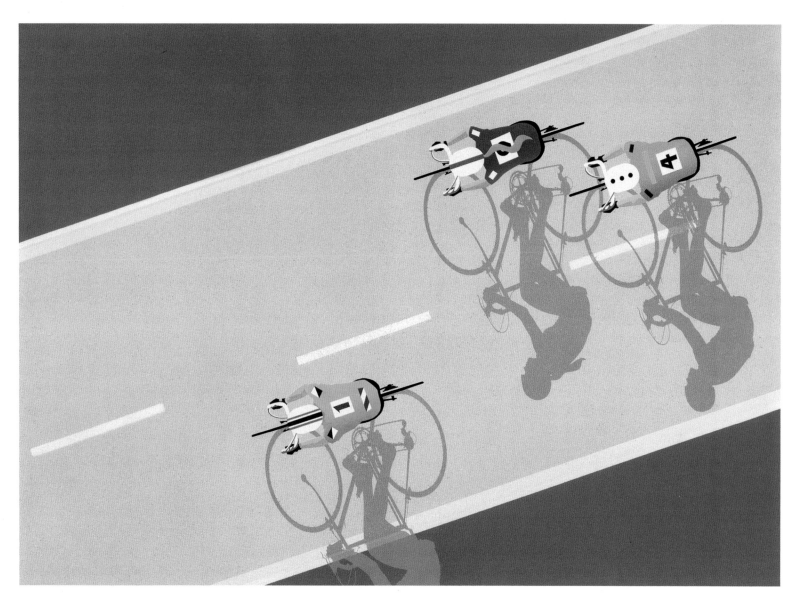

ART DIRECTOR:
SERGIO BELLETINI
DESIGNER:
SERGIO BELLETINI
ILLUSTRATOR:
MICHAEL SCHWAB
AGENCY:
THE MOORE GROUP
CLIENT:
NEUTROGENA
■ 481

ART DIRECTOR:
Hans-Georg Pospischil
ILLUSTRATOR:
Brad Holland
PUBLISHER:
*Frankfurter Allgemeine
Zeitung GmbH*
■ 482–486

■ 482–486 The alarming conditions in New York's public schools, among them juvenile pregnancy, violence and crime, are the subject of an article to which the illustrations *482–484* and *486* belong. "His Lord's Master, the Butler", is the title of an article illustrated by *485*. From the *Frankfurter Allgemeine Magazin*. (GER)

■ 482–486 Die besorgniserregende Situation an New Yorks öffentlichen Schulen ist Gegenstand der Illustrationen *482–484 und 486,* wobei es hier um Schwangerschaften, Hass und Kriminalität geht. *485* gehört zu einem Artikel mit dem Titel «Herr seines Herrn, der Butler.» Aus dem *Frankfurter Allgemeine Magazin.* (GER)

■ 482–486 Les illustrations *482–484 et 486* se réfèrent à la situation préoccupante dans les écoles publiques de New York sur le plan des grossesses d'adolescentes, de la violence et de la criminalité. La fig. *485* illustre un article paru sous le titre de «Maître de son maître, le majordome». *Frankfurter Allgemeine Magazin.* (GER)

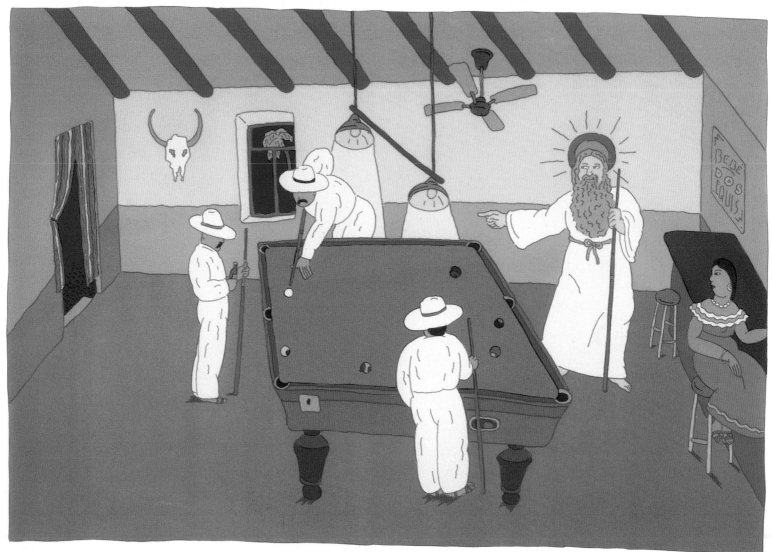

ART DIRECTOR:
Hans-Georg Pospischil

ILLUSTRATOR:
Seymour Chwast

PUBLISHER:
Frankfurter Allgemeine
Zeitung GmbH
■ 487

■ 487 Double spread depicting God in a playing hall of Cuernavaca, Mexico. From an ironic article on clairvoyance in the *Frankfurter Allgemeine Magazin*. (GER)

■ 488 Illustration in the *Frankfurter Allgemeine Magazin* for an air force officer's report on a flight. (GER)

■ 487 Doppelseitige Illustration für einen ironischen Artikel über Hellseherei im *Frankfurter Allgemeine Magazin:* Gott in einer Spielhalle in Cuernavaca, Mexiko. (GER)

■ 488 Illustration für den Bericht eines Luftwaffenoffiziers über einen Flug, im *Frankfurter Allgemeine Magazin*. (GER)

■ 487 Illustration double page pour un article teinté d'ironie sur la voyance dans le *Frankfurter Allgemeine Magazin:* Dieu dans un salon de jeux de Cuernevaca, au Mexique. (GER)

■ 488 Illustration pour le rapport de vol d'un officier de la Luftwaffe. *Frankfurter Allgemeine Magazin*. (GER)

ART DIRECTOR:
HANS-GEORG POSPISCHIL

ILLUSTRATOR:
HEINZ EDELMANN

PUBLISHER:
FRANKFURTER ALLGEMEINE
ZEITUNG GMBH

■ 488

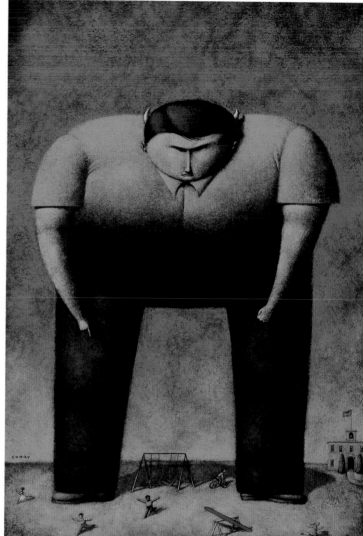

ART DIRECTOR:
FRED WOODWARD
DESIGNER:
JOLENE CUYLER
ILLUSTRATOR:
C.F. PAYNE
PUBLISHER:
REGARDIE'S
■ 489

ART DIRECTOR:
WAYNE FITZPATRICK
DESIGNER:
WAYNE FITZPATRICK
ILLUSTRATOR:
TOM CURRY
PUBLISHER:
*AMERICAN PSYCHOLOGICAL
ASSOC.*
■ 490

■ 489 Nancy Reagan as Henry VIII. Full-page illustration in *Regardie's* magazine. (USA)

■ 490 "School Yard Menace". Bullies are making life miserable for their physically weaker and defenseless victims. Illustration from *Psychology Today*. (USA)

■ 491 From a report in *Medical Economist.* "How long can terror last?" describes the long-lasting psychological effects suffered by a psychiatrist who was attacked by a bear while sleeping in his tent. (USA)

■ 492 The messenger as a symbol of communication. Illustration for an advertisement of TBK, a manufacturer of communications systems. (NOR)

■ 493 Illustration from the magazine *The Physician and Sportsmedicine*. It depicts the quality and usefulness of videos for fitness training. (USA)

■ 494 The fighting between American troops and guerillas in Honduras is the subject of this article in *Regardie's*. (USA)

■ 489 Nancy Reagan als Heinrich VIII. Ganzseitige Illustration aus der Zeitschrift *Regardie's*. (USA)

■ 490 Schulhofrüpel, Kinder, die andere durch körperliche Überlegenheit unterdrücken bzw. quälen, sind Gegenstand dieser Illustration für *Psychology Today*. (USA)

■ 491 Für den Bericht eines Psychiaters, der im Zelt schlafend von einem Bären angefallen wurde und lange unter den psychischen Folgen des Schocks gelitten hat; aus *Medical Economist*. (USA)

■ 492 Der Bote als Symbolfigur für Kommunikation - Illustration für eine Anzeige von TBK, Hersteller von Kommunikationssystemen. (NOR)

■ 493 Illustration aus der Zeitschrift *The Physician and Sportsmedicine*. Es geht um die Qualität und Nützlichkeit von Fitness-Videos. (USA)

■ 494 Der Kampf von US-Einheiten gegen die Guerilla in Honduras ist Thema dieses Beitrags in *Regardie's*. (USA)

■ 489 Nancy Reagen sous les traits d'Henri VIII. Illustration pleine page pour le magazine *Regardie's*. (USA)

■ 490 La brutalité dans les préaux d'école: des millions d'enfants terrorisent des millions de victimes sans défense. Illustration pour *Psychology Today*. (USA)

■ 491 Pour l'histoire d'un psychiatre agressé par un ours alors qu'il dormait sous la tente et qui mit longtemps à se remettre du choc subi. Cette illustration a paru dans la revue *Medical Economist*. (USA)

■ 492 Le messager en tant que symbole de la communication: Illustration pour une annonce de TBK, qui fabrique des systèmes de communication. (NOR)

■ 493 Illustration tirée de la revue *The Physician and Sportsmedicine* où l'on examine la qualité et l'utilité des productions vidéo pour le maintien de la forme physique. (USA)

■ 494 Cet article de *Regardie's* met en vedette l'intervention de l'armée américaine contre les guérilleros honduriens. (USA)

ART DIRECTOR:
ROGER DOWD
DESIGNER:
DEIRDRE MITCHELL
ILLUSTRATOR:
JERRY PINKNEY
PUBLISHER:
MEDICAL ECONOMICS CO.
▼■ 491

ART DIRECTOR:
TINA ADAMEK
ILLUSTRATOR:
EARL KELENY
PUBLISHER:
▼ McGRAW-HILL, INC.
▼■ 493

ART DIRECTOR:
CARL CHRISTENSEN/
MORTEN THRONDSEN
DESIGNER:
MORTEN THRONDSEN
ILLUSTRATOR:
JAMES MARSH
AGENCY:
ANISDAHL/CHRISTENSEN
PUBLISHER:
TBK
▼■ 492

ART DIRECTOR:
FRED WOODWARD
DESIGNER:
JOLENE CUYLER
ILLUSTRATOR:
▼ MARK MAREK
▼■ 494

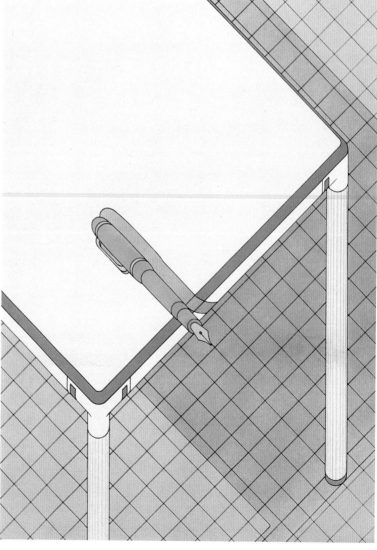

ILLUSTRATOR:
TRISH BURGIO
CLIENT:
TRISH BURGIO
◄■ 495

ART DIRECTOR:
DICK DE MOEI
ILLUSTRATOR:
WERNER HÄBERLING
PUBLISHER:
PENTHOUSE
■ 496

ART DIRECTOR:
TOM KANE
DESIGNER:
TOM KANE
ILLUSTRATOR:
WILSON MCLEAN
AGENCY:
GEER DUBOIS, INC.
CLIENT:
BASF CORP.
■ 499

ART DIRECTOR:
WALDEMAR MEISTER
ILLUSTRATOR:
DIETRICH EBERT
AGENCY:
LEONHARDT & KERN
CLIENT:
WILKHAHN BÜROMÖBEL
◄■ 497, 498

■ 495 By the illustrator Trish Burgio for her own promotion. (USA)

■ 496 "Putting it all on the table" – illustration for an article on poker in the magazine *Penthouse*. (SWI)

■ 497, 498 For a "conference catalog" from Wilkhahn, manufacturer of office furniture. (GER)

■ 499 "Create a new world where lightweight plastics can outfly metals." Ad from BASF, the German chemical concern which produces rugged plastic materials. (USA)

■ 495 Illustration als Eigenwerbung der Illustratorin Trish Burgio. (USA)

■ 496 «Pokern bis auf die Haut» – Illustration für einen Beitrag in der Zeitschrift *Penthouse*. (SWI)

■ 497, 498 Für einen «Konferenz-Katalog» von Wilkhahn, Hersteller von Büromöbeln. (GER)

■ 499 «Die Schaffung einer neuen Welt, in der leichtgewichtiges Plastik Metalle übertrumpft.» Für eine Anzeige von BASF, Hersteller von starkem Plastikmaterial. (USA)

■ 495 Illustration que son auteur, Trish Burgio, utilise pour sa promotion personnelle. (USA)

■ 496 «Le poker jusqu'à la dernière chemise» – illustration d'un article du magazine *Penthouse*. (SWI)

■ 497, 498 Pour un «catalogue conférences» du fabricant de meubles de bureau Wilkhahn. (GER)

■ 499 «Créer un monde nouveau où les matériaux plastique légers dameront le pion aux métaux.» Pour une annonce de BASF, qui fabrique des plastiques renforcés. (USA)

ART DIRECTOR:
Hans-Georg Pospischil
ILLUSTRATOR:
Heinz Edelmann
PUBLISHER:
Frankfurter Allgemeine Zeitung GmbH
■ 500

ART DIRECTOR:
Fred Woodward
DESIGNER:
Fred Woodward
ILLUSTRATOR:
Richard Mantel
PUBLISHER:
Texas Monthly Magazine
► ■ 501

■ 500 "Can't you hear the fright-filled voice?" Double spread based on Munch's well-known painting "The Cry" for an article on the same subject in the *Frankfurter Allgemeine Magazin.* (GER)

■ 501 Illustration for the text of the cowboy song "Little Joe the Wrangler" from the magazine *Texas Monthly.* (USA)

■ 500 «Hören Sie nicht die entsetzliche Stimme?» – doppelseitige Illustration (nach Munchs berühmten Bild) aus einem Beitrag zum Thema Schrei im *Frankfurter Allgemeine Magazin.* (GER)

■ 501 Illustration zum Text eines Cowboy-Liedes, aus der Zeitschrift *Texas Monthly.* (USA)

■ 500 «N'entendez-vous pas cette voix terrifiante?» – illustration double page inspirée du célèbre tableau du Munch pour un texte sur le cri. Illustration figurant dans le *Frankfurter Allgemeine Magazin.* (GER)

■ 501 Illustration des paroles d'une chanson de cow-boy, publiée dans le magazine *Texas Monthly.* (USA)

■ 502 Computer software as the wave of the future is the subject of this full-page illustration. (USA)

■ 503 Illustration for an article in the *Boston Globe* expressing concern for the dwindling supply of fish along New England's coast. (USA)

■ 502 Das Computer Software-Geschäft ist Gegenstand dieser ganzseitigen Illustration. (USA)

■ 503 Illustration für einen Artikel im *Boston Globe*, der sich mit dem abnehmenden Fischbestand vor der Küste Neuenglands befasst. (USA)

■ 502 Illustration pleine page consacrée au marché porteur des logiciels d'ordinateurs. (USA)

■ 503 Illustration pour un article du *Boston Globe* sur la diminution du rendement des pêches au large de la Nouvelle-Angleterre. (USA)

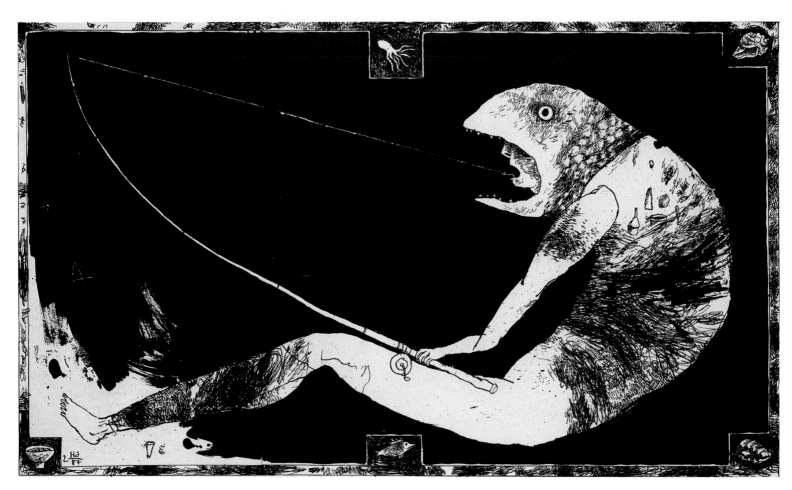

Art Director:
Joe McNeill
Designer:
David Loewy/Steven D. Merin
Illustrator:
John Hersey
Publisher:
CMP Publications
◄ ■ 502

Art Director:
Gail Anderson
Designer:
Gail Anderson
Illustrator:
Henrik Drescher
Studio:
Reactor Art & Design
Publisher:
Boston Globe
■ 503

ART DIRECTOR:
Nancy Kreinhider
DESIGNER:
Dan Maxey
ILLUSTRATOR:
Paul Orlando
AGENCY:
Maritz Inc.
CLIENT:
Maritz Inc.
■ 504

ART DIRECTOR:
Tina Adamek
ILLUSTRATOR:
Matt Mahurin
PUBLISHER:
McGraw-Hill, Inc.
► ■ 506

ART DIRECTOR:
Fred Woodward
ILLUSTRATOR:
Anthony Russo
PUBLISHER:
Rolling Stone Magazine
■ 505

■ 504 Luminous tropical fishes illustrate a calendar promoting travel in the Caribbean. (USA)

■ 505 For an article on a student's death in the magazine *Rolling Stone*. (USA)

■ 506 Illustration for an article on pulmonary diseases in the magazine *Postgraduate Medicine*. (USA)

■ 504 Tropische Leuchtfische, Illustration für einen Kalender, der für Reisen in die Karibik wirbt. (USA)

■ 505 Für einen Artikel in der Zeitschrift *Rolling Stone*, in dem es um den Tod eines Studenten geht. (USA)

■ 506 Illustration für einen Artikel über Lungenkrankheiten in der Zeitschrift *Postgraduate Medicine*. (USA)

■ 504 Poissons lumineux des tropiques. Illustration pour un calendrier invitant au tourisme dans les Caraïbes. (USA)

■ 505 Pour un article du magazine *Rolling Stone* qui parle de la mort d'un étudiant. (USA)

■ 506 Illustration pour un article du magazine *Postgraduate Medicine* qui traite des affections pulmonaires. (USA)

■ 507, 508 From a book entitled *Fashion Illustration Today,* published by Thames & Hudson in London. *507* entitled "The Letter", illustrates an advertisement for New York's *Bergdorf Goodman. 508* is a poster for the Japanese department store New Melsa in Tokyo. (GBR)

■ 507, 508 Aus einem Buch mit dem Titel *Modezeichnungen heute* (deutsche Ausgabe im Verlag Kohlhammer). *507* mit dem Titel «Der Brief» gehört zu einer Anzeige für das New Yorker Kaufhaus *Bergdorf Goodman. 508* ist ein Plakat für das Kaufhaus New Melsa in Tokyo. (GBR)

■ 507, 508 Illustrations figurant dans l'ouvrage *L'illustration de mode aujourd'hui* paru aux Ed. Thames & Hudson de Londres. *507:* «La Lettre», pour une annonce des grands magasins new-yorkais *Bergdorf Goodman. 508:* affiche pour les grands magasins New Melsa de Tokyo. (GBR)

ILLUSTRATOR:
George Stavrinos
PUBLISHER:
Thames and Hudson Ltd.
W. Kohlhammer GmbH
◄ ■ 507

ILLUSTRATOR:
Hélène Majera
PUBLISHER:
Thames and Hudson Ltd.
W. Kohlhammer GmbH
► ■ 508

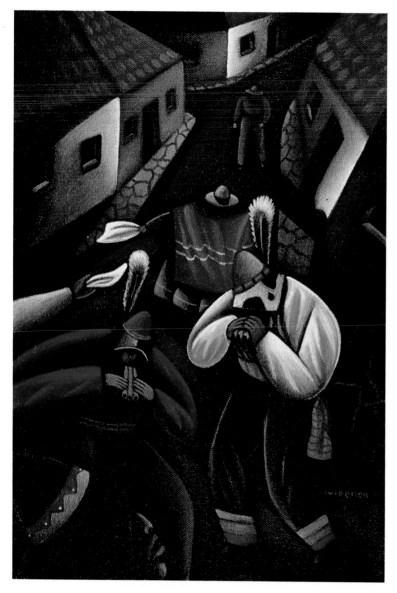

ART DIRECTOR:
STEVEN HOFFMAN
ILLUSTRATOR:
TERRY WIDENER
PUBLISHER:
TIME INC.
■ 509

ART DIRECTOR:
MICHAEL CRONAN
DESIGNER:
MICHAEL CRONAN
ILLUSTRATOR:
MICHAEL CRONAN
AGENCY:
CRONAN DESIGN
CLIENT:
GROUP ONE FILM CO.
■ 510

ART DIRECTOR:
TOM STAEBLER
DESIGNER:
KAREN GUTOWSKY
ILLUSTRATOR:
ROBERT GIUSTI
PUBLISHER:
PLAYBOY ENTERPRISES, INC.
► ■ 511

■ 509 The subject of this illustration is the ritualistic fist fight between the members of two Indian tribes in the Bolivian Andes. From *Sports Illustrated.* (USA)

■ 510 Text and illustration which perhaps leave the viewer questioning the true meaning of the Christmas season. Holiday greetings from a film production company. (USA)

■ 511 The koala bear as a symbol for Australia which is the subject of this article in *Playboy.* (USA)

■ 509 Thema dieser Illustration ist ein ritueller Faustkampf zwischen zwei Indianerstämmen in den bolivianischen Anden. Aus *Sports Illustrated.* (USA)

■ 510 Nonsense-Festtagsgrüsse einer Filmgesellschaft: «An den klaren, kalten Tagen vor den Feiertagen trägt man die Schuhe verkehrt herum und singt alte Lieder.» (USA)

■ 511 Der Koala-Bär als Symbol für Australien, um das es in dem betreffenden Beitrag im *Playboy* geht. (USA)

■ 509 Illustration évoquant un pugilat rituel entre deux tribus d'Indiens des Andes boliviennes. Article paru dans *Sports Illustrated.* (USA)

■ 510 Vœux de fête d'une société de production cinématographique: «Par une journée froide et claire, on s'en va chanter, les souliers à l'envers.» (USA)

■ 511 Le koala emblème de l'Australie. Ce pays est le sujet de l'article de *Playboy* ainsi illustré. (USA)

GIUSTI

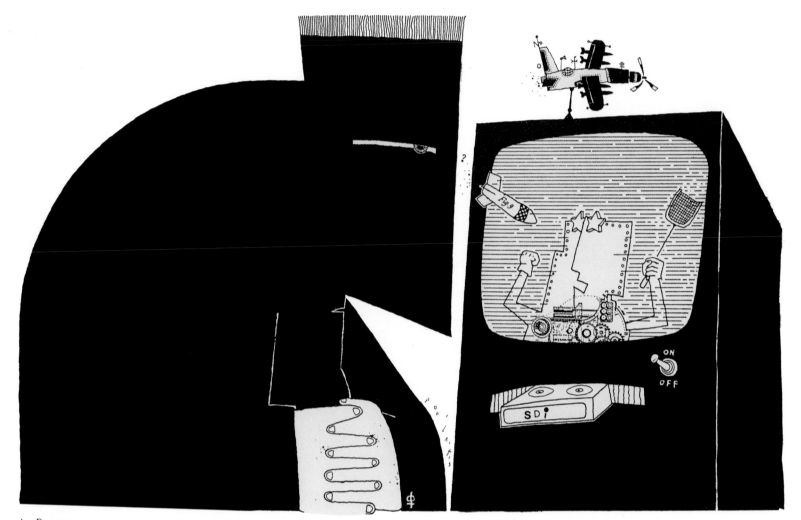

ART DIRECTOR:
WAYNE FITZPATRICK
DESIGNER:
WAYNE FITZPATRICK
ILLUSTRATOR:
DAVID POVILAITIS
PUBLISHER:
THE SCIENTIST
■ 512

ILLUSTRATOR:
BALVIS RUBESS
CLIENT:
BALVIS RUBESS
■ 513

ART DIRECTOR:
HEATHER COOPER
DESIGNER:
HEATHER COOPER
ILLUSTRATOR:
HEATHER COOPER
AGENCY:
HEATHER COOPER
COMMUNICATION BY DESIGN
CLIENT:
GRENVILLE MANAGEMENT &
PRINTING LTD.
■ 514

ART DIRECTOR:
JACKIE MERRI MEYER
DESIGNER:
HARRY NOLAN
ILLUSTRATOR:
JUDY PEDERSEN
PUBLISHER:
WARNER BOOKS
■ 516

ART DIRECTOR:
SUE LLEWELLYN
DESIGNER:
SUE LLEWELLYN
ILLUSTRATOR:
JOSÉ ORTEGA
PUBLISHER:
STEREO REVIEW
■ 517

ART DIRECTOR:
NANCY R. ALDRICH-RUENZEL
DESIGNER:
MICHAEL SCHWAB
ILLUSTRATOR:
MICHAEL SCHWAB
AGENCY:
MICHAEL SCHWAB DESIGN
PUBLISHER:
STEP BY STEP MAGAZINE
◄ ■ 515

■ 515 Self-portrait of the designer Michael Schwab, used as a cover by *Step by Step* magazine. (USA)

■ 516 Illustration for a book cover. (USA)

■ 517 Full-page illustration for an article in *Stereo Review* on the digital revolution from compact disc to digital audio tape and beyond. (USA)

■ 515 Für einen Umschlag der Zeitschrift *Step by Step* verwendetes Selbstporträt des Designers Michael Schwab. (USA)

■ 516 Illustration für einen Buchumschlag. (USA)

■ 517 Illustration für einen Artikel in *Stereo Review* über die «Digital-Revolution», die neusten Entwicklungen auf dem Audiomarkt in Form von Digital-Tonbändern. (USA)

■ 515 Autoportrait du designer Michael Schwab figurant en couverture du magazine *Step by Step*. (USA)

■ 516 Illustration pour une couverture de livre. (USA)

■ 517 Illustration pleine page pour un article de *Stereo Review* consacré à la «révolution numérique» et au passage du disque compact à la cassette audionumérique. (USA)

ART DIRECTOR:
HANS-GEORG POSPISCHIL

ILLUSTRATOR:
CHRISTOPH BLUMRICH

PUBLISHER:
FRANKFURTER ALLGEMEINE
ZEITUNG GmbH

■ 518

■ 518 From an article in the *Frankfurter Allgemeine Magazin* on Chinese cooking. (GER)

■ 518 Aus einem Artikel im *Frankfurter Allgemeine Magazin* über die chinesische Küche. (GER)

■ 518 Pour un article du *Frankfurter Allgemeine Magazin* sur la cuisine chinoise. (GER)

ART DIRECTOR:
MICHAEL MANWARING
DESIGNER:
MICHAEL MANWARING
AGENCY:
MICHAEL MANWARING
CLIENT:
HARDING ASSOCIATES, INC.
■ 519

■ 519 For Harding Lawson,
a company specialized in
environmental analysis and
waste disposal. (USA)

■ 519 Logo für Harding
Lawson, Spezialist für
Umweltanalysen und Abfall-
bewältigung. (USA)

■ 519 Logo pour Harding
Lawson, spécialiste de l'environnement et du traite-
ment des déchets. (USA)

ART DIRECTOR:
PATRICK SOOHOO
DESIGNER:
PAULA YAMASAKI-ISON
AGENCY:
PATRICK SOOHOO DESIGNERS
CLIENT:
PATRICK SOOHOO DESIGNERS
■ 520

■ 520 Corporate logo for a
design studio. (USA)

■ 520 Firmenlogo für ein
Design-Studio. (USA)

■ 520 Etude de logo pour un
studio de design. (USA)

DESIGNER:
MICHAEL BIERUT
PHOTOGRAPHER:
REVEN T.C. WURMAN
AGENCY:
VIGNELLI ASSOCIATES
CLIENT:
*INTERNATIONAL DESIGN
CONFERENCE IN ASPEN*
■ 521

■ 521 Logo symbolizing the
37th Design Conference in
Aspen. (USA)

■ 521 Symbol für die 37.
Design Conference in Aspen,
Colorado. (USA)

■ 521 Emblème de la 37e
Conférence de design
d'Aspen. (USA)

ART DIRECTOR:
*NICOLAS SIDJAKOV/
JERRY BERMAN*
DESIGNER:
BEN WHEELER
AGENCY:
*SIDJAKOV BERMAN GOMEZ &
PARTNERS*
CLIENT:
AUSSIES ENTERPRISES
■ 522

■ 522 Logo for an Austra-
lian fast-food chain spe-
cializing in chicken. (AUS)

■ 522 Logo für eine australi-
sche Hähnchen-Imbiss-
Kette. (AUS)

■ 522 Logo d'une chaîne
australienne de snacks à
base de poulets. (AUS)

ART DIRECTOR:
MICHAEL MANWARING
DESIGNER:
MICHAEL MANWARING
AGENCY:
MICHAEL MANWARING
CLIENT:
RINCON CENTER ASSOCIATES
■ 523

■ 523 For a multi-purpose
waterfront building development. (USA)

■ 523 Für ein am Meer gele-
genes Zentrum für verschiedene Zwecke. (USA)

■ 523 Pour un centre poly-
valent situé au bord de la
mer. (USA)

DESIGNER:
EDUARD CEHOVIN
CLIENT:
INSTITUTE FOR PLANNING AND
ARCHITECTURE, BELGRADE
■ 524

■ 524 Sign for an institute
of planning and architecture
in Belgrade. (YUG)

■ 524 Schrift für ein Institut
in Belgrad für Planung und
Architektur. (YUG)

■ 524 Raison sociale d'un
institut d'urbanisme et d'architecture. (YUG)

ART DIRECTOR:
TAKANORI AIBA
DESIGNER:
TOSHIHIRO ONIMARU
AGENCY:
GRAFIX
CLIENT:
ITO-FARM
■ 525

■ 525 Logo for Ito agricultu-
ral products. (JPN)

■ 525 Logo für Ito-Farm-
Produkte. (JPN)

■ 525 Logo des produits fer-
miërs Ito. (JPN)

ART DIRECTOR:
KAREN BLINCOE
DESIGNER:
RICHARD FISHER-SMITH
AGENCY:
KAREN BLINCOE DESIGN
CLIENT:
PEGASUS
■ 526

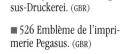

PEGASUS

■ 526 Symbol for the Pegasus printing press. (GBR)

■ 526 Symbol für die Pega-
sus-Druckerei. (GBR)

■ 526 Emblème de l'impri-
merie Pegasus. (GBR)

ART DIRECTOR:
BÜLENT ERKMEN
DESIGNER:
BÜLENT ERKMEN
AGENCY:
REKLAMEVI
CLIENT:
KIRPI
■ 527

■ 527 Emblem for a sport-
ing goods store. (TUR)

■ 527 Emblem für ein
Sportgeschäft. (TUR)

■ 527 Emblème d'un maga-
sin de sports. (TUR)

ART DIRECTOR:
KAZUMASA NAGAI
DESIGNER:
KAZUMASA NAGAI
AGENCY:
NIPPON DESIGN CENTER
CLIENT:
HIMEJI CITY
■ 528

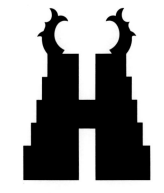

■ 528 Symbol marking the
100th anniversary of Himeji
City, Japan. (JPN)

■ 528 Symbol zum 100jähri-
gen Bestehen von Himeji
City, Japan. (JPN)

■ 528 Symbole du 100e
anniversaire de la ville japonaise d'Himeji. (JPN)

ART DIRECTOR:
Michael Russell
DESIGNER:
Allison Goodman
AGENCY:
Sussman/Prejza & Co., Inc.
CLIENT:
Harold S. Wenal
■ 529–531

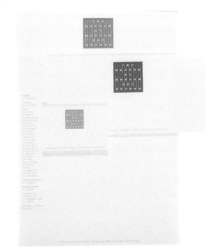

ART DIRECTOR:
MERVYN KURLANSKY
DESIGNER:
*MERVYN KURLANSKY/
ROBERT DUNNET*
AGENCY:
PENTAGRAM
CLIENT:
*MUSEUM OF MODERN ART,
OXFORD*
■ 532-538

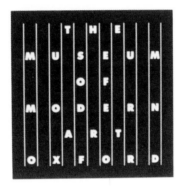

■ 529-531 Over-sized gateway to a shopping center located on a lakeshore. A signboard, and a variation of the symbol for a pavilion on the lake, are also shown. (USA)

■ 532-538 Materials from the corporate identity program of the Museum of Modern Art in Oxford. They include colored pencils, carrier bags, directional signs, logotype for the café, letterhead, mugs, and a logotype for various purposes. (GBR)

■ 529-531 Überdimensionales «Eingangstor» zu einem kommerziellen Zentrum am See sowie Schild und Variante des Symbols für einen Pavillon auf dem See. (USA)

■ 532-538 Aus dem Corporate-Identity-Programm für das Museum of Modern Art in Oxford: Farbstifte, Tragtaschen, Hinweisschilder, Schriftzug für das Café, Briefpapier, Becher und Schriftzug für diverse Einsatzzwecke. (GBR)

■ 529-531 «Porte d'entrée» surdimensionnée d'un centre commercial au bord d'un lac; enseigne et variante de l'emblème pour un pavillon érigé en plein lac. (USA)

■ 532-538 Programme d'identité globale de marque du Museum of Modern Art d'Oxford: crayons couleur, cabas, panneaux d'orientation, logo du café, papier à lettres, gobelets et logo utilisé pour diverses applications. (GBR)

ART DIRECTOR:
Charles S. Anderson
DESIGNER:
Charles S. Anderson/
Sara Ledgard
ILLUSTRATOR:
Charles S. Anderson/
Lynn Schulte
AGENCY:
The Duffy Design Group
CLIENT:
Ralph Lauren «Chaps»
■ 539–544

ART DIRECTOR:
Sara Ledgard 545, 549, 551
Joe Duffy 546
Haley Johnson 547
C. Anderson 548, 550

ILLUSTRATOR:
S. Ledgard/
L. Schulte 545, 549, 551
Joe Duffy/L. Schulte 546
H. Johnson/L. Schulte 547
C. Anderson/L. Schulte 548
Charles S. Anderson 550
AGENCY:
The Duffy Design Group
▶ ■ 545–551

■ 539-544 Examples of the packaging and the promotional material for "Chaps", a line by Ralph Lauren. (USA)

■ 545-551 Logos and emblems: *545* for games by Fallon McElligott; *546* for the Dickson's printing press; *547* for the Calhoun Beach Club; *548* for the Aura Editions; *549* for the World Trade Center in St. Paul; *551* illustrates its application; *550* for a line of *Lee* jeans. (USA)

■ 539-544 Beispiele der Ausstattung und des Werbematerials für die Linie «Chaps» von Ralph Lauren. (USA)

■ 545-551 Logos und Firmenzeichen: *545* für Spiele von Fallon McElligott; *546* für die Dickson's Druckerei; *547* für den Calhoun Beach Club; *548* für den Aura-Verlag; *549* für das World Trade Center in St. Paul, *551* zeigt dessen Anwendung; *551* für eine *Lee*-Jeans-Linie. (USA)

■ 539-544 Exemples des conditionnements et du matériel publicitaire pour la ligne «Chaps» de Ralph Lauren. (USA)

■ 545-551 Logos et marques: *545* pour des jeux de Fallon McElligott; *546* pour l'imprimerie Dickson's; *547* pour le Calhoun Beach Club; *548* pour les Editions Aura; *549* pour le World Trade Center de St. Paul, la fig. *551* en montre l'application; *550* pour une gamme de jeans *Lee*. (USA)

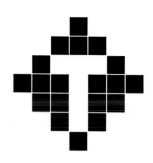

CHICAIGAO

ART DIRECTOR:
JOHN EVANS
DESIGNER:
JOHN EVANS
ILLUSTRATOR:
JOHN EVANS
AGENCY:
SIBLEY/PETEET DESIGN
CLIENT:
SILVERMAN DESIGN CONSULTANT
■ 552

ART DIRECTOR:
ISAAC VICTOR KERLOW
DESIGNER:
ISAAC VICTOR KERLOW
CLIENT:
TLALCALLI REAL ESTATE DEVELOPMENT CORP.
■ 553

ART DIRECTOR:
BART CROSBY
DESIGNER:
CARL WOHLT
AGENCY:
CROSBY ASSOCIATES INC.
CLIENT:
AMERICAN INSTITUTE OF GRAPHIC ARTS
■ 554

ART DIRECTOR:
RON SULLIVAN
DESIGNER:
WILLIE BARONET
AGENCY:
SULLIVAN PERKINS
CLIENT:
KING DOUGLAS PHOTOGRAPHY
■ 555

ART DIRECTOR:
G. RICARDO SORIANO
DESIGNER:
G. RICARDO SORIANO/ REYNALDO CALLEJA
AGENCY:
TRITECH DESIGN STUDIOS
CLIENT:
TREE OF LIFE MINISTRIES FOUNDATION
■ 556

ART DIRECTOR:
MIKE SALISBURY
DESIGNER:
CINDY LUCK/PAM HAMILTON
ILLUSTRATOR:
PAM HAMILTON
AGENCY:
SALISBURY COMMUNICATIONS
CLIENT:
MIKE SALISBURY
■ 557

ART DIRECTOR:
Mike Schroeder
DESIGNER:
Mike Schroeder
ILLUSTRATOR:
Mike Schroeder
STUDIO:
Schroeder Design
CLIENT:
Gary Kelley
■ 558

ART DIRECTOR:
Timothy Horn
DESIGNER:
Timothy Horn
AGENCY:
Timothy Horn Design
CLIENT:
*Monica Stevenson
Photography*
■ 559

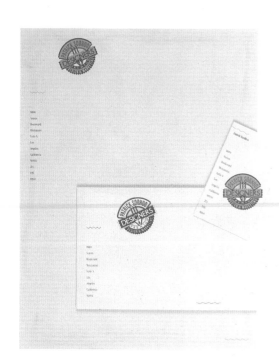

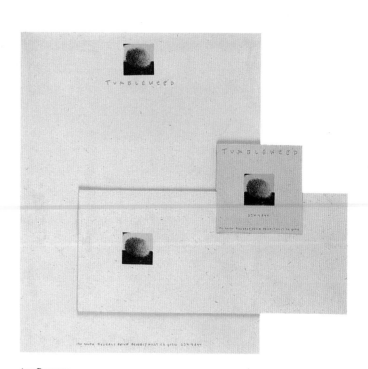

ART DIRECTOR:
Patrick SooHoo/Paula Ison
DESIGNER:
Paula Yamasaki-Ison
AGENCY:
Patrick SooHoo Designers
CLIENT:
Patrick SooHoo Designers
■ 560

ART DIRECTOR:
Michael Brock
DESIGNER:
Gaylen Braun
ILLUSTRATOR:
Tom Keller
AGENCY:
Michael Brock Design
CLIENT:
Tumble Weed Restaurant
■ 561

ART DIRECTOR:
IAN KIDD/KARIN SEJA
PHOTOGRAPHER:
DIETER EUBEL
AGENCY:
IAN KIDD & ASSOCIATES
CLIENT:
VAN GASTEL PRINTING PTY LTD
■ 562

ART DIRECTOR:
JENNIFER MORLA
DESIGNER:
JENNIFER MORLA
AGENCY:
MORLA DESIGN
CLIENT:
MORLA DESIGN
■ 563

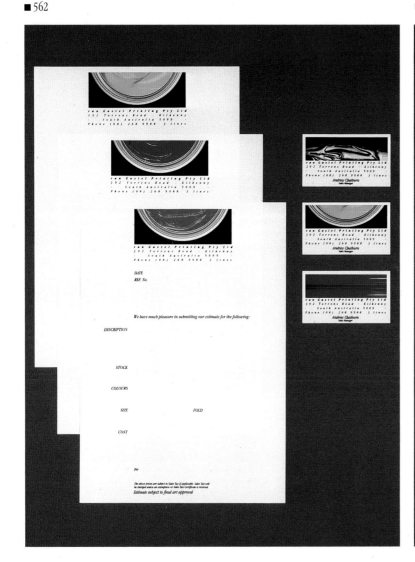

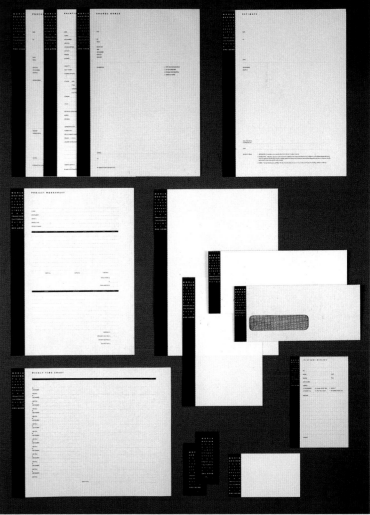

ART DIRECTOR:
HANS BUSCHFELD
DESIGNER:
MANUELA NYHUIS
ILLUSTRATOR:
MANUELA NYHUIS
AGENCY:
FACHHOCHSCHULE KÖLN,
FACHBEREICH DESIGN

■ 564

ART DIRECTOR:
CHARLES S. ANDERSON
DESIGNER:
CHARLES S. ANDERSON
ILLUSTRATOR:
C. ANDERSON/L. SCHULTE
AGENCY:
THE DUFFY DESIGN GROUP
CLIENT:
BROOK'S SHOES
■ 565

ART DIRECTOR:
M. WESTCOTT/M. NAPOLEON
DESIGNER:
M. WESTCOTT/J. PACIONE
ILLUSTRATOR:
K. MURPHY/M. WESTCOTT
AGENCY:
RICHARDSONSMITH INC.
CLIENT:
REEBOK INTERNATIONAL LTD.
■ 566

■ 567 Carrier carton and bottle design for an imported Mexican beer. (USA)

■ 568 Bottle label with a new and unusual styling for an Italian red wine. (USA)

■ 569 Design for the bottle of a Chianti. (USA)

■ 567 Tragkarton und Flaschenausstattung für importiertes mexikanisches Bier. (USA)

■ 568 Flaschenetikett in neuartiger Aufmachung für einen italienischen Rotwein. (USA)

■ 569 Flaschengestaltung für einen Chianti. (USA)

■ 567 Carton de transport et étude de bouteille pour une bière mexicaine d'importation. (USA)

■ 568 Etiquette de bouteille de conception nouvelle pour un vin rouge d'Italie. (USA)

■ 569 Etude de bouteille pour un chianti. (USA)

ART DIRECTOR:
Michael Mabry
DESIGNER:
Michael Mabry/
Noreen Fukumori
ILLUSTRATOR:
Michael Bull
AGENCY:
Michael Mabry Design
CLIENT:
Simpatico Beer
■ 567

Art Director:
Woody Pirtle
Designer:
Woody Pirtle/Alan Colvin
Studio:
Pirtle Design
Client:
Alberini Vineyards
■ 568

Art Director:
Haley Johnson
Designer:
Haley Johnson
Illustrator:
Haley Johnson
Agency:
The Duffy Design Group
Client:
Cocolezzone
■ 569

■ 570, 571 Carrier carton and bottle design for an Australian beer. (AUS)

■ 572 Design of the can for a prestigious export beer produced by New Guinea's largest brewery. (AUS)

■ 573 A nostalgic Australian theme was chosen for the label of this mineral water which is served down under exclusively in restaurants. (AUS)

■ 570, 571 Tragkarton und Flaschengestaltung für ein australisches Bier. (AUS)

■ 572 Dosengestaltung für ein anspruchsvolles Export-Bier der grössten Brauerei Neuguineas. (AUS)

■ 573 Für das Etikett dieses Mineralwassers, das in Australien ausschliesslich in Restaurants ausgeschenkt wird, würde ein nostalgisches australisches Thema gewählt. (AUS)

■ 570, 571 Carton de transport et étude de bouteille pour une bière australienne. (AUS)

■ 572 Boîte pour une bière d'exportation de luxe brassée par la plus importante brasserie de Nlle-Guinée. (AUS)

■ 573 Pour cette eau minérale qui n'est commercialisée en Australie qu'à travers les restaurants, le motif publicitaire est emprunté aux traditions nostalgiques du pays. (AUS)

ART DIRECTOR:
KEN CATO
DESIGNER:
KEN CATO
ILLUSTRATOR:
LENA GAN
AGENCY:
CATO DESIGN INC.
CLIENT:
CASCADE BREWERY
■ 570, 571

ART DIRECTOR:
Ken Cato

DESIGNER:
Ken Cato

ILLUSTRATOR:
Lena Gan

ARTIST:
Neil Moorhouse

AGENCY:
Cato Design Inc.

CLIENT:
South Pacific Brewery

■ 572

ART DIRECTOR:
Barrie Tucker

DESIGNER:
Barrie Tucker

ILLUSTRATOR:
Robert Marshall

AGENCY:
*Barrie Tucker
Design Pty Ltd*

CLIENT:
S. Smith & Son

■ 573

ART DIRECTOR:
Charles S. Anderson
DESIGNER:
Charles S. Anderson
ILLUSTRATOR:
Charles S. Anderson/
Lynn Schulte
AGENCY:
The Duffy Design Group
CLIENT:
Timex
■ 574, 575

ART DIRECTOR:
Andres Hasler/Theo Schnell
DESIGNER:
Andres Hasler/Theo Schnell
AGENCY:
HAS Design AG
CLIENT:
Alinea Watch
► ■ 576

■ 574, 575 Packaging, as viewed both closed and opened, for the *Skiathlom* watch by Timex. (USA)

■ 576 Prospectus, box and solid wooden packaging for *Alinea* watches. The producer thus wants to emphasize the permanence of this watch as opposed to the throw-away variety. (SWI)

■ 574, 575 Geschlossene und geöffnete Packung für *Skiathlom*-Uhren von Timex. (USA)

■ 576 Prospekt, Karton und massive Holzverpackung für Uhren der Marke *Alinea*. Die solide Verpackung entspricht der Positionierung der Uhr als Gegenstück zu Wegwerfprodukten. (SWI)

■ 574, 575 Emballage montré fermé et ouvert pour les montres *Skiathlom* de Timex. (USA)

■ 576 Prospectus, carton et emballage en bois massif pour les montres *Alinea*. La solidité du conditionnement souligne l'aspect durable du produit face aux montres à jeter. (SWI)

ART DIRECTOR:
Charles S. Anderson
DESIGNER:
Charles S. Anderson/
Sara Ledgard
ILLUSTRATOR:
Charles S. Anderson/
Lynn Schulte
AGENCY:
The Duffy Design Group
CLIENT:
First Bank Systems
■ 577

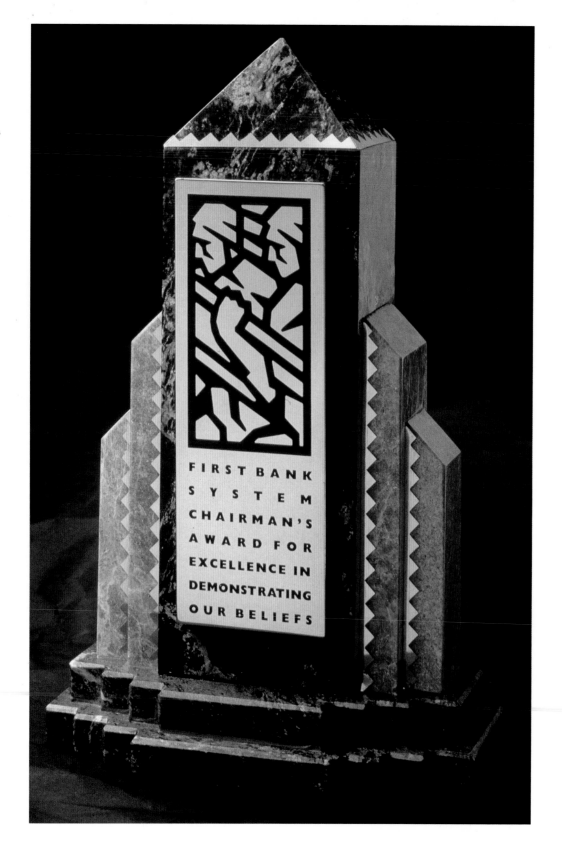

■ 577 Design of an award for presentation by the First Bank Systems. (USA)

■ 577 Gestaltung einer von den First Bank Systems vergebenen Auszeichnung. (USA)

■ 577 Conception du prix dont First Bank Systems récompense les lauréats de ses concours. (USA)

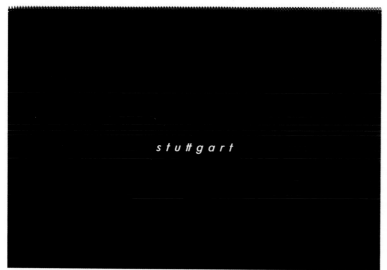

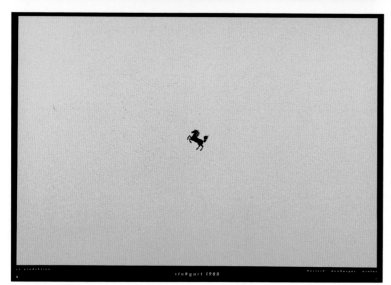

ART DIRECTOR:
CONNY J. WINTER
DESIGNER:
CONNY J. WINTER
PHOTOGRAPHER:
CONNY J. WINTER
CLIENT:
BERTSCH/DOMBERGER/WINTER
■ 578–582

■ 578–582 This wall calendar entitled "Stuttgart" is a co-production of the printer, serigrapher and photographer. The monthly sheets present fashion as photographed in different parts of the city: at the Lauster offices, along a street, on the telecommunications tower, and in the museum Neue Staatsgalerie. (GER)

■ 578–582 Dieser Wandkalender mit dem Titel «Stuttgart» ist eine Co-Produktion von Drucker, Siebdrucker und Photograph. Die Monatsblätter zeigen Modeaufnahmen an verschiedenen Orten in Stuttgart: bei der Firma Lauster, Neckartalstrasse, auf dem Fernmeldeturm und in der Neuen Staatsgalerie. (GER)

■ 578–582 Ce calendrier mural intitulé «Stuttgart» est une coproduction d'un imprimeur, d'un sérigraphe et d'un photographe. Les feuillets mensuels sont illustrés de photos de mode réalisées en divers endroits: chez la maison Lauster, à la Neckartalstrasse, au sommet de la tour TV, au Musée Neue Staatsgalerie. (GER)

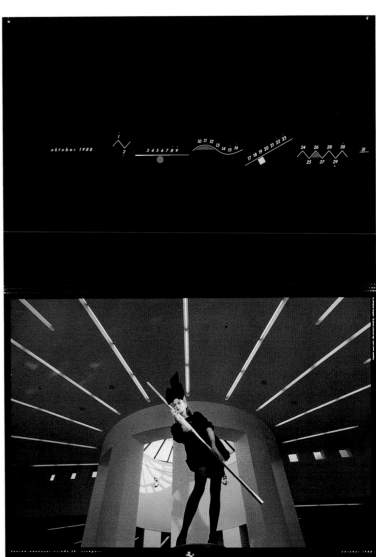

ART DIRECTOR:
KIT HINRICHS
DESIGNER:
KIT HINRICHS/KAREN BERNDT/
GWYN SMITH
ILLUSTRATOR:
SARA ANDERSON
PHOTOGRAPHER:
TERRY HEFFERNAN
COPYWRITER:
PETERSON & DODGE
AGENCY:
PENTAGRAM DESIGN
CLIENT:
AMERICAN PRESIDENT LINES
■ 583–590

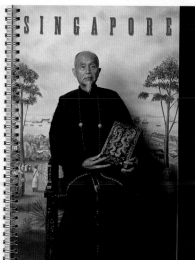

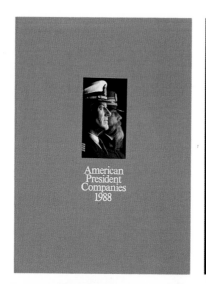

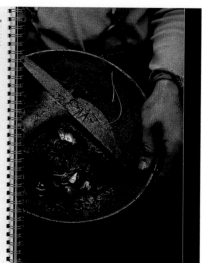

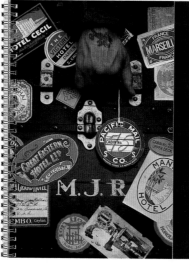

One hundred and forty years ago, the Pacific Ocean was a quieter place. Gold had not yet been discovered. California was a collection of cattle ranches and sleepy towns, and little trade existed between the Pacific Coast and Asia. But in 1848 events took place in California that changed the United States, the Pacific Ocean and the world. American President Lines and its predecessors participated in these events. In 1988 we celebrate our 140th anniversary. To recognize such a landmark, this calendar salutes the events and ideas that shaped our company and your marketplace. By using photographs that reflect the spirit and the style of each period, this year's calendar covers 140 years of service on land and sea. We take pride that APL and affiliates in the American President Companies group have grown and prospered through serving the Pacific, the Indian Ocean and North America–the world's most dynamic trading regions. Today, we look to the future with confidence. We anticipate continued good fortune for all of us blessed with the opportunity to trade in these vital markets.

American President Lines 1988 Calendar

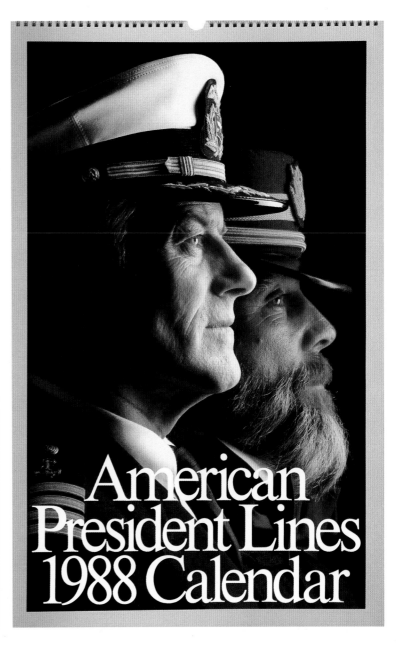

American President Lines 1988 Calendar

■ 583-590 Cover and double spreads from an agenda as well as the transparent overlay from a wall calendar of the American President Companies. Significant events from the last 140 years of the shipping industry are illustrated in both. They include the California Gold Rush of 1849; direct postal service with Singapore and other countries of the Pacific in 1917; the worldwide Pacific Mail Service which began in 1920; and the homecoming of the warships "Liberty" and "Victory" at the end of World War II. (USA)

■ 583-590 Umschlag und Beispiele der Doppelseiten aus einer Agenda und Deckblatt mit Transparentpapier eines Wandkalenders der American President Companies. Das Thema sind Ereignisse aus 140 Jahren, die für die Entwicklung der Reederei von Bedeutung waren: Das Goldfieber in Kalifornien 1849; direkte Postverbindung mit Pazifikländern, u.a. mit Singapur 1917; der weltweite Service der Pacific Mail, der 1920 begann; die Heimkehr der Schiffe «Liberty» und «Victory» Ende des zweiten Weltkriegs. (USA)

■ 583-590 Couverture et exemples des doubles pages d'un agenda, ainsi que la page de couverture transparente d'un calendrier mural d'American President Companies. Ces deux imprimés ont pour thème l'histoire de cet armement sur 140 ans: la ruée vers l'or de Californie en 1849; la liaison postale directe avec les pays riverains du Pacifique, dont Singapour, en 1917; le service international Pacific Mail inauguré en 1920; le retour des navires «Liberty» et «Victory» à la fin de la Seconde Guerre mondiale. (USA)

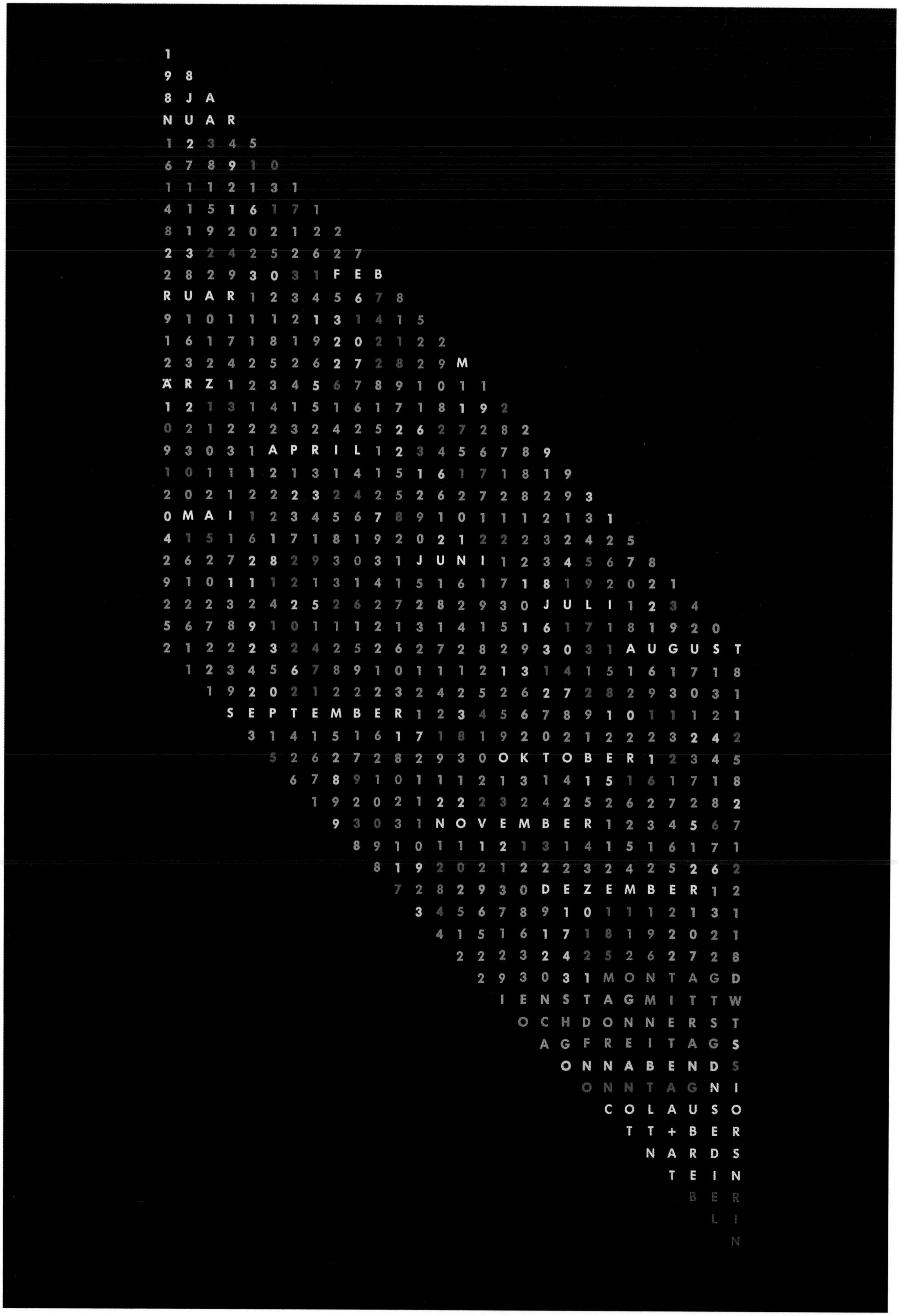
1
9 8
8 J A
N U A R
1 2 3 4 5
6 7 8 9 1 0
1 1 1 2 1 3 1
4 1 5 1 6 1 7 1
8 1 9 2 0 2 1 2 2
2 3 2 4 2 5 2 6 2 7
2 8 2 9 3 0 3 1 F E B
R U A R 1 2 3 4 5 6 7 8
9 1 0 1 1 1 2 1 3 1 4 1 5
1 6 1 7 1 8 1 9 2 0 2 1 2 2
2 3 2 4 2 5 2 6 2 7 2 8 2 9 M
Ä R Z 1 2 3 4 5 6 7 8 9 1 0 1 1
1 2 1 3 1 4 1 5 1 6 1 7 1 8 1 9 2
0 2 1 2 2 2 3 2 4 2 5 2 6 2 7 2 8 2
9 3 0 3 1 A P R I L 1 2 3 4 5 6 7 8 9
1 0 1 1 1 2 1 3 1 4 1 5 1 6 1 7 1 8 1 9
2 0 2 1 2 2 2 3 2 4 2 5 2 6 2 7 2 8 2 9 3
0 M A I 1 2 3 4 5 6 7 8 9 1 0 1 1 1 2 1 3 1
4 1 5 1 6 1 7 1 8 1 9 2 0 2 1 2 2 2 3 2 4 2 5
2 6 2 7 2 8 2 9 3 0 3 1 J U N I 1 2 3 4 5 6 7 8
9 1 0 1 1 1 2 1 3 1 4 1 5 1 6 1 7 1 8 1 9 2 0 2 1
2 2 2 3 2 4 2 5 2 6 2 7 2 8 2 9 3 0 J U L I 1 2 3 4
5 6 7 8 9 1 0 1 1 1 2 1 3 1 4 1 5 1 6 1 7 1 8 1 9 2 0
2 1 2 2 2 3 2 4 2 5 2 6 2 7 2 8 2 9 3 0 3 1 A U G U S T
1 2 3 4 5 6 7 8 9 1 0 1 1 1 2 1 3 1 4 1 5 1 6 1 7 1 8
1 9 2 0 2 1 2 2 2 3 2 4 2 5 2 6 2 7 2 8 2 9 3 0 3 1
S E P T E M B E R 1 2 3 4 5 6 7 8 9 1 0 1 1 1 2 1
3 1 4 1 5 1 6 1 7 1 8 1 9 2 0 2 1 2 2 2 3 2 4 2
5 2 6 2 7 2 8 2 9 3 0 O K T O B E R 1 2 3 4 5
6 7 8 9 1 0 1 1 1 2 1 3 1 4 1 5 1 6 1 7 1 8
1 9 2 0 2 1 2 2 2 3 2 4 2 5 2 6 2 7 2 8 2
9 3 0 3 1 N O V E M B E R 1 2 3 4 5 6 7
8 9 1 0 1 1 1 2 1 3 1 4 1 5 1 6 1 7 1
8 1 9 2 0 2 1 2 2 2 3 2 4 2 5 2 6 2
7 2 8 2 9 3 0 D E Z E M B E R 1 2
3 4 5 6 7 8 9 1 0 1 1 1 2 1 3 1
4 1 5 1 6 1 7 1 8 1 9 2 0 2 1
2 2 2 3 2 4 2 5 2 6 2 7 2 8
2 9 3 0 3 1 M O N T A G D
I E N S T A G M I T T W
O C H D O N N E R S T
A G F R E I T A G S
O N N A B E N D S
O N N T A G N I
C O L A U S O
T T + B E R
N A R D S
T E I N
B E R
L I
N

ART DIRECTOR:
NICOLAUS OTT/BERNARD STEIN
DESIGNER:
NICOLAUS OTT/BERNARD STEIN
AGENCY:
NICOLAUS OTT/BERNARD STEIN
CLIENT:
NICOLAUS OTT/BERNARD STEIN
◄ ■ 591

ART DIRECTOR:
DAN REISINGER
DESIGNER:
DAN REISINGER
AGENCY:
DAN REISINGER
CLIENT:
ISCAR LTD.
■ 592–595

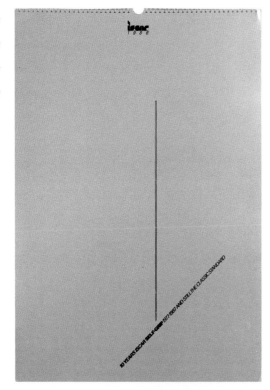

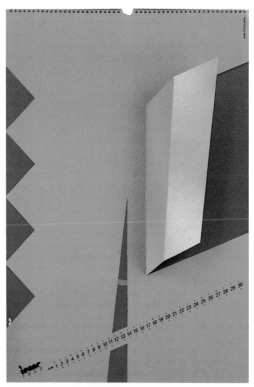

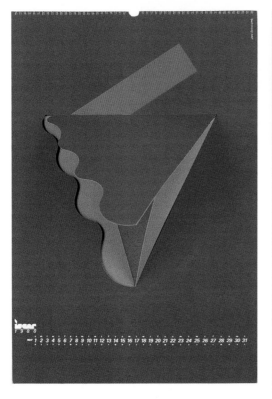

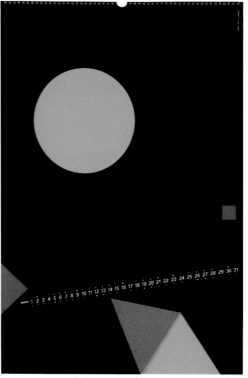

■ 591 The German designers Nicolaus Ott and Bernard Stein promote their own team with a new form of calendar displaying an entire year. (GER)

■ 592–595 Three-dimensional sheets from a wall calendar for the metal tools company Iscar Ltd. (ISR)

■ 591 Ganzjähriger Kalender in neuer Form als Eigenwerbung für das deutsche Graphiker-Team Nicolaus Ott und Bernard Stein. (GER)

■ 592–595 Dreidimensionale Blätter aus einem Wandkalender für den Metallkonzern Iscar. (ISR)

■ 591 Un calendrier de conception nouvelle réalisé en autopromotion par les graphistes allemands Nicolaus Ott et Bernard Stein. (GER)

■ 592–595 Feuillets tridimensionnels d'un calendrier mural du groupe métallurgique Iscar. (ISR)

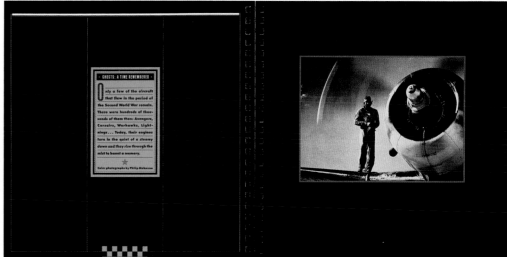

ART DIRECTOR:
JENNIFER MORLA
DESIGNER:
JENNIFER MORLA
PHOTOGRAPHER:
PHILIP MAKANNA
COPYWRITER:
PHILIP MAKANNA
AGENCY:
MORLA DESIGN
CLIENT:
GHOSTS
■ 596–602

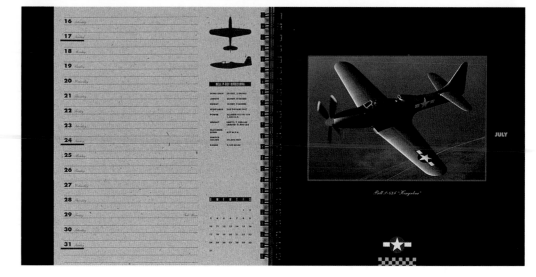

■ 596–602 Pages from a desk agenda put out by Ghosts, a publishing company. They illustrate aircraft from the Second World War which in the meantime have become history. The sheets for the calendarium are narrower than those for the photographs and are printed on a paper with a marked wood structure. (USA)

■ 596–602 Beispiele der Seiten aus einer Tischagenda, herausgegeben vom Ghosts-Verlag. Das Thema sind Flugzeuge aus der Zeit des Zweiten Weltkriegs, die inzwischen Geschichte geworden sind. Die Blätter für das Kalendarium sind weniger breit als die Photoseiten und auf holzhaltigem, strukturiertem Papier gedruckt. (USA)

■ 596–602 Exemples des pages d'un agenda de bureau publié par les Editions Ghosts, avec pour thématique les types d'avions utilisés durant la Seconde Guerre mondiale et devenus historiques. Les feuillets du calendrier sont de format réduit par rapport aux pages photo et imprimés sur papier structuré. (USA)

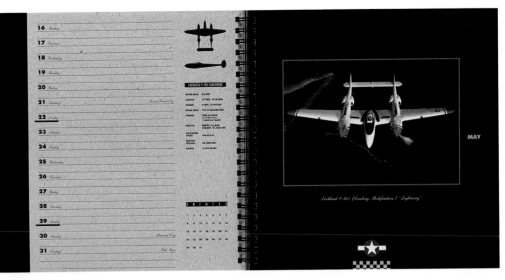

MAY

16 Monday
17 Tuesday
18 Wednesday
19 Thursday
20 Friday
21 Saturday   Armed Forces Day
22 Sunday
23 Monday
24 Tuesday
25 Wednesday
26 Thursday
27 Friday
28 Saturday
29 Sunday
30 Monday   Memorial Day
31 Tuesday   Full Moon

LOCKHEED P-38L LIGHTNING

WING SPAN	52 FEET
LENGTH	37 FEET, 10 INCHES
HEIGHT	9 FEET, 10 INCHES
WING AREA	327.5 SQUARE FEET
POWER	TWO ALLISON V-1710-111/-113, 1,600 H.P. EACH
WEIGHT	EMPTY: 12,800 LOADED: 21,600 LBS
MAXIMUM SPEED	414 M.P.H.
SERVICE CEILING	44,000 FEET
RANGE	2,600 MILES

Lockheed P-38L (Cooling Modification) "Lightning"

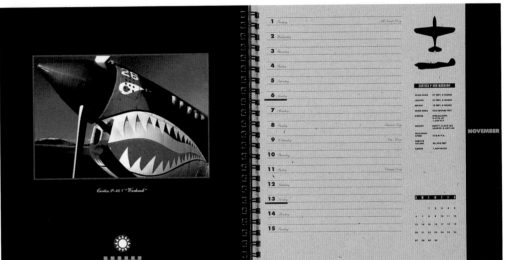

NOVEMBER

1 Tuesday   All Saints Day
2 Wednesday
3 Thursday
4 Friday
5 Saturday
6 Sunday
7 Monday
8 Tuesday   Election Day
9 Wednesday   New Moon
10 Thursday
11 Friday   Veterans Day
12 Saturday
13 Sunday
14 Monday
15 Tuesday

Curtiss P-40 N "Warhawk"

CURTISS P-40N WARHAWK

WING SPAN	37 FEET, 4 INCHES
LENGTH	33 FEET, 4 INCHES
HEIGHT	12 FEET, 4 INCHES
WING AREA	236 SQUARE FEET
POWER	ONE ALLISON V-1710-81, 1,360 H.P.
WEIGHT	EMPTY: 6,000 LBS LOADED: 8,850 LBS
MAXIMUM SPEED	378 M.P.H.
SERVICE CEILING	38,000 FEET
RANGE	1,400 MILES

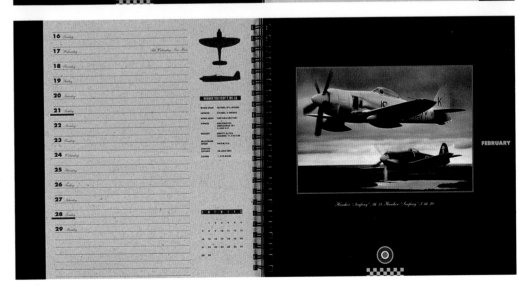

FEBRUARY

16 Tuesday
17 Wednesday   Ash Wednesday, New Moon
18 Thursday
19 Friday
20 Saturday
21 Sunday
22 Monday
23 Tuesday
24 Wednesday
25 Thursday
26 Friday
27 Saturday
28 Sunday
29 Monday

HAWKER SEA FURY F.MK.20

WING SPAN	38 FEET, 4¾ INCHES
LENGTH	34 FEET, 7 INCHES
WING AREA	280 SQUARE FEET
POWER	ONE BRISTOL CENTAURUS 18/ 2,450 H.P.
WEIGHT	EMPTY: 8,700 LOADED: 11,930 LBS
MAXIMUM SPEED	460 M.P.H.
SERVICE CEILING	35,800 FEET
RANGE	1,170 MILES

Hawker "Seafury" Mk.11 Hawker "Seafury" S.Mk.20

■603 Front side of the cover for a recording by Miles Davis entitled "Tutu". (USA)

■604 Cover for a recording by Robbie Nevil as issued by Manhattan Records. (USA)

■605 Record cover for poetic songs by Rosko. (USA)

■606 For a record issued by CBS with a recording by the Japanese pianist Makoto Ozone. (USA)

■607 Cover for a record by Madonna. (USA)

■603 Vorderseite der Hülle für die Schallplatte «Tutu» von Miles Davis. (USA)

■604 Hülle für eine bei Manhattan Records erschienene Platte mit Aufnahmen von Robbie Nevil. (USA)

■605 Plattenhülle für poetische Songs von Rosko. (USA)

■606 Für eine bei CBS erschienene Platte mit Aufnahmen des japanischen Pianisten Makoto Ozone. (USA)

■607 Hülle für eine Schallplatte von Madonna. (USA)

■603 Recto de la pochette du disque «Tutu» réalisé par Miles Davis. (USA)

■604 Pochette d'un disque de Robbie Nevil édité par Manhattan Records. (USA)

■605 Pochette pour des chansons poétiques de Rosko. (USA)

■606 Pour un disque CBS du pianiste japonais Makoto Ozone en concert. (USA)

■607 Pochette pour un disque de Madonna. (USA)

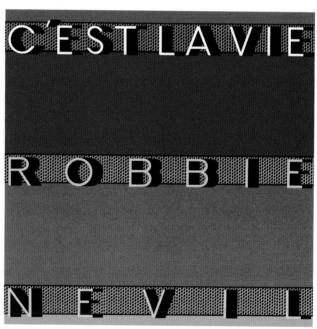

ART DIRECTOR:
EIKO ISHIOKA
DESIGNER:
EIKO ISHIOKA/SUSAN WELT
PHOTOGRAPHER:
IRVING PENN
AGENCY:
EICO DESIGN INC.
PUBLISHER:
WARNER BROS. RECORDS INC.
◀◀■603

ART DIRECTOR:
PAULA SCHER
DESIGNER:
PAULA SCHER
AGENCY:
KOPPEL & SCHER
PUBLISHER:
MANHATTAN RECORDS
◀■604

ART DIRECTOR:
ALLEN WEINBERG
DESIGNER:
ALLEN WEINBERG
PHOTOGRAPHER:
NICK FAIN
STUDIO:
CBS RECORDS, INC.
PUBLISHER:
CBS RECORDS, INC.
◀◀■605

ART DIRECTOR:
ALLEN WEINBERG
DESIGNER:
ALLEN WEINBERG
PHOTOGRAPHER:
DUANE MICHAELS
STUDIO:
CBS RECORDS, INC.
PUBLISHER:
CBS RECORDS, INC.
◀■606

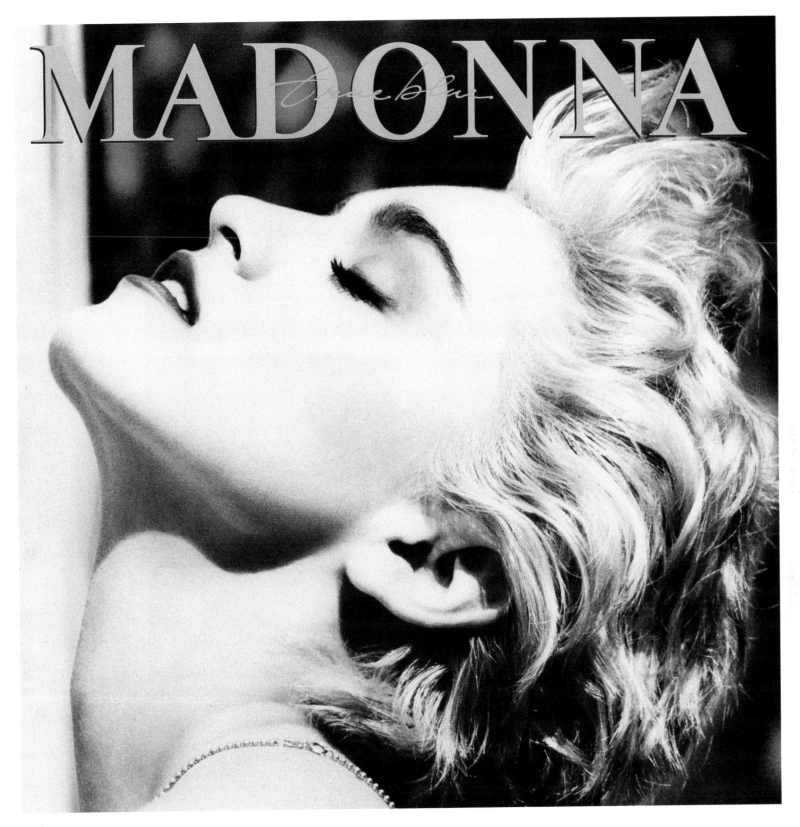

ART DIRECTOR:
JERI MCMANUS HEIDEN/
JEFF AYEROFF
DESIGNER:
JERI MCMANUS HEIDEN
PHOTOGRAPHER:
HERB RITTS
STUDIO:
WARNER BROS. RECORDS, INC.
CLIENT:
MADONNA
PUBLISHER:
SIRE RECORDS CO.
■ 607

ART DIRECTOR:
Tony Lane/Nancy Donald
DESIGNER:
Nancy Donald
ILLUSTRATOR:
Nancy Donald
STUDIO:
CBS Records, Inc.
PUBLISHER:
CBS Records, Inc.
◄◄■ 608

ART DIRECTOR:
Allen Weinberg
DESIGNER:
Allen Weinberg
PHOTOGRAPHER:
Chip Simons
STUDIO:
CBS Records, Inc.
PUBLISHER:
CBS Records, Inc.
◄■ 609

ART DIRECTOR:
Christopher Austopchuk
DESIGNER:
Christopher Austopchuk
PHOTOGRAPHER:
Chip Simons
STUDIO:
CBS Records, Inc.
PUBLISHER:
CBS Records, Inc.
◄◄■ 610

ART DIRECTOR:
Jeri McManus Heiden
DESIGNER:
Jeri McManus Heiden
PHOTOGRAPHER:
William Coupon
ILLUSTRATOR:
Elizabeth Brady
STUDIO:
Warner Bros. Records
PUBLISHER:
Warner Bros. Records
◄■ 611

■ 608 Record cover for romantic songs as interpreted by Wendy and Lisa. (USA)

■ 609 For a record issued by CBS. (USA)

■ 610 Cover for a recording by The Radiators as issued by CBS Records, Inc. (USA)

■ 611 For a record with songs from South Africa, the homeland of Miriam Makeba. "Sangoma" is the designation for a person who is possessed by the ghost of his ancestors. (USA)

■ 612 Cover made from a mat paper revealing a strongly marked wood structure, for a Polish jazz recording. (POL)

■ 613 For a record issued by CBS. (USA)

■ 614 For a record by the Charmant de Sable Orchestra issued by Igloo. (BEL)

■ 615 Cover for the jazz record "Homage to Coltrane". (FRA)

■ 608 Schallplattenhülle für romantische Lieder der Interpreten Wendy und Lisa. (USA)

■ 609 Für eine bei CBS erschienene Schallplatte. (USA)

■ 610 «Gesetz der Fische» – Schallplattenhülle für Aufnahmen von The Radiators. (USA)

■ 611 Für eine Platte mit Liedern aus Südafrika, Miriam Makebas Heimat. «Sangoma» ist die Bezeichnung für eine Person, die vom Geist ihrer Vorfahren besessen ist. (USA)

■ 612 Hülle aus stumpfem, stark holzhaltigem Papier für eine polnische Jazz-Platte. (POL)

■ 613 Für eine bei CBS erschienene Platte. (USA)

■ 614 Für Aufnahmen des Orchesters Charmant de Sable erschienen bei Igloo. (BEL)

■ 615 Für eine Jazz-Platte: Hommage an Coltrane. (FRA)

■ 608 Pochette de disque pour un récital de chansons romantiques par Wendy et Lisa. (USA)

■ 609 Pour un disque édité par CBS. (USA)

■ 610 «Loi des poissons» – pochette d'un disque enregistré par The Radiators. (USA)

■ 611 Pour un disque de chansons d'Afrique du Sud, la patrie de Miriam Makeba. Le terme «Sangoma» désigne une personne possédée par l'esprit des ancêtres. (USA)

■ 612 Pochette en papier mat à forte teneur en bois, pour un disque de jazz polonais. (POL)

■ 613 Pour un disque édité par CBS. (USA)

■ 614 Pour un disque de l'orchestre Charmant de Sable. édité par Igloo. (BEL)

■ 615 Pochette pour le disque «Hommage à Coltrane». (FRA)

DESIGNER:
Lech Majewski
ILLUSTRATOR:
Lech Majewski
PUBLISHER:
Poljazz
◄◄■ 612

ART DIRECTOR:
Christopher Austopchuk
DESIGNER:
Christopher Austopchuk
PHOTOGRAPHER:
Chip Simons
STUDIO:
CBS Records, Inc.
PUBLISHER:
CBS Records, Inc.
◄■ 613

ART DIRECTOR:
Patrick Regout
DESIGNER:
Patrick Regout
ILLUSTRATOR:
Patrick Regout
PUBLISHER:
Igloo
◄◄■ 614

ART DIRECTOR:
Bernard Amiard
DESIGNER:
Bernard Amiard
PUBLISHER:
Owl Records
◄■ 615

"THE SORT OF BOOK THAT COULD START A REVOLUTION!" —Erica Jong, Vanity Fair

A LESSER LIFE

THE MYTH

OF WOMEN'S

LIBERATION

IN AMERICA

"UTTERLY CONVINCING...Every American needs to think deeply about the questions Hewlett raises." —Washington Post Book World

SYLVIA ANN HEWLETT

THE PULITZER PRIZE NOMINEE

INTERVALS

ROD McKUEN

ART DIRECTOR:
JACKIE MERRI MEYER
DESIGNER:
CARIN GOLDBERG
PUBLISHER:
WARNER BOOKS
■ 616

ART DIRECTOR:
JOSEPH MONTEBELLO
DESIGNER:
WILLIAM GRAEF
PHOTOGRAPHER:
WILLIAM GRAEF
AGENCY:
WILLIAM GRAEF
PUBLISHER:
HARPER & ROW
■ 617

■ 616 Cover for a paperback about women's emancipation in the United States. (USA)

■ 617 Lacquered cover for a book published by Harper & Row, New York. (USA)

■ 618 Catalog for an exhibition of paintings from the Guggenheim collections. (AUS)

■ 616 Umschlag für ein Taschenbuch zum Thema der Frauenemanzipation in den USA. (USA)

■ 617 Lackierter Umschlag für ein bei Harper & Row erschienenes Buch. (USA)

■ 618 Für den Katalog einer Ausstellung mit Werken aus den Guggenheim-Sammlungen. (AUS)

■ 616 Couverture pour un livre de poche consacré à l'émancipation des femmes aux Etats-Unis. (USA)

■ 617 Couverture vernissée pour un livre paru aux Editions Harper & Row. (USA)

■ 618 Pour le catalogue d'une exposition réunissant des œuvres provenant des collections Guggenheim. (AUS)

DESIGNER:
JOHN SPATCHURST
AGENCY:
SPATCHURST DESIGN ASSOCIATES
PUBLISHER:
*ART GALLERY OF
NEW SOUTH WALES*
■ 618

THE MODERNS

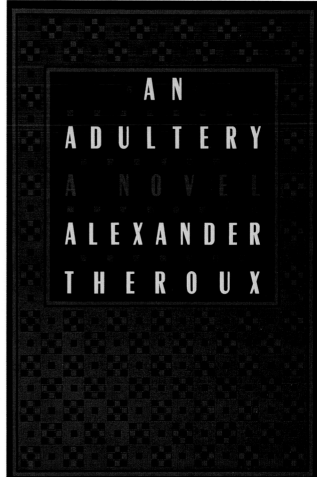

ART DIRECTOR:
GÜNTHER SCHMIDT/
ANGELIKA NODLER
ILLUSTRATOR:
GÜNTHER SCHMIDT/
ANGELIKA NODLER
■ 619

ART DIRECTOR:
FRANK METZ
DESIGNER:
PAULA SCHER
AGENCY:
KOPPEL & SCHER
■ 620

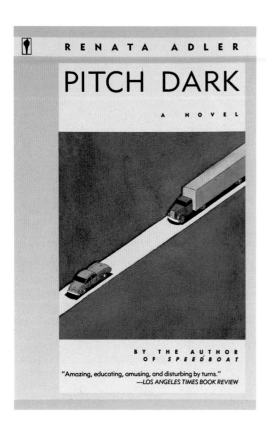

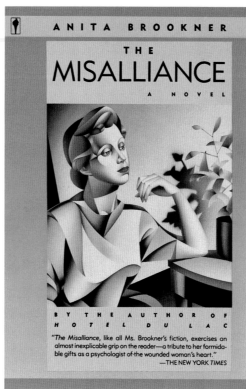

ART DIRECTOR:
APRIL GREIMAN
DESIGNER:
APRIL GREIMAN
ILLUSTRATOR:
APRIL GREIMAN
AGENCY:
APRIL GREIMAN, INC.
PUBLISHER:
AIGA/WATSON GUPTILL
■ 621

ART DIRECTOR:
JOSEPH MONTEBELLO
DESIGNER:
JULIE METZ
ILLUSTRATOR:
STEVEN GUARNACCIA 619, 621
JOHN JINKS 620
PUBLISHER:
HARPER & ROW
◄■ 622-624

■ 619 For a book containing stories and illustrations which relate to dreams. (GER)

■ 620 For a novel published by Simon & Schuster. (USA)

■ 621 Cover of the AIGA's design annual. (USA)

■ 622-624 Covers for a series of paperbacks published by Harper & Row. (USA)

■ 619 Für ein Buch mit Geschichten und Illustrationen zum Thema Traum. (GER)

■ 620 Für einen Roman mit dem Titel «Ein Ehebruch». (USA)

■ 621 Umschlag eines Design-Jahrbuchs der AIGA. (USA)

■ 622-624 Umschläge für eine bei Harper & Row erschienene Taschenbuchreihe. (USA)

■ 619 Pour un recueil de récits illustrés sur le thème du rêve. (GER)

■ 620 Couverture pour le roman «Un Adultère». (USA)

■ 621 Couverture d'un annuel de design de l'AIGA. (USA)

■ 622-624 Couvertures pour une collection de poche parue aux Editions Harper & Row. (USA)

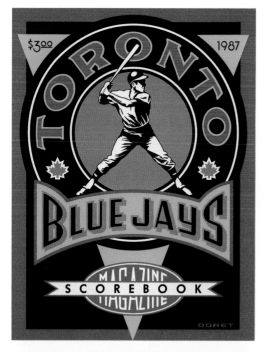

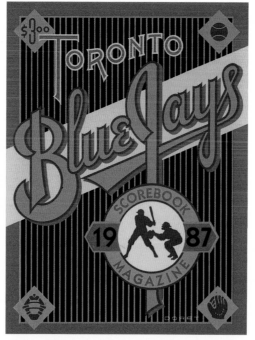

ART DIRECTOR:
Shari Spier

DESIGNER:
Michael Doret

ILLUSTRATOR:
Michael Doret

AGENCY:
Michael Doret, Inc.

PUBLISHER:
*Controlled Media
Communications*

■ 625–632

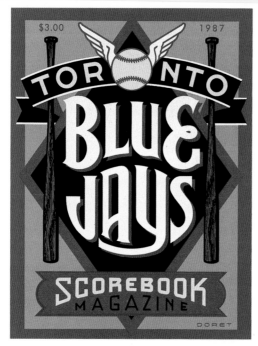

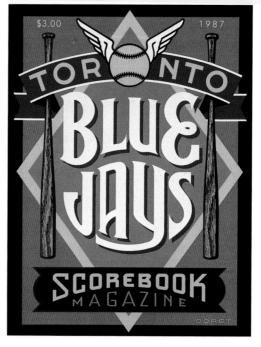

ART DIRECTOR:
Thom Marchionna/Jill Savini
PHOTOGRAPHER:
Bruce Ashley
AGENCY:
Apple Computer/
Creative Services
PUBLISHER:
Apple Computer
■ 633

So Far

THE FIRST TEN YEARS OF A VISION

■ 625-632 Covers for a series of books for the Toronto Blue Jays baseball team in which the season's scores and other data can be recorded. (CAN)

■ 633 Dust jacket for a book commemorating the 10th anniversary of Apple Computers. (USA)

■ 625-632 Umschläge für eine Reihe von Büchern, in denen sich die Ergebnisse der Baseball-Mannschaft Blue Jays aus Toronto eintragen lassen. (CAN)

■ 633 Schutzumschlag eines zum zehnjährigen Bestehen von Apple Computers herausgegebenen Buches. (USA)

■ 625-632 Couvertures d'une série d'ouvrages permettant au lecteur d'inscrire les résultats de son équipe de base-ball favorite, les Blue Jays de Toronto. (CAN)

■ 633 Jaquette d'un ouvrage publié pour le dixième anniversaire des ordinateurs Apple. (USA)

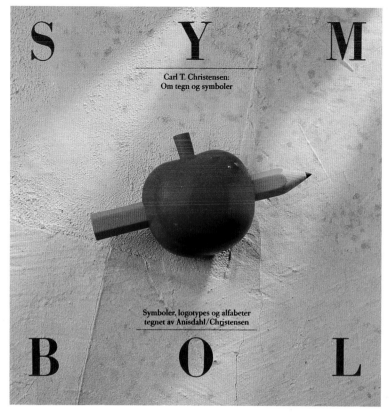

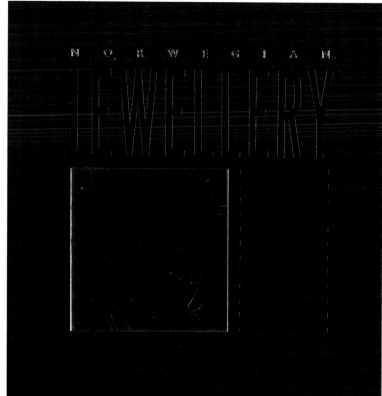

ART DIRECTOR:
CARL T. CHRISTENSEN
DESIGNER:
CARL T. CHRISTENSEN
PHOTOGRAPHER:
TERJE MARTHINUSEN
AGENCY:
ANISDAHL/CHRISTENSEN
PUBLISHER:
ANISDAHL/CHRISTENSEN
■ 634

ART DIRECTOR:
JUNN PAASCHE-AASEN
DESIGNER:
JUNN PAASCHE-AASEN
ILLUSTRATOR:
TERJE AGNALT
PUBLISHER:
ROYAL NORWEGIAN MINISTRY OF FOREIGN AFFAIRS
■ 635

ART DIRECTOR:
HIROYUKI HAYASHI
DESIGNER:
KIYOHISA NAKANO
AGENCY:
GRAFIX INTERNATIONAL
PUBLISHER:
NAMCO LTD.
► ■ 637

■ 634 Cover for a book of the Anisdahl/Christensen Agency which shows symbols, trademarks, etc. (NOR)

■ 635 Catalog for a Japanese exhibition of modern Norwegian jewelry. (NOR)

■ 636 Dust jacket for a book on exhibition design published by the Madison Square Press. (USA)

■ 637 Cover with the character of a relief for a Japanese reference book on computer games. (JPN)

■ 638 "Outfits – Clothing, Accessories, Perfumes". For a statistical documentation published by the Spiegel Verlag. (GER)

■ 634 Umschlag für ein Buch der Agentur Anisdahl/Christensen mit Symbolen, Schutzmarken etc. (NOR)

■ 635 Für den Katalog einer Ausstellung modernen norwegischen Schmucks in Japan. (NOR)

■ 636 Schutzumschlag für ein Buch über die Planung und Gestaltung von Ausstellungen. (USA)

■ 637 Umschlag mit Reliefcharakter für ein japanisches Nachschlagewerk über Computer-Spiele. (JPN)

■ 638 Für eine statistische Dokumentation des Spiegel-Verlags über Kleidung, Accessoires und Parfums. (GER)

■ 634 Couverture d'un livre de l'agence Anisdahl/Christensen consacré aux emblèmes, marques déposées, etc. (NOR)

■ 635 Pour le catalogue d'une exposition de bijoux norvégiens modernes au Japon. (NOR)

■ 636 Jaquette d'une étude sur la conception et la mise en œuvre d'expositions. (USA)

■ 637 Couverture en relief pour un manuel de jeux informatiques publié au Japon. (JPN)

■ 638 Pour une documentation statistique des Editions Spiegel relative à la mode, aux accessoires et aux parfums. (GER)

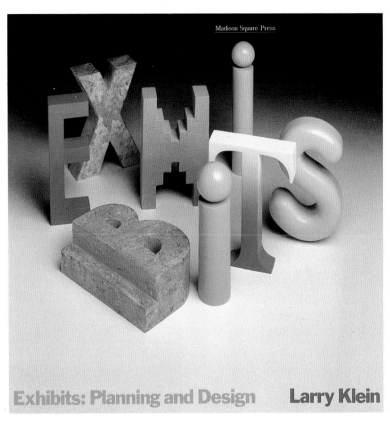

ART DIRECTOR:
WALTER BERNARD
DESIGNER:
WALTER BERNARD
PHOTOGRAPHER:
MATTHEW KLEIN/NICHOLAS FASCIANO (CONSTRUCTION)
AGENCY:
WBMG INC.
PUBLISHER:
MADISON SQUARE PRESS
■ 636

ART DIRECTOR:
ERICH KRÜTZFELDT
DESIGNER:
HOLGER MATTHIES
PHOTOGRAPHER:
HOLGER MATTHIES
PUBLISHER:
SPIEGEL-VERLAG
▼ ■ 638

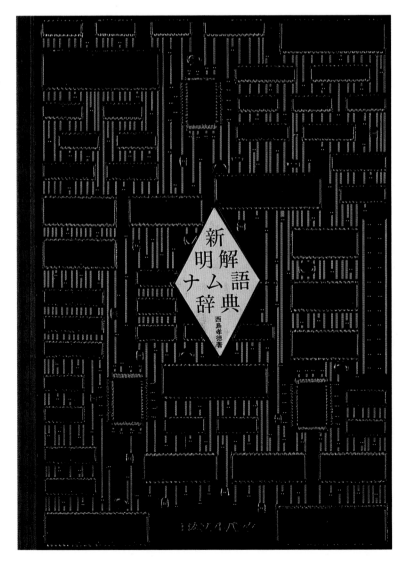

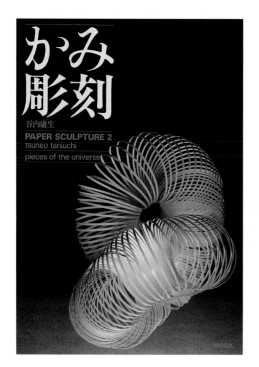

かみ
彫刻

谷内庸生
PAPER SCULPTURE 2
tsuneo taniuchi
pieces of the universe

ART DIRECTOR:
TSUNEO TANIUCHI
DESIGNER:
TSUNEO TANIUCHI
PHOTOGRAPHER:
YUKISUKE FUSHIMI/
TOSHIHARO MUROSAWA
STUDIO:
TSUNEO TANIUCHI
PUBLISHER:
GENKO-SHA CO. LTD.
■ 639-642

■ 639-642 Cover and
double spreads from a
Japanese book on origami,
the art of paper folding. (JPN)

■ 639-642 Umschlag und
Doppelseiten aus einem
japanischen Buch über
Papierskulpturen. (JPN)

■ 639-642 Couverture et
doubles pages d'une mono-
graphie japonaise sur les
sculptures en papier. (JPN)

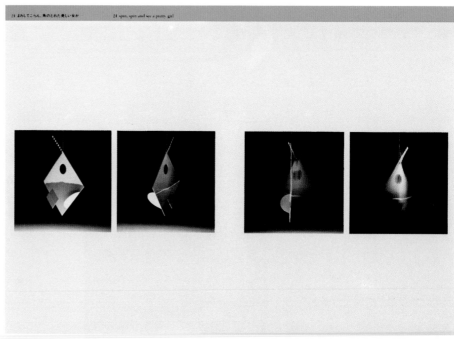

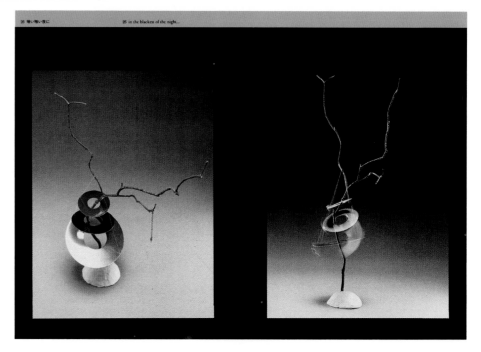

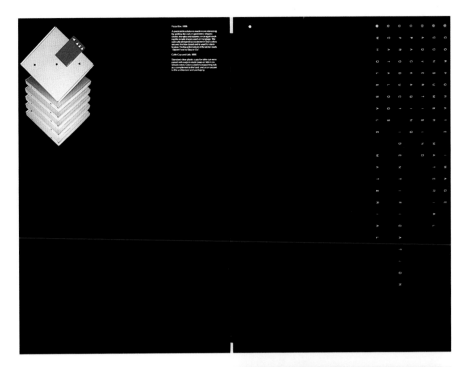

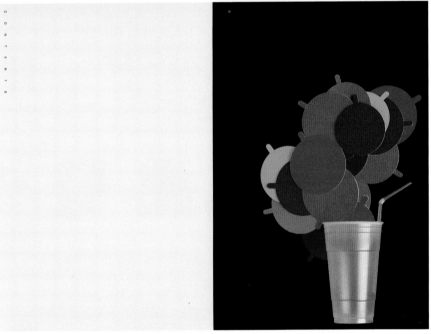

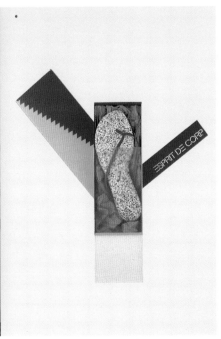

ESPRIT'S GRAPHIC WORK 1984-1986

ART DIRECTOR:
TAMOTSU YAGI
DESIGNER:
TAMOTSU YAGI
PHOTOGRAPHER:
ROBERTO CARRA
STUDIO:
ESPRIT GRAPHIC DESIGN
PUBLISHER:
ESPRIT DE CORP.
■ 643-646

■ 643-646 Slipcase and double spreads from a large-sized book describing the graphic images of Esprit, the successful clothing firm which has recently expanded into other markets such as food products. (USA)

■ 643-646 Schuber und Doppelseiten aus einem grossformatigen Buch über die graphische Seite der erfolgreichen Bekleidungs-firma Esprit, die jetzt auch in andere Märkte wie z.B. Nahrungsmittel eingestiegen ist. (USA)

■ 643-646 Emboîtage et doubles pages d'un ouvrage au grand format présentant l'image graphique d'Esprit, un grand de la confection qui vient de se diversifier en s'assurant une part du marché de l'alimentation, entre autres. (USA)

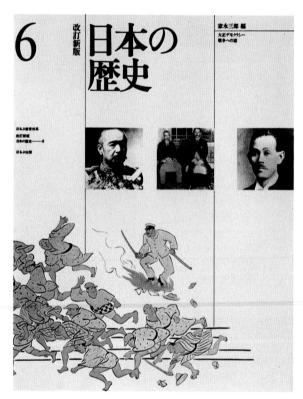

ART DIRECTOR:
MINORU NIIJIMA
DESIGNER:
MINORU NIIJIMA/CHIAKI AIBA
STUDIO:
MINORU NIIJIMA DESIGN
PUBLISHER:
HOLP PUBLISHING CO. LTD.
■ 647–650

STARS&STRIPES

By Kit Hinrichs

A Celebration of the American Flag by 96 International Designers and Artists

ART DIRECTOR:
KIT HINRICHS
DESIGNER:
KIT HINRICHS/
CHRIS HILL (COVER ART)
AGENCY:
PENTAGRAM DESIGN
PUBLISHER:
CHRONICLE BOOKS
■ 651

■ 647–650 For a series of books on Japanese history. (JPN)

■ 647–650 Für eine Reihe über die Geschichte Japans. (JPN)

■ 647–650 Pour une série historique sur le Japon. (JPN)

■ 651 The Star Spangled Banner and its interpretation by 96 well-known designers and artists. The book was conceived by the American Institute of Graphic Arts. (USA)

■ 651 Interpretationen des Sternenbanners von 96 Top-Designern und Künstlern. Organisator des Buches war das American Institute of Graphic Arts. (USA)

■ 651 Ouvrage présentant 96 interprétations de la bannière étoilée par des designers et artistes de grand renom, à l'instigation de l'American Institute of Graphic Arts. (USA)

WINTER

a novel of a Berlin family

LEN DEIGHTON

ART DIRECTOR:
Carol Carson
DESIGNER:
Jon Valk
ILLUSTRATOR:
John Rush
PUBLISHER:
Alfred A. Knopf
■ 652

Mary Ellen Jordan Haight

8-Shakespeare and Compa

WALKS
IN GERTRUDE STEIN'S
PARIS

ART DIRECTOR:
Clane Graves
DESIGNER:
Clane Graves/Roy T. Clark
AGENCY:
Formaz
PUBLISHER:
Peregrine Smith Books
■ 653

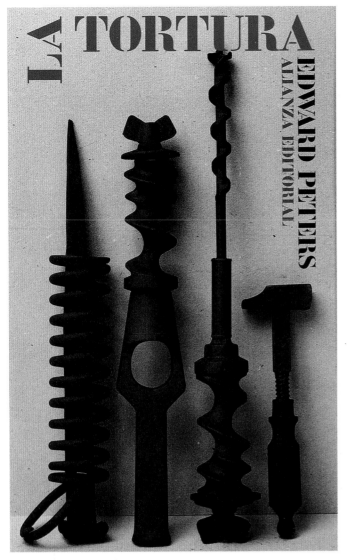

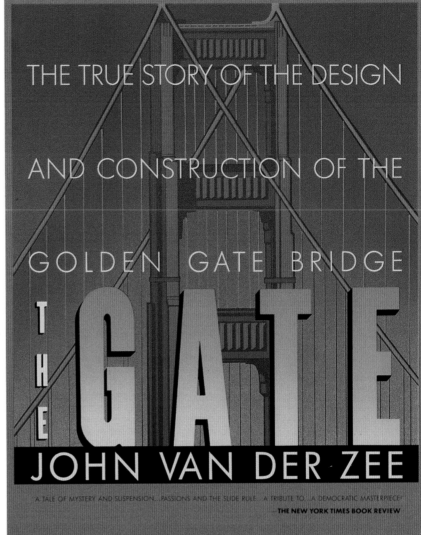

ART DIRECTOR:
Daniel Gil
DESIGNER:
Daniel Gil
PHOTOGRAPHER:
Daniel Gil
PUBLISHER:
Alianza Editorial, S.A.
■ 654

ART DIRECTOR:
Frank Metz
DESIGNER:
Paula Scher
AGENCY:
Koppel & Scher
PUBLISHER:
Simon & Schuster
■ 655

■ 652 For a novel about a Berlin family as published by Alfred A. Knopf. (USA)

■ 653 Cover for a paperback describing five literary walking tours through Paris. (USA)

■ 654 For a paperpack published by Alianza. (SPA)

■ 655 Cover for a book relating the history of the Golden Gate Bridge as published by Simon & Schuster. (USA)

■ 652 Für einen bei Alfred A. Knopf erschienenen Roman über eine Berliner Familie. (USA)

■ 653 Umschlag für ein Taschenbuch, das fünf literarische Wanderungen durch Paris beschreibt. (USA)

■ 654 Für ein bei Alianza erschienenes Taschenbuch. (SPA)

■ 655 Planung und Bau der Golden Gate Bridge werden in diesem Buch geschildert. (USA)

■ 652 Pour le roman d'une famille berlinoise publié aux Editions Alfred A. Knopf. (USA)

■ 653 Couverture d'un poche retraçant cinq itinéraires littéraires à travers le Paris de Gertrud Stein. (USA)

■ 654 Pour un poche des Editions Alianza. (SPA)

■ 655 Cet ouvrage paru chez Simon & Schuster narre l'histoire de la construction du pont sur la Golden Gate. (USA)

ART DIRECTOR:
Francesco Giona
ILLUSTRATOR:
Pier Paolo Cornieti
PUBLISHER:
Priuli & Verlucca
■ 656

■ 656 "Of Laughing Rice". Cover and inside page of an illustrated Italian cookbook. (ITA)

■ 656 «Vom lachenden Reis» – Umschlag und Innenansicht eines illustrierten Kochbuches. (ITA)

■ 656 «Du riz qui rit» – couverture et page intérieure d'un livre de cuisine italien. (ITA)

VERZEICHNIS

SUBSCRIBE TO GRAPHIS: FOR USA AND CANADA

MAGAZINE	USA	CANADA
☐ GRAPHIS (One year/6 issues)	US$ 79.00	CDN$ 99.00
☐ 1987 Portfolio (Case holds six issues)	US$ 11.00	CDN$ 15.00

☐ Check enclosed
☐ Please bill me (My subscription will begin upon payment)
☐ Students may request a 25% discount by sending student ID.
IMPORTANT! PLEASE CHECK THE LANGUAGE VERSION DESIRED:
☐ ENGLISH ☐ GERMAN ☐ FRENCH
Subscription fees include postage to any part of the world.
Surcharges: US$ 57.00 (CDN$ 75.00) for Airmail,
　　　　　　US$ 22.50 (CDN$ 30.00) for Registered Mail.

NAME

TITLE

COMPANY

ADDRESS

CITY

STATE/PROV. 　　　　　　　　POSTAL CODE

COUNTRY

PROFESSION

SIGNATURE 　　　　　　　　DATE

Please send coupon and make check payable to:
GRAPHIS US, INC., 141 LEXINGTON AVENUE, NEW YORK, NY 10016, USA.
Guarantee: You may cancel your subscription at any time and receive a full refund on all unmailed copies. Please allow 6–8 weeks for delivery of first issue.

REQUEST FOR CALL FOR ENTRIES
Please put me on your "Call for Entries" list for the following title(s).
Please check the appropriate box(es).
☐ GRAPHIS PHOTO ☐ GRAPHIS POSTER ☐ GRAPHIS DESIGN
☐ GRAPHIS PACKAGING ☐ GRAPHIS DIAGRAM ☐ GRAPHIS ANNUAL REPORTS
By submitting material to any of the titles listed above, I will automatically qualify for a 25% discount toward the purchase of the title. 　　　　GDA 88

BOOK ORDER FORM: FOR USA AND CANADA

ORDER YOUR GRAPHIS ANNUALS NOW!

BOOKS	USA	CANADA
☐ Graphis Design Annual 88/89	US$ 65.00	CDN$ 85.00
☐ Graphis Photo 88	US$ 65.00	CDN$ 85.00
☐ Graphis Diagram	US$ 65.00	CDN$ 85.00
☐ Graphis Annual Reports	US$ 65.00	CDN$ 85.00
☐ Graphis Poster 88	US$ 65.00	CDN$ 85.00
☐ Graphis Design Annual 87/88	US$ 59.50	CDN$ 79.50
☐ Photographis 86	US$ 59.50	CDN$ 79.50
☐ Graphis Posters 86	US$ 59.50	CDN$ 79.50
☐ 42 Years of Graphis Covers	US$ 49.50	CDN$ 60.00

☐ Check enclosed
☐ Please bill me (Mailing costs in addition to above book price will be charged)

NAME

TITLE

COMPANY

ADDRESS

CITY/STATE/PROV.

POSTAL CODE 　　　　　　　　COUNTRY

PROFESSION

SIGNATURE 　　　　　　　　DATE

Please send coupon and make check payable to:
GRAPHIS US, INC., 141 LEXINGTON AVENUE, NEW YORK, NY 10016, USA.

REQUEST FOR CALL FOR ENTRIES
Please put me on your "Call for Entries" list for the following title(s).
Please check the appropriate box(es).
☐ GRAPHIS PHOTO ☐ GRAPHIS POSTER ☐ GRAPHIS DESIGN
☐ GRAPHIS PACKAGING ☐ GRAPHIS DIAGRAM ☐ GRAPHIS ANNUAL REPORTS
By submitting material to any of the titles listed above, I will automatically qualify for a 25% discount toward the purchase of the title. 　　　　GDA 88

SUBSCRIBE TO GRAPHIS: FOR EUROPE AND THE WORLD

MAGAZINE	BRD	WORLD	U.K.
☐ GRAPHIS (One year/6 issues)	DM 146,–	SFr. 118.–	£ 45.00
☐ 1987 Portfolio (Case holds six issues)	DM 24.–	SFr. 19.–	£ 8.00

☐ Check enclosed (for Europe, please make SFr.-checks payable to a Swiss bank)
☐ Please bill me (My subscription will begin upon payment)
☐ Students may request a 25% discount by sending student ID.
IMPORTANT! PLEASE CHECK THE LANGUAGE VERSION DESIRED:
☐ ENGLISH ☐ GERMAN ☐ FRENCH
Subscription fees include postage to any part of the world.
Surcharges: SFr. 84.00/DM 102,00/£ 34.50 for Airmail,
　　　　　　SFr. 30.00/DM 36,00/£ 12.00 for Registered Mail.

NAME

TITLE

COMPANY

ADDRESS

CITY 　　　　　　　　POSTAL CODE

COUNTRY

PROFESSION

SIGNATURE 　　　　　　　　DATE

Please send coupon and make check payable to:
GRAPHIS PRESS CORP., DUFOURSTRASSE 107, CH-8008 ZÜRICH, SWITZERLAND
Guarantee: You may cancel your subscription at any time and receive a full refund on all unmailed copies. Please allow 6–8 weeks for delivery of first issue.

REQUEST FOR CALL FOR ENTRIES
Please put me on your "Call for Entries" list for the following title(s).
Please check the appropriate box(es).
☐ GRAPHIS PHOTO ☐ GRAPHIS POSTER ☐ GRAPHIS DESIGN
☐ GRAPHIS PACKAGING ☐ GRAPHIS DIAGRAM ☐ GRAPHIS ANNUAL REPORTS
By submitting material to any of the titles listed above, I will automatically qualify for a 25% discount toward the purchase of the title. 　　　　GDA 88

BOOK ORDER FORM: FOR EUROPE AND THE WORLD

BOOKS	BRD	WORLD	U.K.
☐ Graphis Design Annual 88/89	DM 138,–	SFr. 112.–	£ 45.00
☐ Graphis Photo 88	DM 138,–	SFr. 112.–	£ 45.00
☐ Graphis Diagram	DM 138,–	SFr. 112.–	£ 45.00
☐ Graphis Annual Reports	DM 138,–	SFr. 112.–	£ 45.00
☐ Graphis Poster 88	DM 138,–	SFr. 112.–	£ 45.00
☐ Graphis Design Annual 87/88	DM 138,–	SFr. 112.–	£ 45.00
☐ Photographis 86	DM 138,–	SFr. 112.–	£ 45.00
☐ Graphis Posters 86	DM 129,–	SFr. 105.–	£ 42.00
☐ 42 Years of Graphis Covers	DM 98,–	SFr. 85.–	£ 35.00

☐ Check enclosed (For Europe, please make SFr. checks payable to a Swiss Bank)
☐ Amount paid into Graphis account at the Union Bank of Switzerland, Acct No 3620063 in Zürich.
☐ Amount paid to Postal Cheque Account Zürich 80-23071-9 (Through your local post office)
☐ Please bill me (Mailing costs in addition to above book price will be charged)

NAME

TITLE

COMPANY

ADDRESS

CITY 　　　　　　　　POSTAL CODE

COUNTRY

PROFESSION

SIGNATURE 　　　　　　　　DATE

Please send coupon and make check payable to:
GRAPHIS PRESS CORP., DUFOURSTRASSE 107, CH-8008 ZÜRICH, SWITZERLAND

REQUEST FOR CALL FOR ENTRIES
Please put me on your "Call for Entries" list for the following title(s).
☐ GRAPHIS PHOTO ☐ GRAPHIS POSTER ☐ GRAPHIS DESIGN
☐ GRAPHIS PACKAGING ☐ GRAPHIS DIAGRAM ☐ GRAPHIS ANNUAL REPORTS
By submitting material to any of the titles listed above, I will automatically qualify for a 25% discount toward the purchase of the title. 　　　　GDA 88

GRAPHIS PRESS CORP.
DUFOURSTRASSE 107
CH-8008 ZÜRICH
SWITZERLAND

GRAPHIS U.S., INC.
141 LEXINGTON AVENUE
NEW YORK, NEW YORK 10016
U.S.A.

GRAPHIS PRESS CORP.
DUFOURSTRASSE 107
CH-8008 ZÜRICH
SWITZERLAND

GRAPHIS U.S., INC.
141 LEXINGTON AVENUE
NEW YORK, NEW YORK 10016
U.S.A.